Not the Price of Admission

Healthy Relationships After Childhood Trauma

Laura S. Brown, Ph.D. ABPP

ISBN-13: 978-1517683405
ISBN-10: 1517683408

Table of Contents

Forward—And Onward

I had planned to spend Memorial Day weekend of 2015 working on the last chapter of a book that I had nearly completed during the previous months. I was going to send it off for reviews and comments and savor the experience of creation before taking some time to revise, edit, and publish later in the year.

That was this book. I didn't spend the weekend writing. Instead, I walked into my home that Friday evening after dinner with friends to find that thieves had been in the house. They stole many things that could be replaced, but took the one thing that I knew I could not simply order another one of from Amazon—my manuscript. I had carefully backed the book up on a flash drive and a laptop. The thieves took both devices.

One sleepless night later, I sat exhausted and grief stricken, wondering how I could possibly recreate the book. I don't make notes or an outline. Instead, I write books by gestating them in my brain, then dump the material into the keyboard over an intensive writing session. The ideas for the book had migrated to the page; I had no idea if I could ever find them again.

I tried to begin the grieving process. But I did not, could not, accept yet that I had no other options. I decided to hope against hope that I could lure the thieves into ransoming my flash drive back to me. I had an idea of who had invaded my home. The neighborhood I live in, known for being free spirited and open, has been plagued by a group of methamphetamine addicts who case houses for unlocked doors, break into cars, and steal packages off porches. I was fairly certain that they had been the ones in my house.

I took a picture of the stolen flash drive off the internet and used it to make posters, which I put up around the neighborhood. I targeted places where I knew that these folks went for cigarettes, sugar, and alcohol, and offered a no-questions-asked reward for the return of the "lost" flash drive.

My hunch proved correct. Five days later, a knock on my door introduced me to a disheveled young white man, misery streaming out of every pore of his being, who had a copy of the poster and the flash drive in his hand. He told a yarn about how he had supposedly found the drive on the ground near a local convenience store. I paid the ransom, thanked him profusely for returning the book to me, wished him well, and recovered this beloved child of my brain (which I promptly backed up into the cloud and three different geographically distributed portable devices!).

Had the manuscript not been returned, I knew that I would have to move through my grief and re-write this book. I might never have been able to find my original words. But I was strongly motivated to produce this book. For that motivation, which sustained me over the four painful days that the book was missing, I have a very special collection of people to thank. My commitment to my clients and to all the people I know who have struggled with relationships after childhood trauma were what kept me in touch with hope and the desire to write again. The folks who have honored me with their presence in my therapy office for the last four decades are the primary inspiration for this book, as they have been for much of my writing.

Though on the morning after the theft most of me wanted to simply give up and go into a place of despair, I was inspired by the courage and willingness of the people with whom I work. They do hard things on days when they are exhausted, grief stricken, and frightened by the echoes of their past, when they are struggling with the difficult realities of their present lives whose seeds were planted by childhood abuse and neglect. How could I have integrity as a therapist asking people to take risks to heal from much more enormous losses if I was unwilling to get up off the ground and move forward after the theft? I couldn't—and as a therapist, integrity is everything. So I wept and sat down once again to try to talk with you all about your right to have a good-enough, safe-enough, loved-enough life that works. I wrote very little that day.

Wonderfully and strangely, the void that briefly opened by the felt-like-forever loss of this book created a fertile space into which new ideas and energy flowed. In the brief period between theft and recovery, I found myself sitting down between therapy sessions making notes about things I wanted to remember to include, and interrupting supervision meetings with my interns to run into my office and jot down an idea that had emerged as we discussed a client's struggles with relationships. The thieves gave me the strange gift of realizing that this book would be there no matter what even though I went through painful hours to see that.

So thank you, all of you, for being my reason to write. Thank you for teaching me with your struggles. Thank you for inspiring me with your courage. Special thanks to the six of my clients who read a nearly-finished draft of this book and gave me excellent and valuable feedback.

Attention: Some Hard Stuff Ahead

A few words before we dive in. One piece of feedback from clients is that reading this book should not be done in one sitting. My early readers, who are wise people who've spent a lot of time on their own healing work, advised me to tell you to take your time, go slowly, take breaks. One person read a few pages, put it down, and then picked it up again, for several months, then went back and re-read the book in its entirety a second time. This book stirs things up.

There are also blunt and sometimes graphic descriptions of the kinds of truly bad things that adults do to children, and that were done to some of you. My early readers told me two things about that content. First, it was helpful to several of them because it told the truth about their experiences. They also said, and asked me to tell you, that reading that material may feel distressing. Or you might find yourself numbing out when you read it. That's because this stuff is painful to read and may push on your own memories of trauma. Give yourself ample time and plenty of permission to respond to that material in whatever way works best for you. Take what helps you from this book. The rest won't matter.

Tracy Bryan, Psy.D., who is both a writer and a skilled and compassionate wounded healer of complex trauma, made this book read more fluidly. David Brown also provided editorial feedback and the valuable eye and perspective of someone who's not a psychologist. Mrs. Kitts, who taught grammar to both David and me between 1965 and 1969, wherever you are, your North Carolina accent sounded frequently in my head as I wrote, edited, and re-wrote this book. Thanks to all of you.

Lynn Brem took the cover photo and bravely climbed all over the lava one evening as the sun was setting. Denise Brem once again produced a powerful cover for my book. She also taught me how to make the internal formatting more pleasant for the reader's eye and easier for me to make that happen. Who knew you could learn something new about a program you've been using for two decades?

One final thank you. Most of this book was written at a house on the Big Island of Hawai'i that sits along the Kapoho tide pools. Being able to sit and write with the ocean in all of its changing nature directly in front of me, and being free to take breaks among the fish and coral of this unique protected reef, has made these hard topics flow more easily from brain to keyboard. Linda and Kirk Flanders, who have been instrumental in making parts of this reef into the Wai'opae Marine Life Conservation District, created a lovely space. Thanks, folks, for sharing your home with strangers like me. And thanks to the people of Hawai'i, who in their spirit of aloha have generously shared their aina (homeland) with all of us who began as their colonizers.

About the Cover Photo

The picture on the cover was taken at a spot on the beach at Kalapana in lower Puna, on the east side of the Big Island of Hawai'i. This beach, once one of the island's famous black sand beaches, was covered—along with the towns of Kalapana, Kaimu, and Queen's Gardens—in an eruption in 1990 from the nearby Kilaue'a volcano, known as the goddess Pelé to Hawai'ians.

In the 25 years since the lava flowed, life has returned to the beach. New life has pushed through the apparently impenetrable lava rock. Plants that have found their way through the rock are very much like you, the people reading this book, whose life has emerged green and vital through what appeared to be devastation.

CHAPTER 1
Ready for the Thing Called Love

*"Waiting for the punch line, thinking that the joke's on you,
like good is too good to be true."*

Maia Sharp

If for you, good is too good to be true in a relationship, then you grew up in a family where there was, at the very best, no danger. There was merely insufficient love and care. At the worst, you grew up in a household where your physical, sexual, emotional, and/or spiritual safety were repeatedly put at risk by some or all of the adults around you. These versions of childhood experience are painfully common even though they're made invisible by the world around us. There are rarely clear battle scars on the bodies of people who grew up in these war zones. Even when those scars are easy for others to see, it's rare for people around you to know how you incurred these warrior marks. No one gives out purple hearts or raises monuments to the unknown survivors of childhood trauma.

Since the 1970s, research conducted on rates of childhood maltreatment in the general population (meaning not just people seeing therapists) has found that at least one-third of adults in the United States have had one or more less-than-optimal—and at times outright dangerous—experiences in their childhood. That's a lot of invisible purple hearts walking around the planet. This research doesn't even begin to touch the experiences of people whose lives or bodies were not threatened or violated, but who lived in an emotional desert where connection and affection were mostly absent. This book is for all of you.

Childhoods like yours are full of powerful emotional lessons that teach children, without any words, that emotionally-meaningful relationships are perilous. These lessons convey the twisted truth that relationships always come with large, painful, and continuing price tags attached. Being emotionally close to other humans feels unsafe, even when emotional closeness is what you passionately desire. If you're reading this book, there's a good chance that you've gone through life enacting this belief in the danger of love.

You've put up with abuse and exploitation, with low-quality emotional contact, with distance, and with all sorts of less-than-desirable situations. You've let yourself be made crazy at times to hold onto a connection that you're terrified of losing. You've spent your life convincing yourself that the best you could expect in a relationship was to be tolerated, not truly and fully loved. You've spent hours anxiously wondering if the next encounter with someone who matters to you might be the last. You're rarely certain that a connection is solid. Your truth is that nothing good lasts.

In trying to have some sense of control in a world that has felt chronically lacking control, you've repeatedly—but rarely consciously—done things to bring the other shoe down and get things over with. You're certain that the shoe will drop eventually, so you pull it down. As we'll discuss later in this book, none of this is evidence of weakness or a lack of self-control. Your fears, your stumbles, your difficult relationships arise from powerfully biologically mediated patterns of attachment that require hard work and intention to bypass.

When you were very young your brain learned to associate attachment with danger, pain, fear, or confusion. As a consequence of this very problematic pairing you've been confused forever by the outcomes of your attempts to have emotionally nourishing relationships You've thought that you were doing the right thing, whatever that was, and you were surprised by people responding in ways that seemed to tell you you'd been doing it wrong. You've felt defeated.

You've believed, without ever saying these words, that paying hard prices was the only way you could get anyone to relate to you in other than the most superficial of manners. You've rarely felt secure in an emotionally-meaningful relationship. You've sought connection, and it has failed to help you. You've tap-danced like crazy when you felt as if you were at risk of losing a relationship. You've kept trying, kept looking for cues that you're doing it right, kept giving and pleading—often to little avail. There were rules, you were sure of it. You didn't know what the rules were, and it seemed as if no one was willing to throw a rulebook in your direction. Or they gave you the rulebook, and when you followed it, told you, "Oops, I didn't really mean those rules, did I?"

This book is a sibling to *Your Turn for Care: Surviving the Aging and Death of the Adults Who Harmed You,* which I wrote in 2012. That book focused on dealing with your relationships today with the adults who had undermined your welfare and safety when you were little. The intersection of caregiving with the legacy of abuse is a topic that seemed urgent to address because so many of the survivors of childhood trauma I knew were facing that challenge without much by support.

When I notice this kind of vacuum of resources, it frequently leads to the birth of a book. The seed for this book was planted in a similar way. To no one's surprise, many of the difficult dynamics I touched on regarding dealing with aging and dying abusers also had relevance for other life issues faced by survivors of less-than-adequate childhood care. People read *Your Turn for Care* and wrote to me to ask whether I had suggestions for a similar book to help them with people who hadn't abused them when they were kids, people they were trying to relate to today. Thanks, folks. I listened to you.

It turns out that many excellent books about relationships written for people who had good-enough childhoods didn't quite do it for survivors. Those books skipped the step of explaining why emotionally-meaningful connections of all kinds presented core challenges that the self-help strategies simply don't address. The neurobiology of trauma—the ways in which childhood abuse and neglect and disrupted attachment affect, not simply your psyche, but the biology of your response to other human beings when you get close to them—calls for a different set of skills, including compassion for self, in order to get the relationships you want and deserve. For survivors of childhood trauma, the human complexity of emotional intimacy is exponentially larger. It's not impossible to deal with; it's simply bigger than can be imagined by people who don't understand or never experienced childhood trauma. We're imagining it here.

The fact that emotionally-meaningful relationships—friendships, romantic relationships, and workplace relationships—feel confusing, scary, and difficult for many survivors is something that I know about only too well. My life and work have taught me that difficulties with self-care, boundaries, self-empowerment, and self-compassion don't emerge only when survivors have to address whether or not to care for an aging abuser or deal with the death of the adults who had made their childhood difficult. The dynamics you learned in families of origin, and the neural networks laid down in early attachment relationships, showed up in any relationship that mattered to you, anything that was emotionally-meaningful, anything where your human desire for connection was in play. When your early experiences fell below the line of adequacy in some way, adulthood and emotional connection were like a wilderness without maps—or worse, with maps that led you into confusion or danger.

Conundrums inherent in emotionally-meaningful relationships that arise from childhood experience create dilemmas for survivors throughout life. While people who've had adequate or better childhood experiences do not skip challenges in relationships, pitfalls are multiplied and sometimes quite different in shape and form for you, a person whose adult caregivers were below adequate in their behaviors.

Problematic childhood experiences with the adults who raised you have lasting effects, many of them painful—on your conscious, non-conscious, and biological paradigms for how to engage in emotionally-meaningful relationships. Relationship patterns set in motion by failed adult caretakers from your childhood persist. Sometimes as a survivor you understand that this is what you're dealing with. Sometimes you can stand back and have compassion for yourself. More often, you blame yourself and feel shame. That is, after all, what you've been taught to do by childhood experiences in which relationship problems were ascribed by the adults around you to something wrong in you, not to failures in their care for you. Sometimes you are bewildered, wondering if you have a sign painted on your back telling others to misuse, exploit, and abuse you. One persistent experience for survivors is that you find you pay all kinds of prices to be in relationships.

This book is an exploration of the root causes of struggles that many survivors have with emotionally-meaningful relationships. It's also a discussion of ways of transforming those struggles. Hacking the code of emotionally-meaningful relationships is challenging for adult humans in the best of circumstances; humans are unable to read one another's minds. But in your family you were frequently expected to perform this feat of clairvoyance and punished when you could not.

We are actually quite challenging for one another. We are different from one another, and rarely in perfect sync. We make and drop connections like a cell phone line. This normative collection of challenges fuels an industry of relationship self-help books, workshops, and retreats for people seeking better relationships, usually with romantic partners (although those of you working in large organizations will likely have attended retreats and workshops whose aim is to improve the emotionally-meaningful relationships in the workplace as well).

Sing, Sing a Song

Before there were self-help books, poets and troubadours sang for centuries of the vicissitudes of emotional connection. It's why we have torch songs, and the enormous repertoire of "loved and lost" lyrics, and music in every genre about how someone did us wrong. It's why Emile deBeque sings the elegiac "once you have found her, never let her go," lyrics in South Pacific, and why Sondheim's character Desireé sings "Send in the clowns," the poignant ballad of having missed an emotional window of opportunity.

The drama of love and connection, though sung in many different melodies, is a universally human one. I was a singer before I was a psychologist. My performances were saturated with lyrics of pain and passion that are central to the human experience of attachment, love, and connection. Writing about this topic has turned on the jukebox that lives in my head, because those lyrics often succinctly describe challenges that survivors face when trying to forge connections with other humans. So bear with me, please, as I quote (and sometimes mangle) the words of Rogers and Hammerstein, Joni Mitchell, Leonard Cohen, and the other musical poets of love and broken heartedness. Sometimes I think that if I simply sat all of my clients down with Leonard Cohen's collected works, I would be able to retire from my practice. But not everyone heals through music—so here's a book that's not nearly as eloquent, but tries to say the same things.

It's the Attachment

While emotionally-meaningful relationships of all kinds can kick anyone's behind, survivors face special challenges. This is because the adults who raised you gave you less-than-adequate attachment experiences. Your relationships difficulties are not caused by something about you that's uniquely, personally, and utterly screwed up. One of the common effects of the kind of attachment wound that we'll be discussing, which can happen even in the absence of overt abuse or neglect, is that kids blame themselves for the painful nature of their relationships with the caregivers from their childhood, then proceed to blame themselves for all relationship difficulties. Those people feel terminally unique, different from others in bad ways.

This book offers a window into how common your struggles are, and how normal you are for an attachment-wounded person. I hope you'll see yourself here so you can look in the mirror with enhanced understanding and compassion. Shame and self-blame don't thrive well in the light shining from the lamp of knowledge. When you know that you are neither alone nor uniquely flawed, it's harder to pin all of the problems you've had in relationships on something inherently wrong about you simply because you find emotionally-meaningful relationships to be such a mine field.

Looking for Love in All the Hard Places

We come into the world hardwired to seek attachment and connection with the humans around us—a point I'll visit repeatedly because it's so central to our discussion. Ironically and dangerously for those of you whose caregivers were the source of terror, infants and children are driven to seek connection with caregivers when frightened. This is the terrible paradox driving children into the arms of adults who hurt them. This paradox is the neural and emotional root of survivors' difficulties with emotionally-meaningful relationships.

From childhood on humans spend their lives trying to figure out how to make attachment and connection nourish, sustain, calm, and center them. This is, after all, what the attachment system of the brain is meant to do. Our infant brains drive us to naturally seek out connection when we are fearful. Simply because your experiences of attachment have been less than adequate or dangerous doesn't change that brain circuitry and what it drives you to do.

When we have been well loved, or simply loved well enough by the people who cared for us before we had language, we get sane and reasonable information about the complex and intricate world of emotionally-meaningful relationships. Our understanding is informed by healthy self-love and self-compassion. There is congruence between what the brain is wired to do and actual experiences with other human beings. Good-enough care in childhood doesn't make relationships a walk in the park. It does, however, provide helpful roadmaps, as well as the neurobiological substrate associating connection with safety.

People who were well and consistently loved in childhood generally believe themselves to be essentially loveable. It's the first lesson learned by babies who are loved well enough, and it's a lesson that sticks with them for life. There was congruence between their wired-in need to seek connection and the safe-enough care given by the adults around them.

These folks unconsciously expect others to treat them with love, respect, and care. They believe that love endures, even when someone is angry, sad or temporarily unavailable. When they're treated disrespectfully or callously, these well-enough-loved folks rarely assume that they've done something to deserve ill treatment. They don't heap blame on themselves if a relationship goes through a tough time; one fight does not mean a breakup is looming. They know that love is solid, not fragile, persistent, and not contingent on perfection.

When relationships end, well-enough-loved people are able to grieve. They're unlikely to unfairly blame themselves. They feel the pain of loss. Then they are able to move forward, choose differently, and find friendships, partners, and spouses who are able to love them as they are. They learn from their errors, in part because they don't code errors as evidence of deep character flaws, which is an interpretation that many survivors make. Making yourself the one and only problem doesn't solve anything. It leads to anxiety, self-hatred, and difficulty in learning from mistakes.

Well-enough-loved folks can usually understand errors in relationships as their own quirks, not huge and insuperable barriers. They can acknowledge that they are imperfectly skillful in the complex dance of intimacy and connection. Like an athlete in training, well-enough-loved people can review the "game film" of a difficult situation and observe themselves with sufficient compassion to learn and make changes.

Well-enough-loved people mostly love others that way, too. They don't expect perfection—they know that's a myth. They don't hunt for unicorns in the forest of relationships. They're quite happy with unmythical beasts. They're capable of offering humor and compassion to friends and lovers who are human and who stumble and sometimes step on their emotional toes. They can get angry when someone does something that is not okay. They're irritated by the umpteenth time that someone forgets to follow through on a commitment. They're upset when someone lies to them. They can hit a wall when things are too hard for too long. But they are unlikely to hold onto the anger or upset as a protective distancing device, or to use anger punitively or for the sake of revenge.

These folks generally trust their perceptions and intuitions about people. They can sense betrayal and respond to it appropriately. They know it's okay to say that someone is doing them wrong. They've never been required to choose between attachment and safety or between attachment and personal integrity. People who had good-enough care before they had language know that they deserve to be treated with fairness and respect if they've behaved in a fair and respectful manner themselves. For them, attachment and safety are bound up together in one nourishing package.

Emotionally-meaningful relationships will nonetheless have challenges and heartache, and will create both intense joy and immense confusion for people who were loved well-enough even with all of this capacity in their emotional repertoire. Life is a flawed system, this whole business of relating to one another—but it's what we've got. It's an opal in its matrix—gorgeous, ever-changing, fragile in some ways, and yet solid. Life is unpredictable (like the theft of this book when it was in embryo). Yet those loved well enough approach life and love with optimism and hope even when they've had periods of loss and pain.

Love Hurts

Very few of these capacities and beliefs have been available to you if you had less-than-adequate-experiences with primary caregivers in your childhood. If you've experienced disruptions and wounds to attachment in early life and/or abuse and neglect growing up, if one or some of your caregivers was more interested in how you were a mirror on the wall reflecting back their wonderfulness than they were in your well-being, if you could never predict how that person would respond to you from moment to moment, or if any part of this was true for you, then you were handed a completely erroneous and confusing guide to attachment, love, and connection. Emotionally-meaningful relationships feel like a million-piece puzzle, and not a fun one. Damage done by the missteps or failures of caregivers to your capacities for attachment reverberate throughout your life, particularly with regard to emotionally-meaningful relationships. For you, love often does hurt.

As I was finishing this manuscript I attended a presentation by a scientist, Regina Sullivan, who studies the brains of infant rats so as to better understand infant humans. She said something profound that made me sit up and pay attention. As she spoke about her baby rats, I had echoes reverberating through my head about the people I know who grew up with dangerous caregivers. She told the audience of trauma experts that adult caregivers control the brains of infants and small children. Adults, through their actions, regulate the brains of infants and children. Adults control temperature and access to food, and they also control what happens in the brain's attachment system by how they relate to infants and children.

Adults control the brains of infants and small children. Think about that for a moment. Consider the power of that statement. Your struggles with emotionally-meaningful relationships are not your fault or your flaw. They are the result of your newborn brain being controlled by adults who were dangerous, thoughtless, and disengaged, doing things that messed very badly with your circuitry. There are things you can do to repair those circuits. You didn't mess them up. The task of repair is not simple, and it can be done.

For you, love and connection have been equal parts longed for and terrifying, difficult and shaming. Love reveals old wounds that have never healed, even as you allow yourself to entertain the wish that this time love might heal you. Despair and hope battle it out for control of your relationship life. Each new connection, each fresh friendship, can be fraught with difficulty. Moving to a new job, a new town, or a new street is challenging because you were too preoccupied as a child by the effects of what was happening at home to be able to pay attention to social cues. You know that there are rules to the social game. When you were young, you were too busy soothing your anxiety or being depressed, dissociated, or terrified to be able to pay attention to those social rules.

Each new potential emotionally-meaningful relationship with another adult—friend, lover, or co-worker—is a new opportunity both to seek fulfillment of fantasies of finally being fully accepted or, more likely, to suffer the fear of finally being completely crushed. Even relationships with kids are hard. You worry that your daughters and sons will discover that their parent is worthless and reject you. This can make it difficult for you to set boundaries with them when they misbehave or become adolescents. Each new person who matters to you is an opportunity for you to re-enact painful patterns that seem to show up despite your best efforts to behave differently. Each new relationship loss, each misstep in connection along the way, can turn on old themes of self-criticism and shame. Each new apparent failure can become an opportunity to revisit narratives of inadequacy and self-hatred, as well as inner beliefs that no one is to be trusted no matter how nice they may seem initially.

It's hard for you to trust your judgments about other people. Sometimes you trust too much, and sometimes you trust too little. In many of your emotionally-meaningful relationships you feel a bit like a tenant on a month-to-month agreement with a landlord who won't tell you what the grounds are for eviction until you're out on the lawn with your possessions. Your inner sense that you're only there as long as the other person will put up with you creates a deep vein of anxiety under the surface of your interactions. No matter how much or how often others reassure you of their care and commitment, you look for the little cues telling you that the end is near—because you learned, before you had words, that the end of connection is always on its way. Connection and danger are neurologically wired together for you instead of connection being the thing that soothes fear. You're continuously checking the emotional weather because once a storm comes in, you believe that it's there to stay.

Being in a relationship that feels like it might be a good one looks like a scary ride that's fun for some other people but not for you. Survivors of difficult childhood attachment experiences keep wondering what the price of admission is to that ride. To be in a relationship, do you have to give up your safety, boundaries, values, and identity? Do you need to walk on eggshells or constantly apologize for being human? Do you have to ignore signals inside yourself saying that something's wrong and never voice your discomforts? Must you never be angry? Never express disappointment? Be always the mirror on the wall saying, "Yes, you are the fairest"?

You scurry, you scramble, trying to read between the lines. What feat of emotional magic or trickery do you have to perform to get this one not to leave? Not to be mean to you? Not to show you disgust or contempt? Not to get tired of you? How can you sneak some of your needs through the back door, where they won't be visible enough for this new person to see them and reject you for having them? What can you do to get this person to sometimes—though not always—because you are a realist, after all—be loving and tender to you if your spouse, respectful and decent if your friend? And if they are decent, respectful, or kind, must you tread lightly, ask little, simply be extremely grateful for what you have so that they don't realize the truth that you're too difficult, too much, and not worth it after all? Or even worse, must you cringe enough so that you're prepared for the emotional blow when they realize that you're really not worthy?

Sounds terrible, doesn't it? It's no wonder that many survivors of less-than-adequate attachment experiences find themselves giving up on the hope that they will ever experience love, care, and genuine connection with people in any realm of their lives. The perceived price of admission has been too high, paid too often, and has felt too inevitable. The pain of risking finding out that the abusive, neglectful, difficult, or disturbed adults of your childhood were right—that no one will ever love you, like you, want to hang out with you—becomes unbearable. So you exit the stage. You get a dog. You make your life smaller. You tell yourself that you can be content with this until, without warning, the possibility of love, intimacy, friendship, and connection shows up again, and you find it nearly impossible to resist hope. You get back on the ride once more, vowing to make it different this time, yet not really knowing how.

This book is about getting off that ride and getting onto a path leading toward emotionally-meaningful relationships that can work for you and be part of the process of healing your attachment wounds. **You don't have to spend your life paying a price for what happened to you when you were little.**

It's not simple to reverse the course that you were put on, but it's doable. You're already able to work hard at relationship and connection. When you were little you were doing most of the work with the grownups in your life that really was their job to do. The solutions you came up with then have gotten you this far, but they don't work very well any more in these quite different circumstances. You need help to develop capacities that will actually get you what you want. This kind of transformation can even be done inside of an existing relationship. It's not easy, yet people *can* change their covert agreements about what emotional prices they're willing to charge or to pay. You may be pleasantly surprised by how willing people are to love you, or how surprised and saddened they are that you've believed that they required a price from you.

Emotional intimacy, love, and attachment are our human birthrights. We are primates, born needing connections with others of our species. We wither and sometimes die without those connections. We count on connection to keep us safe. When we lose a deep connection, our hearts physically ache and sometimes seize up and spasm. When adults who raised you unjustly exposed their serious failures, you enter adulthood with wounds to your psyche and kinks in your wiring. Sometimes you know what those wounds are. Sometimes you only discover them when someone gets close enough to you to pull off whatever is covering them. While I was writing this book I met a woman who told me that she was unable to know the depth of her wounds until she was 50. When she finally dove in she cried for most of a year. Old wounds start to ache again when you allow someone to get close to you in the same way that old scars ache in damp weather.

This is the push-pull nature of emotional intimacy for survivors. You desire closeness because you are human. You are terrified of it because the source of your wounds has been other humans, the adults who you loved with all of your open, vulnerable, child's heart, and who in return wounded that heart repeatedly. You want connection and love. Connection and love confuse you. You think you have to live on crumbs or learn to live hungry. You're starving, so you gobble anything you can, even if it makes you ill.

You don't have to live on crumbs, and you don't have to stuff yourself until you're sick when the real thing shows up so that you can get as much as possible before it's yanked away. There's a way to get to the banquet table without paying more than everyone else sitting there and to enjoy the meal, knowing that there will be more when you're hungry again.

They fuck you up, your mum and dad.
They may not mean to, but they do.
They fill you with the faults they had
And add some extra, just for you.

Philip Larkin, *High Windows*

The abusive, neglectful, impaired, depleted, or dangerous adults who raised you taught you, by how they treated you, that there would be a price to relationships. This is because they exacted a price for your attachment to them. Their motives were many and rarely were consciously known to them. Some of them wounded you by accident and some by design.

Some of these people were, most likely, inheritors of generations of people who also had a distorted perspective on humanity and attachment. These difficult caregivers, living with their own legacies of pain, did not necessarily mean for you to suffer, too. They simply were unable or unwilling themselves to figure out how to heal from their own attachment wounds. In some instances they actually thought they were protecting you from heartache by "helping" you to become impervious or detached, to act as if you were invulnerable emotionally, to develop a cynical take on other humans, or to enter life devoid of hope, being "realistic" rather than open to possibility. These caregivers schooled you in their own wounded beliefs that the price of admission to emotional intimacy was always going to be too high. They tried, overtly and covertly, to talk you out of ever wanting it.

Some of those caregivers were too caught up in caring for their own insides, scratching their own emotional itches, to care about how you felt or what happened to you. They were too drunk, too lost in untreated mental illness, too violent or cruel or sexually perverse or self-focused, to give a good goddamn. These caregivers betrayed you and lied to you. They tricked you into thinking that they offered attachment and connection. Your small child self struggled to stay connected to them no matter what because you were human. Infants and children do their little level best to be connected to adults and to love those adults no matter what. If it only even vaguely looks and feels like attachment, infants will attach, even if what you're attaching to is itself dangerous and toxic.

Your troubled caregivers frequently gave you very specific directions, sometimes unspoken but no less clear, as to the price of admission for connection with them—connection that you absolutely required, connection that you could not choose to go without. You were required to tolerate violations of your body. You learned not to protest when they called you vile names, not to flinch when they beat you, not to ask questions when they left you alone and cold and hungry while they were on a binge, not to scream when they took you for a careening drunken drive in the car without a seatbelt, not to complain when they failed to respond to your normal childhood needs.

You had to soothe them when they were anxious, to listen while they ranted manically. You cheered them up when they were depressed. You flattered them and told them what wonderful people they were. They taught you that the only way to have connection was to give up important aspects of yourself and your safety. They taught you that there was a price that you had to keep paying and paying. Love was for rent, and the rent could be raised anytime, collected any moment. You learned to expect the unexpected. You knew that the sky *was* falling.

So it's no wonder that survivors of any form of problematic childhoods struggle with emotional intimacy. What is consistently impressive to me, as a therapist whose good fortune it has been to work with so many of you for the last 40 years, is the persistence, creativity, and hope that many survivors bring to the arena of emotionally-meaningful relationships. Thrown in with predators, you are courageous. Licking wounds and grieving, you have come into my office feeling defeated—and yet have risen up again and again. You have fought for your birthright of good-enough relationships with others. The power of the human urge to attach—to "only connect"—is profound. It's a force of nature to which I bow in respect.

The confusion you often feel when your emotionally-meaningful relationship seems to be with a decent, compassionate, not-like-your-family human being is another legacy from being raised by adults who failed miserably at the job. You ask yourself, "Is this the real thing?" And if so, what do you do with it? Is there truly no other shoe, no Lucy holding the football to pull away from you at the last nanosecond? Do these people really mean what they say? Where's the hidden agenda that you must figure out?

When not caught in a reenactment of childhood experiences, survivors frequently have no idea how to behave or what to expect. You may unconsciously start to search for small clues that tell you that this new person is, indeed, just like all the rest. You pull out familiar ways of paying for connection even as the other person wonders why you don't believe that they do, truly, want to connect with you—simply connect—with no hidden painful prices.

Like many survivors of less-than-adequate attachment experiences you hire a therapist because you find yourself somehow blowing up every relationship you're in. Or you go to therapy because you've been left behind and betrayed and sometimes abused or endangered by every emotionally-meaningful relationship that you've had, friends and lovers alike. Sometimes you have a painful pattern of getting people to leave before they leave you, controlling what feels like an inevitable process of loss. A tragic pattern of leaving the good ones behind before they "figure out who I really am" often dogs the emotional footsteps of survivors of less-than-adequate attachment experiences. The feeling of being damned no matter which choices you make can feel defeating. But being damned to loneliness feels too true for you to ignore.

Or you find yourself being used, abused, and exploited everywhere you turn. You're the one at work who finishes other peoples' projects. You're the one left to clean up the dishes after the potluck, the one nominated for the crappy jobs. You don't understand why that happens. You wonder if there's a target on your back saying, "Kick me." You end up feeling as if you're doomed to repeat the pain of your childhood. Maybe, you think, your caregivers were right. People are cruel, you'd better get used to it. But you don't want to get used to it. You don't want your caregivers to be right. So you calculate how much more of a price you're able to extract from yourself, and you try again.

All Access Pass

You don't have to live like this. I'm here to tell you that your worst fears and despair need not be true. You can have love and connection without paying prices. This doesn't mean that good-enough relationships are all rainbows and unicorns and sappy love songs. Far from it. Attachments between humans, intimate relationships, friendships, and all the permutations of how we connect, are never perfect and are sometimes obnoxiously difficult. People who are well loved and are connected with others who are well loved still have conflicts, still experience moments or days or weeks or months of emotional distance and distress, still have their share of difficult encounters, still get irritated by the other person, still end relationships or behave badly. They still lose those they love to illness or death or distance. They are not strangers to grief.

The difference is what folks who were well-enough-loved as children do with these experiences. Each problematic encounter is treated as its own thing. It's not evidence of something else or the predictor of something else that ultimately leads to a negative judgment about the self. A bad relationship with a former friend, spouse, or co-worker is simply an unpleasant experience that one hopes not to repeat. Negative encounters with others are not seen as lessons to remind people of their place in the world. They are simply what they are—one bad time with one person who perhaps turned out not to have been a very good choice. They are not evidence that one must pay a higher price simply to have someone in your life. They are just bad times.

A fight with your spouse is only what it seems to be: a fight about that pile of clothing that's left out once again, not the first sign that you're about to be abandoned because you were either the one failing to put your pile away or the one opening your mouth to indicate unhappiness with the pile. A friend or partner having a bad month isn't cause for the despairing assumption that feels truer than true that things are about to go badly from now on, or for putting yourself entirely aside to bring that person back to feeling good. It's simply the normal ups and downs of human experience. A loss is cause for sadness, not self-blame.

The reasonable emotional cost of attachment is—or should be—that sometimes we feel distress because we differ and are in conflict with one another. A reasonable cost of attachment is that sometimes we're angry with someone close to us who has behaved in a way that is not okay and that we want that person to stop acting that way. A reasonable cost, when a relationship is lost or someone dies, is that we feel grief. Grief is, in fact, one of the most powerful indicators of the presence of love. The presence of grief felt cleanly, without accompanying self-hatred or self-blame, is the evidence of love.

But the cost of attachment is not—and should not be—the requirement to get rid of your self, to make yourself small, or to make the relationship all about pleasing and soothing the other person at the expense of your own welfare. The price of connection isn't that you have to be in danger. You don't have to bargain away your safety in order to have connection. The price isn't about feeling out of control of behaviors that seem to chase other people away. Those are unfair prices, psychic loan shark prices. No longer paying those inflated and unfair prices is what this book is all about.

In these pages we will explore several things. First, we'll look at how a childhood in which you are subjected to less-than-adequate attachment experiences creates challenges to emotional intimacy for survivors. We'll consider common relationship patterns that emerge from these wounds to the psyche and look at some of the underlying neurobiology of attachment. Then we'll explore the difficult—and yet entirely possible—task of changing patterns so that you can increase your capacity to find and keep the quality of love and care that we all deserve.

None of this is simple. The terrible gift of being abused, neglected, or exploited by caregivers in your childhood is a persistent confusion that makes what's good feel dangerous and suspect and what's bad feel familiar. Change entails learning to tolerate difficult sensations and emotions, to embrace the terror of ambiguity, and to disrupt non-conscious loyalties to old family narratives about how life and love will go for you.

Been There, Done That, Have the T-Shirt

All of this is doable. I know, and not just because I've been a therapist for my entire adult life. I've been there myself. I was raised by people whose wounds affected their ability to parent well. They each carried their own emotional burdens—ones that they placed on their kids because they had no idea of how not to do so. They were not malicious. They nurtured our intellectual capacities and musical talents, and encouraged us to think critically. They gave us a strong sense of our heritage. They were civic-minded, people who gave to their communities, people who cared about social justice and the common good. They were simply hurt and impaired themselves in the realm of engendering secure attachment.

Keeping my mother emotionally regulated became the entire family's task, especially after a debilitating bout of post-partum depression put her in a psychiatric hospital when I was six-and-a-half years old. Because she never spoke of her childhood history of physical abuse, which I learned only from her mother and younger sister when I was myself an adult, and because her time in a psychiatric hospital occurred in 1959, long before the link between childhood trauma and depression was known, she never had a chance to genuinely heal. She simply got less symptomatic from being given electroconvulsive treatments.

She became avoidant, as is true for many trauma survivors, terrified of a recurrence. She threw herself into her work, which for many years protected her from her own insides. After that terrible and frightening time in her own life she did not want to ever have to be "uneasy," as she finally said to me toward the end of her life. I did my best when I was a child never to let her know anything that was troubling me if I could help it.

But when we took normal childhood risks, my mother became frightened, and my father got scared. He was what dog people call a "fear-biter." When he was scared, he symbolically bit us with his anger. My mother was everything to him, and he would do anything for her. When we failed to appreciate her caregiving efforts sufficiently, she took to her bed, more depressed—and he got mad. When she seemed to give more attention to my brother than to him, my brother became his target. When they had a bad encounter with each other, I found myself on the receiving end of his verbal abuse. He couldn't be angry with her until the very end of their lives when he was too ill to contain himself. He deflected his fear into anger, and his anger onto one of the kids. Love felt contingent on keeping the balls of my mother's happiness well-juggled.

As a psychotherapist, and as an adult who has compassion for suffering human beings, I get it. Tears of compassion for him well up in my eyes when I think about how scary this all was for him. He was only 32 with three little kids, one of them a newborn, when my mother, the love of his life, fell into her depression. He was emotionally alone in the world but for her. He was psychologically unsophisticated, lacking in self-awareness. He was a man of his time and place in the world. He tried to soothe himself when his beloved wife fell into an emotional abyss and keep his family intact.

His children were one of the means by which he soothed himself. Some of the ways he soothed himself with us were good ones. I knew the laws of thermodynamics when I was seven because I was his companion on long walks, where he taught me things that were relevant to his work as an engineer. I baked cakes because he baked cakes. I soothe myself with food because he did. "We're eaters," he would say to me when he snuck home something yummy but unhealthy.

We all tried hard in our ways, my brothers and I. We got good grades and high scores on standardized tests, we won awards and excelled in many endeavors. We could be bragged about. Ultimately it seemed that nothing was ever quite enough for them. Each of us was a child with unique desires, opinions, and imperfections. Each of us grew up, developed minds of our own and disagreed with them. Each of us has paid some prices.

The therapist I am had its beginnings in that little girl who would sit for what seemed to be forever at the table in a darkened kitchen as her mother poured out words of fear and sadness to her. My clients think I'm patient. Maybe— and both my clients and I have those two- and three-hour-long kitchen table "sessions" to thank for that patience.

So I know, not only from the work I do, but also from living my own life, that this transformation process is possible. It's not easy in any way. Anyone who tells you that you can take six simple steps and have great relationships is either deluded or lying to you. Being able to have good quality encounters with other human beings is a skill. It requires continuous practice so that the neural networks associated with love and attachment can be transformed over time from their previously well-worn grooves into new ones that aren't about trauma, abandonment, and loss. These new neural networks will be more fragile, and need more care and tending than the old ones.

The old neural networks will not be gone. They will need to be gently thanked and set aside, repeatedly, in favor of the new ones, because they will continue to attempt to assert themselves. You know that feeling you get when you can hardly stand to be in your body when you're in conflict with someone you're in an emotionally-meaningful relationship with? You know that urge to just shut down and go away and get it over with so that you don't feel like tearing your face off? That's those neural networks of your less-than-adequate attachment doing their thing in your body. They might be retired, but they haven't moved to wherever people you know go when they're not on a job any longer.

Having the relationships you deserve also requires learning to tolerate certain kinds of distress as aspects of normal life. These are feelings that, in your childhood, were usually the harbingers of something very bad about to happen. You'll have to learn to be around other people when they're unhappy and know that this is not evidence of coming doom. To stop paying unreasonable prices, you have to be willing to learn to soothe your insides while someone close to you is unhappy or even angry. You'll have to acquire the capacity to trust that the relationship will not be damaged if you do not leap into the breach and immediately make things good for everyone else. You'll have to learn to embrace ambiguity, to be able to get through not knowing what's happening and not being in constant contact with the other person. To stop paying prices you have to rediscover and rebuild your capacities to accurately assess other people. These are capacities you were born with that got messed with by damages to attachment. You need to learn to respond to your assessments of others in light of that present-day information. You'll have to stop seeing other people through the lens of your childhood. Just because someone reminds you of the father who violated you doesn't mean that this new person will, too.

A Few Words About Where I'm Coming From

Before we go much further into the "what to do about this" section of the book, here's some information about how I think about things. Empowerment is central to my theory of what makes therapy work and healing happen. Making informed decisions, and knowing the biases that this author brings to her work, are both empowering. This way you can decide if you want to take me seriously without treating me like I'm Oz the Great and Powerful.

I've been doing this work since 1970 when I got my first job at a psychiatric hospital, and I've been a practicing psychologist since 1979. I didn't consciously intend to work with trauma. When I began my practice, I didn't know my family trauma history, although I did know of my parents' distress, and I certainly knew about my heritage as an Eastern European Jew whose grandparents had fled danger. I simply knew that when I sat with people and listened carefully to their stories, histories of trauma emerged repeatedly. I fell backwards into being a trauma therapist, for which I am grateful beyond words. I'm especially thankful to the clients I worked with between 1979 and 1984, the years in which my clients were all teaching me about trauma while I flew on sheer intuition.

Today, mental health professionals know that a history of childhood trauma and/or problematic attachment experiences with caregivers—two things that frequently go hand in hand—are implicated in many of the problems that bring people to therapy. Sadly, this personal history is also the first step for some survivors on paths to incarceration, chronic illness, and shorter life expectancy. Trauma—especially childhood trauma—also brings people to the doors of 12-Step recovery programs, and to jobs as first responders and law enforcement officers, clergy, teachers, and, of course, psychotherapists. Helping professions are populated by people who learned to help others because being helpful and highly attuned to the moods of others was what kept them safe and alive.

I practice, teach, and write about feminist therapy, which is an approach that looks at people's experiences of power and powerlessness in the context of sex, gender, social class, ethnicity, sexual orientation, and other components of identity in which disempowerment and maltreatment frequently occur. I consequently believe that the problem in general is not an individual human being's flaws and errors. Rather, the problems that we all face can be found entrenched in larger systems in society that work to keep people undereducated, underemployed, and disenfranchised. These systems pit people against one another: poor Euro-American people against people of color, native-born people against immigrants, the temporarily able-bodied against people with disabilities, and on and on. My standpoint says that we are empowered when we are able to become one another's allies working toward greater equality of opportunity and resources.

Because experiences of childhood maltreatment are viewed through the lenses created by our many and intersecting components of identity, the challenges we face in creating love and connection in adult life are often flavored by those facets of self. Gender and sexuality are big players because that's where our romantic and sexual selves are expressed—but also because some of the ways in which children are given the message that there are terrible prices they must pay for admission to connection have to do directly with narratives of gender and sexuality, and with sexual abuse, or with violence against children who are gender nonconforming.

Research by psychologist Kimberly Balsam has shown that if you are lesbian, gay, bisexual, genderqueer, or transgendered you are more likely to have been a target of abuse in your family than were your heterosexual or gender-conforming siblings. If you were sexually abused you are more likely to have become sexually active too young, at a time when it was difficult for you to keep yourself sexually safe. People living with HIV are much more likely than those who don't have the virus to have a history of childhood sexual abuse. If you are a woman who was sexually abused, you are more likely to have become pregnant when you didn't want to, and to have been pregnant in adolescence. These are extraordinary prices that are placed on the bodies of some children.

Culture also plays a very large role. We all have a culture we're a part of that conveys to us what's "normal" and how life should be. Those cultures that have been the targets of systematic destruction and hatred, such as those where people have been colonized or enslaved, are ones in which despair is constantly fighting against hope. These are the cultures in which intergenerational legacies of trauma and oppression sometimes manifest themselves in less-than-adequate parenting practices because resources—both material and emotional—are scarce and so often threatened. If you were taught that people like you can't gain access to power, happiness, or safety in life, it's harder for you to know that you can have those things and not be a traitor to your group. It can be hard to see that there are people in your group who, despite oppression, have loved and parented their children well and created as much safety as possible.

While this is not universally true for cultures that have been targeted, intersections of poverty and oppression can often create families in which trauma gets handed down from generation to generation. Poor people are at greater risk of trauma from outside of their immediate relationships—more risk of police violence, environmental injustice, inadequate healthcare, and sub-standard education. These are well-established facts about disparities due to poverty. All of these factors can affect the capacity to parent well in someone who is vulnerable emotionally. None of these factors is itself a barrier to effective and loving parenting—they just make it harder.

Then there is the effect of the biology of trauma in cultures that have been collectively traumatized. To slightly change the quote from the Torah, (the first five books of the Jewish Bible), the sins *perpetrated* on the parents are often passed down to the third and fourth generations, through damaged lives and epigenetic changes. *Epigenetic changes* are changes in gene expression due to trauma exposure that are passed along to offspring. These changes have recently been found definitively both in descendants of Holocaust survivors and also in offspring of indigenous people forced into residential schools in their childhood. Bad things done to your elders changed what they biologically passed down to you.

Not surprisingly, growing up in a family system in which children must compete with one another and the adults for the apparently scarce resources of love and safety creates vulnerability to seeing the world as a place where each of us must strive alone for our needs, stepping over others if we must in order to survive. Happily, many people who grow up in such difficult families refuse to believe that this state of affairs is what they're stuck with. Thus, many social justice activists are also people who grew up in emotionally difficult families and/or in cultures with histories of oppression, genocide, and discrimination. But rarely do those folks understand that social justice includes justice for themselves. They swallow the bitter fruit of injustice in their important relationships, seeing themselves as less worthy than the people for whose rights and opportunities they labor.

I believe that you deserve justice—and we all do. By this I mean that you deserve, as much as any other human, to have fair living and working conditions in which you are not the target of exploitation, harassment, or verbal abuse—that you deserve, as much as anyone else, a safe enough world in which to live, safe enough water and air to drink and breathe, and good enough care for your body and soul. My bias is that no one gets justice by denying it to someone else. I don't think that justice is license. Justice isn't about the right to do or say whatever one wants or to harm others because one has been harmed. "An eye for an eye leaves the whole world blind."

Rather, justice is a collective endeavor. Nelson Mandela taught this to the world with his Truth and Reconciliation Commission. So don't be afraid that seeking justice for yourself is going to deprive someone else. And don't think that revenge equates to justice. Justice expands from the presence of justice, and the more of it there is the more it grows for everyone. This view of the world as having enough of the good for all of us flies in the face of what many of you learned in the families where there was a chronic scarcity of the good stuff.

Don't Know Much (Yet) About Attachment

The next part of this book is a short course on the topics of attachment and complex trauma. My goal is for you to be able to make sense of yourself and of the enduring effects of childhood maltreatment on your functioning. You don't have to take anything I say on faith. My suggestions about what to do will make more sense to you if you have the information that's informing my thinking. I'm distilling a huge amount of scientific and professional literature into shorter, more usable formats. If you'd like to check out some of my sources yourself, there is a Resources section at the end of this book that includes references, both written and online, to information that supplements what I'm writing.

Like any author writing for a general audience about the specialized knowledge of her discipline, I have picked and chosen from what I consider to be the most helpful scientific literature. However, like all fields of scientific inquiry, psychological science is constantly changing and growing. Remember when we used to pound on pillows to get rid of our anger? Then we learned that doing this only rehearsed anger, instead of dissipating it. The science of psychology and the behavioral sciences is not static. One study doesn't show us anything for sure, although it might get a lot of headlines in the media. In fact, the latest study getting those headlines was the one showing that lots of studies that once got headlines turned out to have results that couldn't be reproduced.

I have biases, and they color my choice of what I read and find helpful. There are some thinkers in the field of behavioral science with whom I entirely disagree, so I'm not citing them here. They could be right and the people to whom I listen could be wrongheaded, as could I. Simply because I like what I think doesn't make it right. I thus strongly encourage you to use your own critical thinking and judgment to evaluate what I say. Not all mental health professionals will agree with all of my opinions, and some of what I say may seem foolish to you. Although it's not my intent, some of my perspectives may violate your values. If that's the case, take what's useful and leave the rest, as people say in the 12-Step world.

Above all, know that what I write here is meant to evoke, nourish, and strengthen your own inner wisdom. In those moments when you feel stuck, see if you can find one small powerful thing you can do in that moment to change things, even a little. And you can do one small thing to get less stuck, more free, pay less of a price.

The reason why you and other survivors struggle with relationships, connection, and love is that somewhere inside of yourself you sense that these are risky situations. They were terribly risky in your childhood. You aren't wrong about that. And it's today now. It's the 21st century. What follows is not meant as a substitute for your own wisdom. Rather, it is to help that wisdom become loud enough that you listen to it when it emerges to ground you in the present day. Today can be different. Today can be a place where you do not pay the price of admission for love, connection, and attachment.

I illustrate some of the points in this book with stories, all of which are amalgams of the lives of three, four, or more people. I've changed important factors such as gender, ethnicity, sexual orientation, and age as much as possible to disguise the people who inspired those stories. Some of these people are folks whom I've met in the course of my work. Others of these are friends and colleagues. If you work with me now, or did in the past, you might recognize yourself here simply because your struggles and healing experiences have taught me a lot of what's in this book. It's you, and it's also very much not you, populating these examples.

Some Terms and Definitions

There are words I frequently use in this book. Here's what I mean by these terms.

I will refer to "adult survivors" or "survivors" to mean anyone who, as a child, was a target of maltreatment, abuse, or neglect for whatever reason. I also include in this group those persons whose experiences were more subtly abusive or neglectful. In other words, I'm including all of you whose experiences were of being raised in conditions of some degree of emotional, physical, sexual, and/or spiritual absence of safety, consistency, and quality of relatedness from your adult caregivers. These parameters of my definition make you a very heterogeneous group of people, with a range of challenges in your life. Ultimately, these distinctions aren't as important as what you share, which involved the experience of not being adequately cared for, of not having good-enough attachment, of being not safe-enough emotionally and/or physically in childhood, as well as the reality of knowing that at your core, you have had little to no experience with safe, consistent, and secure attachment and connection.

When I refer to "emotionally-meaningful relationships," I am referring to the range of relationships in which people are emotionally open to and vulnerable with one another. These relationships may be romantic or sexual, and they need not be; an intimate relationship can be with a friend, with a spiritual advisor, with a mentor, or with your yoga teacher. What is core to this construct is that these are relationships in which we can risk being seen and known, and in which all humans—both survivors and others—play out lessons learned in early life about love and attachment.

The Book of Love Is Long and Boring

So why one more book about how to have relationships? Excellent question, dear reader. After all, there are hundreds and hundreds of books about how to have relationships, and at least a few that I think are excellent and science based. I have included those in the Resources section at the end of this book. So I, too, wondered, "Why one more book?" I re-read hundreds of pages of relationship advice founded in the best psychological science, hoping to get a break from this self-imposed writing assignment. Maybe someone had covered the topic, and I could find a better use for my time than sitting in front of a computer for another thousand or so hours.

It turns out that most of what is written about relationships assumes certain emotional knowledge and capacities. These are skills that are extremely difficult for many survivors to access. The person who I consider to be today's best thinker about the role of attachment in relationships is Sue Johnson. She wrote *Hold Me Tight* and is one of the creators of emotion focused therapy (EFT) for couples. She gets closest to the particular concerns of people with complex trauma and other experiences of childhood maltreatment. But according to my best experts—my clients—she doesn't get quite close enough. *Hold Me Tight* is a book for everyone, not only survivors. There's not a focus on being survivors of really awful childhoods trying to have relationships.

The absence of focus on your specific problems can leave survivors at risk of feeling once again like failures. You decide that you're incompetent in the domain of relationships because you can't easily follow advice and prescriptions that are helpful for folks who were well-enough loved. Sometimes an excellent book about relationships can feel shaming. Let's start where you are. You're a survivor, paying high prices to be in relationships and not knowing how to apply all the great advice in the other books. Let's take a look at how you got here, so that you can find your way out of the tunnel of not-love. Giving up on paying the unfair price of admission to connection and love means that you have to learn to live radically in the present. This is a challenge for survivors because so many of you live relationally in the past. So let's explore how to get back into the time machine and be here, now.

CHAPTER 2
Time Passages

"Well it's just now and then, my line gets cast into these time passages."

Al Stewart

Our Inner Time Travelers

My colleagues Kathy Steele, Onno van der Hart, Suzette Boon, and Ellert Nijenhuis, all scholars of complex trauma and dissociation, have written eloquently about how children in appallingly impossible and dangerous situations learn to survive by separating themselves into discrete and disconnected pieces. They describe the development of what they call the "apparently normal part of the personality," or ANP. The ANP is the mask that survivors wear comfortably in superficial—and emotionally not particularly meaningful—interactions in the world, performing tasks like going to school or work. They differentiate ANPs from "emotional parts of the personality," or EPs. These are the parts of self that are frozen like a fly in amber in the emotions, perceptions, and experiences of the past. EPs are the places you go to when you say to yourself that you're feeling "little," when you berate yourself mercilessly, when you seem unable to stop being flooded with overwhelming emotions that you know are larger than what is happening now but cannot scale back. EPs are the expressions of the neural networks formed by less-than-adequate attachment experiences in childhood. You didn't make them up. They grew in place to help you survive your earliest years.

EPs run a big percentage of survivors' relational lives. They show up in emotionally-meaningful relationships full of predictions and certainties about how you'll be perceived and treated by others, and what you have to do. Or they'll notice things and shut you up because they believe that if, like the child in the story, they say "The emperor has no clothes," bad things will happen and relationships will end. When your primary consciousness in a given moment derives from being swept up in the flood of an EP, you are no longer your adult self. You are transported back in time to your unhappy or dangerous childhood. Survivors' relationships with people in their lives are governed largely by their EPs, the young parts of you who believe that there are always prices—and sometimes very high ones—to pay for any kind of connection.

While everyone can feel a little young or internally disconnected, the phenomenon of having ANPs and EPs is pronounced and problematic for people who've experienced attachment trauma. This division of self is sharpest for people whose response to being subjected to the very worst kinds of childhood horror has been to develop dissociative identity disorder (DID—formerly known as multiple personality disorder) in order to survive. The ANPs and EPs of the person living with DID are often so separated from one another that they take over conscious control of the body without other parts having a conscious awareness of what has happened. The costs of DID can get very high, especially when an EP acts in ways that are markedly incongruent with the apparent age and values of the body that the EP inhabits. But it is more common than not for survivors who do not have DID to also have this divided—and sometimes disorganized—sense of self that sends them time-traveling emotionally.

For example, your best friend seems distracted and distant when you get together for coffee. Your be-a-friend ANP, which walked you in the door, starts to fade in the presence of the faint hints of distressed emotion wafting off your friend. You quickly begin to feel panicky. Even though you'd been looking forward to seeing her to share your latest struggles and successes, you find a way to make yourself scarce and leave earlier than planned with an excuse of some work project. An EP has been evoked by your friend's demeanor and has taken you back in time to your relationship with the mother who repeatedly told you what a "selfish jerk" you were for interrupting her angry diatribes about your father. The "take-care-of-other-people's-feelings" EP, which slipped in and took over the experience, thus "knew" that your friend was feeling that way about you. Why else would she be distracted and distant, the mood states that were the usual prelude to your mothers' screeds against you?

After weeks of shame-filled avoidance and unanswered voicemails from her later, you finally find out that you met your friend for coffee after she had awakened that morning to a leak in her roof that had ruined her favorite chair and that she was feeling badly about how distracted she was with you. You want to believe her. That's the kind of person you know her to be—at least, your ANP knows that about her. Decent, caring, taking responsibility for herself, that's your friend. Yet you're still not entirely sure that her mood didn't have something to do with you. Your EPs are the ones in charge of relationships. After all, you (aka your EP) say to yourself, if that was happening, she needed you to listen to her, and you weren't. You were prattling on and on about yourself—and back in time you travel. The fact that she's apologizing to you for being distracted and distant doesn't matter much, yet. The EP and its neural networks grow stronger when we rehearse those narratives once again.

EPs can be unfrozen from the past. They can be transformed and integrated into a more whole self that lives mostly in the present. At this point some of you are protesting the notion of radical present-time living—particularly those of you who grew up in chaotic, unpredictable households and thus became the masters of careful advance planning, owners of the *Worse Case Scenario Handbook*, and experts in the use of Excel spreadsheets, *Getting Things Done* systems, and various other types of organizational devices. "Don't we have to plan for the future? See under ant/grasshopper, anticipating disaster, being prepared, past as prologue, etc., etc."

Take a deep breath, little ants. I'm not saying not to be thoughtful nor to skip making plans about things over which you have control and choice. I'm not saying not to put money in the 401K if you can, or not to have an earthquake/hurricane/tornado kit or six months of income in the bank if you can, or not to back up your important documents in different places. Those are all things that adequately-attached people do. It's wise to make choices today so that you can be as materially safe as possible in the future.

But survivors of childhoods in one of the circles of hell have learned to assume that emotional life is full of interpersonal earthquake/hurricane/tornados coming, if not every second, then right around the corner. All emotional weather is dangerous weather. That was your life when your deep non-conscious understanding of human beings was forming. You grew up in the disaster zone. You haul out survival kits at the first vibration of the emotional earth, the first sighting of a cloud in the relational sky, or the first breath of interpersonal wind in the trees. You stop looking at what's happening now—a large truck going by, a normal rainstorm, a slightly more-energetic-than-usual breeze—and go directly into disaster survival mode. Your friend's distracted and distant mood feels like a warning that you're about to be ditched for the sin of wanting attention. For you it's not what it is, which is simply information about another human having a less-than-wonderful day happening in close proximity to you.

You come to these conclusions *not* because you are selfish and self-centered and think it's all about you. (I heard some of you starting to think that.) Far from it. You see yourself as so disposable that you cannot begin to imagine that other people in your life would care if you weren't there. In your own mind, you're an irritant, a supplicant—not a desired and valued equal.

This all makes perfect sense for *then*. *Then*, the place in space and time where you were a child, was a series of disaster movies. Once you had that figured out, you created your emotional disaster survival kit and used it constantly. One of the terrible legacies of growing up in an emotional fault zone or tornado alley is that it then becomes difficult to see that you might not be living there any longer. Your EPs inhabit that disaster zone. They have difficulty recognizing the milder and more temperate climes of the present. You're wonderful in a crisis because you've been experiencing a lot of life as a crisis since the emotional hurricanes of your childhood world.

Often when life is calm and good, you can't recognize it for what it is. Sometimes you perplex yourself by finding yourself stirring up the winds so that you can be back in a familiar emotional weather system. "Everything was going so well. Why did I have to go and do that?" Your EPs developed in the context of problematic attachments offered to you by the adults who raised you. Lessons learned that young are powerful, but they don't come with language. Consequently, those lessons, although powerful and controlling of your choices, often make no sense. They simply feel right, deep in your neurons where they are encoded. You feel as if survival depends on behaving in this way. So you repeatedly do what was smart in the past, but is a problem for people in your life today.

Or you might be the person whose disaster survival kit consisted of a blindfold and earplugs—"Wake me up when it's over." You notice that you can't tell that you're back in a disaster zone until the hurricane has blown the roof off and the storm surge has flooded your house. Then, and only then, you notice that you've been cold, wet, and blown around emotionally for a long time. You were so exhausted by the chronic danger in your childhood that you became numb to it unless and until it ratcheted up to life-threatening proportions. Your little central nervous system couldn't tolerate being activated into terror that often, so you became able to go from numb to terrified in a split second.

Today, you don't let yourself know that things really are bad when they are. Then when you get it, you go into hyper-alert mode. You go from zero to one thousand in the blink of an eye, which disconcerts you and the people you're trying to relate to. This pattern also makes it even more difficult to accurately assess what's happening in the here and now because your system is flooded with stress hormones. This flooding makes it very difficult to engage the thinking parts of your brain.

I Gotta Get Out of This Place

Joe's story exemplifies the "Get it over with, it's only going to end anyhow" storyline of wounded attachment. He was about to marry the love of his life. "So why am I thinking about going out and cheating on him," he asked, sitting in his therapist's office with his head in his hands, his shoulders hunched in a posture of shame. "He's the best thing that ever happened to me. He loves me, he understands my moods and doesn't take them personally. His family loves me. If I go out and fuck this new guy I met at that workshop, they're all going to hate me. Why am I throwing this all away to get laid?"

Joe's ANP and even a few of his EPs knew that his fiancé, Soren, was a wise choice in the present. Soren had been raised with relatively secure attachment, and he had the wisdom and compassion necessary to see through Joe's own painful emotional storms and not personalize them or see their relationship as doomed to fail.

Soren also had boundaries, a bottom line, and a realistic view of the man he loved. He knew that Joe had been repeatedly unfaithful to partners before they met, leaving a trail of destroyed relationships and angry exes behind him. So when their relationship looked like it was getting serious, he had given Joe the bottom line—"No sexual cheating." Joe consequently knew without having to guess or mind-read that to cheat was to damage the relationship badly— perhaps terminally. There were many other things Joe could do that would be hard on Soren, but none of them were firing offenses.

Joe's EPs were in a state of panic as the wedding day approached. They were waiting for the proverbial other shoe to drop and attempting to take charge by pulling that shoe down first and doing the one thing that Soren had clearly stated to be a deal-breaker. Those young emotional parts of Joe could not believe that the cost of Soren being loving and committed to him was as simple as Joe being sexually faithful. There had to be a catch, somewhere.

Joe had learned that there had always been a catch, being raised by a father with untreated bipolar disorder and a streak of meanness. His father's moods and rules seemed to change with the weather and the level of neurotransmitters in his synapses. The anxiety of waiting for the inevitable can sometimes generate behaviors that ensure that it will happen. Joe had learned as a child that if he provoked his father when the rage was just beginning to build, the beatings would be shorter and less energetic. Plus, he would feel a sense of control. Those days, he thought he knew why his dad was hitting him.

Joe could feel himself on the verge of provoking an outcome again. He loved Soren, and was terrified of losing him. But because he was certain, deep inside of himself, that he would lose Soren someday, his EPs were "helping" him. Their goal was to get the loss over with before Joe had more time and love sunk into the relationship, and more grief to anticipate.

Of course, none of this loss, grief, and misery was truly inevitable. It's not for you—if this is your story—and not for Joe. Joe had done enough therapy and other healing work at this point that he was able to identify and interrupt his EPs' activities and get himself into the present. He developed a relationship safety plan to protect himself from soothing his anxiety by getting anywhere close to having sex with this new man. (We'll discuss relationship safety plans in detail later in this book.) He planned to spend more time painting, which he had learned would calm him down and reduce anxiety, and less time sitting in front of his computer scanning social media, which dysregulated him. He made a commitment to himself to avoid seeking opportunities to meet or talk with the other man, and he deleted the new guy's contact information from all of his devices. He unsubscribed from the dating app that he had loaded onto his phone several months earlier when he was telling himself that he was "Just curious about what all my single friends were talking about." He told himself the truth.

Joe also asked Soren to attend a session with him and told him what was going on. Soren was upset, and yet also glad that Joe had stopped at the point of only thinking about cheating. He was mostly angry that Joe had tried to blow up their relationship, and he refused to cooperate with him on that project. Soren reminded Joe that he could think anything he wanted so long as he never had sex with anyone else. "I didn't ask you not to have thoughts or feelings about having sex with another guy. That's unreasonable, and crazy and impossible. I told you never to act on it if you wanted me as your mate. That's reasonable, and it's an agreement we both have to keep."

Joe had to stay firmly in the present, listen carefully to the specifics of what Soren was saying, and remind himself repeatedly that Soren was Soren and not his father. When upset with Joe, his father would arbitrarily withdraw or withhold things from him on the grounds that he had broken some rule that he had never heard about until that moment.

This profound commitment to present-time living is at the core of many of the strategies we'll discuss for having the quality of love and attachment that you want and deserve. To stop paying the price of admission to love and connection, you need to be able to differentiate between the past and now, between the family you grew up in and the adult world of connection and attachment that you're endeavoring to live in today. There are a variety of methods for staying as firmly in the present as possible that we'll explore later.

Don't You Ever Feel Like You're Less Than

Notice, carefully, that I do not—and never will—suggest to you that you can or should achieve perfection. It's particularly important to underscore that point for survivors. For many of you, your relationship to your own imperfection has frequently been less than loving and compassionate. **Perfection is impossible and unattainable**, not because you are damaged or incompetent or whatever self-hating label you've put on yourself.

It's impossible and unattainable because you are human. If you're not sure (and I've met quite a few survivors, particularly those who were targets of childhood abuse and neglect, who weren't entirely sure that they were human), you can send in your DNA to one of those places that'll test it, but I'd wager my entire retirement savings that the results will come back at least 99% homo sapiens (maybe a little bit Neanderthal if your family came from Northern Europe or Denisovian if your heritage is Asian). I'm only slightly joking here. Because some of you were not treated as a human ought to be, you grew up unsure that you were human.

Humans learn by falling down and getting back up and then falling down and getting up again. Have you ever watched a baby learn to stand up and walk? It's a good thing that we're so close to the ground and so well padded when we're little.

In her lovely book, *The Gifts of Imperfection,* Brené Brown discusses the value of embracing the reality that we are truly human. I have learned from you telling me about your attempts to read it that this simple book can be very hard for survivors to read, beginning with the title. You've been led to believe that the reason your childhood was so painful was that you were imperfect in ways that were intolerable for the adults who raised you. Falling down and getting up was not seen as normal, but as some kind of major problem for your caregivers. You can see no gifts in being flawed, only risk and sorrow and disruptions to connection.

Yet embracing imperfection, living life in the full humanity of yourself, is absolutely necessary for living a life without a knot in your gut. It's a secret that people who were raised with good-enough attachment know, one that allows them to feel safe-enough even during difficult times in their relationships with others. The secret's out. You can know this, too. Humans are inherently not A+ students. We are inherently average. We sometimes fail. And that's okay, it's fine; it's really safe-enough more of the time than not.

One of the terrible and untruthful emotional lessons of growing up as you did is that you came to believe that you had to be perfect. Perfection was necessary so that the bad stuff would stop happening, or the good stuff might show up again. You would try and try, and when whatever you were doing seemed not to work, you tried and tried again. You had only a few strategies to choose from because less-than-good attachment leads to less flexibility and more difficulties with expanding past the one or two strategies that occasionally did work when you were young. Failures of apparent perfection had painful and sometimes dangerous consequences for you.

Often you hit despair and gave up after too many allegedly failed attempts, having developed the learned helplessness that is common in the lives of many survivors. Learned helplessness is the psychological result of being trapped and unable to change your painful situation, no matter what you do. You figured out that you could do nothing that would work, so you stopped. You may have adopted a stance of never trying at all because you told yourself that there was no point. But all along you were given—directly or otherwise—a model of aspiring to perfection. You were handed a paradigm telling you that if only you could do (fill-in-the-blank) correctly, then your father wouldn't violate you sexually, or your mother wouldn't scream at you, or you wouldn't dread coming home from school wondering what would be happening in the house. If you could be perfect, you would be okay. You would be safe, maybe, if only for a little while.

It was a terrible, powerful lie—the lie that any of this had to do with how or who you were or weren't. It was a lie that if you had only been perfect, you would be loved enough, safe enough, attached enough. You should have been afforded all of the love, safety, and attachment any human infant deserves simply by virtue of showing up on the planet. The notion that safety must be earned is a lie. The notion that you must sacrifice safety in order to have attachment is a terrible lie, a toxic and dangerous lie.

Here's the truth. What was happening to you when you were little had nothing to do with any real or imagined failures on your part. No matter that some or all of the adults in your life were telling you, both directly and indirectly, that you were indeed the problem. **You were not the problem—I promise.** Children are supposed to be difficult, selfish, fearful, needy, demanding, out-of-control, messy, snot-nosed, oppositional, disruptive. **All of those things are true about children.** They are just fine, okay, normal things about being a child, not descriptions of something wrong or of intolerable imperfection.

In fact, these are all things that are true to some degree about humans at all stages of our lives. Good-enough parents aren't thrilled when their kiddo displays one of these behaviors. And they don't stop talking to them for years, beat them up, abuse them verbally, use them sexually, withhold food or medical care, keep them from going to school, or leave them in a so-called timeout for two weeks when they're not thrilled with what the kid just did. They supply logical consequences mixed with compassion and sometimes, a little humor. They convey to their kid that she or he is still loved, always loved, and safely attached.

But your EPs don't know that you're not the problem. They have no understanding of the fact that imperfection is the human condition, and that children are childlike. They are frozen in the past, where lying rules were treated like the truth. Bringing your EPs out of their frozen past state and into the present requires living by new rules. **The first of those is that perfection is impossible for all human beings.**

I know I'm being scary to some of you now, saying these things. I promise I'm not trying to be frightening, and this is not dangerous. I am certain of this fact—as certain as that the earth is round and water is wet. Take a deep breath. Read on.

By qualifying my statements about what is possible I am also not saying, "You, damaged person, you can get some of this good stuff, but not all of it, so be grateful for what you can get." That's your EP experiencing me through the old distorted lens of "She's just being nice now, but really she knows that I'm worthless."

Not so. What I'm really saying is the opposite of what you fear I'm saying. **I'm saying that having the good stuff is as possible for you as for anyone else, since no one gets a perfect version of love and connection.** To get the good stuff, the real stuff, or to see that it's already here, you've got to make deep changes within yourself and your view of how to operate in the world. You can start by giving up perfection as a goal.

These last two sentences might sound unfair or like I'm blaming you for your difficulties in relationships. That's your EP speaking again, dear reader. Notice how quickly those EPs latch onto comments about you and swoop you down the wormhole of time, back to the lying rules of the family system where they were formed. So let me offer additional clarity about my purpose in saying that you will need to change. You will need to change your relationship to yourself. It sucks, and there it is. The answer is not in finding Mr/Ms Right, or in never having friendships, or in contenting yourself with superficial and meaningless connections, or in trying ever harder. Unlike *The X-Files*, the truth is *not* out there. It's here, in you. Here's the map to the treasure.

You've Got to Carry That Weight

The truth is that the power to heal and transform is within each of us. You have the power to make your life become closer to what you want, closer to your dreams and imaginings. You can get help turning that power on from therapists, spiritual leaders, communities, friends (both human and otherwise), from a divine being if you believe in one, from art or music or martial arts, from anyone or anything that reminds you of your inherent worth. It may take years of healing work to activate that power. It's not like in the movies where people get fixed in one powerful, cathartic session (there's a reason why that's called fiction, folks). You're going to spend those years on the planet anyhow, so why not spend them taking back as much of your innate capacities for love and connection as you are able?

Ultimately, no matter where or from whom you get help and support, the power to transform your life is yours as an adult, and it *is* available to you. This isn't always good news to people who have had to shoulder emotional responsibilities long before they should have. More than 20 years ago, a woman with whom I was working forcefully and vociferously objected to my alleged good news about her power within by reminding me that she was sick and tired of being the responsible one, and she was ready for someone to be responsible for her. She had grown up in a family that trafficked its children for labor and prostitution. Some of her earliest memories were of taking care of even younger children's wounds after an adult had done terrible things to them. She had often gone hungry. Her body had been repeatedly violated and harmed. She had been the one who helped her younger siblings to escape into a pretty good foster family. She had been responsible. No one had ever really been responsible for her in any kind of deep or emotionally-meaningful way.

She taught me that before we embrace the power to change our lives as adults, it's sometimes necessary to spend time creating the space to grieve the theft of the opportunity to be a cared-for, safe child in the arms of adults who were responsible to and for you. She, and some of you, too, had never had that. The adults who raised her were dangerous and criminal, the worst of the worst. That grief, which surprised her with its size and force, was a prerequisite to her finally celebrating her ability to be responsible to and for herself. If you're where she was right now, you may at times find this book difficult to read because I will continue to invite you to find that internal power and capacity. Like her, you may need to spend some time to be angry and sad about what was stolen from you before you can reach toward the present. You might want to read the chapter about grief first, and come back to the rest of the book later.

Here's my commitment to you as we explore this painful territory together. **I will never, ever blame you for your wounds. I will never, ever say that you are at fault for the difficult encounters you have had in your attempts to find connection and love. I *will* ask you to look at your part in things because that's where your power lies—in seeing yourself with compassionate eyes and making changes. I will not ever blame you.** I'm not sugarcoating things because I am committed to telling you the truth.

This is what I know to be true. You're not the source of your problems. You're not helpless to change things now. You were helpless with regard to the emotional miseducation you received about attachment and connection. You were helpless about how your neural networks of attachment were formed and distorted. **You're not helpless now**. Today, as an adult, you have power that is never available to children. You have choices today that no child has.

I *will* ask you to examine your part of your difficult interactions. I will do so only so that you can better understand the effects of your early wounds. The goal is not to rub your nose in your missteps, but to be empowered to make choices that give you more of the outcomes you desire and deserve. We cannot change what we cannot see. We are unable to transform that for which we feel no responsibility. You are not the problem in your life. You are, however, the solution to that problem. This book is an attempt to place some power in your hands so that you are more able to get more of the life you deserve.

Here's what is fundamentally true for me. I stand here in awe of your courage, your persistence, and your willingness. I also stand here to say that the power to change your difficult dynamics with other people well enough, imperfectly enough, is in your hands—in the hands of a creative, persistent, courageous, luminous human being. That would be you, dear reader. I'm sure of it. You have stumbled and fallen, as has every human. You have not yet learned, perhaps, to look at that stumbling and falling and skinned emotional knee with compassion. Know that it is with the eye of compassion that I approach you in this book. This means that I do not judge what you do when you struggle and fall. I am curious about it, about how you fall and how you have gotten back up so that you, too, can be curious and creative. I am willing to describe what I've seen and to place your difficulties into the context of what was done to you when you were little so that you make sense to yourself, as you make sense to me.

As Leonard Cohen writes, "We mostly fall, we mostly run…and every now and then we try…to heal the damage that's been done." We do damage not because we are evil. We do it by accident. We fall into people, we bruise them emotionally, because we are full of humanity. And you're trying to heal those wounds rather than blame them on the person you fell into. That's a very big thing that sets you apart from the people who failed in caring for you when you were little.

I could probably stop right here. The rest of this book truly is commentary. Cohen has captured the essence of being human and the perils of striving toward connection. He has also famously said, "There is a crack in everything—that's where the light gets in." All humans, survivors and not, are full of these cracks, of that humanity. Kintsugi is the Japanese art of repairing broken pottery with gold. The cracks make the pottery more beautiful and more valuable. Taking back your life from childhood trauma and having relationships that nourish you means presenting yourself to the world as a piece of kintsugi, not as a damaged vessel. I invite you to see your cracks, not as your ugliness or damage, but rather as the place from which your light can be seen, the places where the gold of your healing process shines.

CHAPTER 3

Aching Broken Hearts

"All you need is love."

John Lennon

Humans are primates. This short sentence sums up in a few words why attachment is central to our development. Being a primate explains why wounds to attachment and relationship are so powerful and long lasting for us. Primates are with rare exceptions intensely social creatures. Among primates, humans are some of the most social. Our chief rivals for this position are our genetically closest relatives, the bonobos, who spend much of their time nurturing relationship through friendly and sexual touch. Infants of many species are strongly biologically driven to seek attachment to adults at birth. Humans appear to be among the most driven of all species where attachment and connection are concerned.

Humans are hardwired from birth to seek connection with others of our species and with species that relate to us, such as dogs. Being connected gives us feelings of safety and comfort. It allows the developing infant brain to calm down in moments of fear. Attachment soothes pain, so much so that we feel pain less when we are in physical touch with, or even close proximity to, someone to whom we are attached.

In the absence of connection, or when that connection is disrupted early in our lives, we struggle to survive. There's a reason why it's considered a form of torture to subject a human to isolation from others—why solitary confinement in prisons leads to severe psychological distress. Humans are all "people who need people."

We humans are also dependent in our attachments to caregivers for much longer than any other primate, or perhaps any other species on the planet. Only female elephants and certain species of whales appear to remain as connected to their parents as humans. The evolution of the human species over millions of years created creatures with very large brains that are not fully formed at birth. Because of this long post-natal period of brain development, human infants and children require care from the adults that is unmatched in length by any other species. This necessary long period of dependency allows our large brains to fully develop, and thus engenders all of the things that make us human—language, art, science, abstract thought, spirituality.

Research on brain development indicates that human brains—particularly that part of the brain that makes us most human, our orbital prefrontal cortex—do not finish developing until our mid-20s. Brain development is massively affected by the quality of attachment experiences offered to us by our adult caregivers. The care we do or don't receive creates neural networks that inform how we understand attachment and relationships. In the absence of adequate attachment, some neural networks wither, and others grow.

As human children we *need* adults in our lives to care for us and to put our welfare first until we are able to fend somewhat for ourselves. It's not a want. It's a need, like air, water, and food. Human children need adults to feed us, keep us warm or cool enough, educate us in the ways of relating to other humans, teach us how to protect ourselves, and to assess risk in physical, moral, spiritual, and interpersonal realms. The part of our brains that tells us we're in danger, the amygdala, doesn't even start to function until humans are six months old. Until that time we are 100 percent dependent on the adults around us to know when we're in danger and keep us safe. This job of protecting the young of our species is one of the few things that most students of human behavior will agree on as being completely hardwired into humans by evolutionary forces.

In *Your Turn for Care*, I described this required relationship between adults and children as the human "contract for care." It is the unspoken rule of species survival. Humans cannot give birth and walk away in a week or two, or a year or 10 years. We have to do more for our young than keep them fed. Adults must do some very specific things for the infant brain to develop to its full capacities and for the new human to live long enough to keep the species going. Adults must relate. They must attend to the child, interact with the child, teach the child how to put words to emotional experiences, and model how to manage vulnerability. They must teach the child how to trust and when to be suspicious. They must train children to become members of the human tribe, to know the rules by which humans play.

Love You and Lose Again

If you are a survivor, you were raised by people who were impaired in some way in their ability to engage in this most important human task. They broke the contract for care. They did not make you central. Perhaps they exploited your normal childhood vulnerability to believing what adults say. Maybe they took advantage of you needing comfort and connection even though the one to whom you had to go for that comfort was scaring or hurting you. Or they simply were unable to show up for the task of giving you the attachment experiences that you needed because they were themselves too affected by emotional distress, physical illness, and/or inadequate resources.

At the same time that they were breaking this basic human contract for your care, they were simultaneously teaching you that it was your job to keep your relational agreements with them as well as others. They expected loyalty from you even when they hadn't any to you. They taught you that you had to pay a price to be in relationships by exacting prices from you that children can't pay without suffering damage to their developing senses of self and capacities to be in relationships of any kind.

The rules of relating to other humans have thus been a continuing source of confusion for you. You haven't wanted to be like the adults who raised you. You knew intuitively that they had committed violations of core human tasks and values. You wanted to be someone who could be counted on: loyal, committed, engaged, and decent. So you haven't known that it's okay to say "enough already" or "no." You haven't been able to figure out that you don't have to be the only person holding up the bargain in a relationship. You don't quite grasp why it's perfectly moral to drop your end when other people drop theirs. You've overridden your inner warning signals too many times and trusted people who were dangerous to you. Or you're on the other end of the spectrum, thinking that you hear a tsunami warning when it was just the siren of a distant ambulance going by, and you've kept people at a distance in order to feel even a little bit safe. You haven't known when to say "enough, already." You haven't known how to be safely connected.

Like a Bird on a Wire

There are several other hardwired human phenomena that give infants the best possible chance for the lengthy period of brain maturation to take place. One of these is sheer cuteness, what scientists refer to as "neoteny." Big eyes, chubby cheeks, big round heads—all of the things that make kittens, puppies, infants (and Mini Cooper cars) adorable—are there for an evolutionary purpose. Humans are generally irresistibly drawn to this combination of features. We want to coo over and cuddle the creature exhibiting them. We start to respond this way while we're still little ourselves. Remember times you've seen a toddler relating this way to an infant?

Thus, when the little owner of those features hasn't stopped crying for what seems like forever, or has just thrown up on your favorite shirt, or has broken a precious piece of art that you forgot to place out of reach, your initial reactions of anger and aggression are normally quickly quelled by how cute the crying, throwing up, not-yet-coordinated creature who's doing these things is. Neoteny protects little creatures from adults' worst impulses. Normally, non-infant humans simply cannot resist being good to little, round, big-headed, big-eyed creatures. As one of my friends once said of her daughter who was very much in the stage of saying "no" to her at every possible moment, "If they weren't so cute we'd have to kill them. But we don't, of course."

Notice "normally." In the families where you grew up, this human norm was often violated. One or more of the adults who had the responsibility for your care when you were little were inhumanly impervious to neoteny, or were so impaired in their capacities that they were unable to respond consistently in the evolutionarily correct fashion to your normal infant and child behaviors and needs. Or they sexualized your cuteness. They mistook their arousal for an invitation from you to behave in ways that children never wish to act. Kids flirt, but for cuddles and affection, never for sex. These adults' impairment had consequences for you then. Their errors continue to reverberate today in your wounded understanding of what makes relationships happen.

The Closer I Get to You

As it turns out, the Beatles were close to right about love being all we need. Humans need love and connection in order to survive. We need it delivered in healthy ways and regular doses in order to thrive. Survivors learn the terrible prices of admission to relationships because they're given problematic experiences with the attachment system. The attachment system is the next basic evolutionary strategy for developing the human brain. An entire rich and complex body of research in behavior and neuroscience has grown up in the last 70 years around this phenomenon, culminating in attachment theory (AT).

Attachment theory chronicles the ways in which humans learn about relationships and develop relational self-concepts and paradigms. We do this through experiences of connection and disconnection with the people who care for us when we are small. When caregivers respond appropriately to infants and behave in ways that are good-enough (a concept first named by one of the founding thinkers of AT, Donald Winnicott), infants develop a sense of the world and others in it as safe and of themselves as good.

Healthy attachment assists in the development of the brain, particularly the orbital prefrontal cortex where much of our ability to regulate emotion is situated. It gives us a solid foundation for becoming functional humans. Attachment systems are interpersonal ones, so attachment happens in the space between the infant and the caregiver. Attachment systems are also neurological ones. There are specific places in human brains that are responsible for wiring in attachment as it's happening.

Because their caregivers are human and thus imperfect, infants also learn that even the best caregiver will not always meet a need or understand a communication. Good-enough isn't the same as perfect. When these missteps and missed communications occur, as they inevitably will, the good-enough caregiver repairs the breach in a way that communicates love and care to the infant. Good-enough caregivers don't blame or shame the infant. They do assist children in distinguishing between "me" and "not-me." Children need to hear, "Daddy didn't understand that you were thirsty. I'm sorry, sweetie. Here's that sippy cup." Not, "Goddamn it, how was I supposed to know that you were thirsty? Shut up!"

Infants who are well-enough cared for begin to understand that they are not the caregiver and the caregiver is not them. They realize that's okay, because even in these moments of misses, the caregiver is still as present and available as is humanly possible. In disconnection there is reconnection. The caregiver will do her or his best to meet the child's needs and fulfill the contract for care. The caregiver isn't ashamed or self-hating for having been imperfect, and isn't punishing the child for exposing his or her completely human inability to read the mind of someone who is at best barely verbal yet.

Many of us have seen (and some of you have been) the adult holding a crying baby, soothingly saying, "I don't know what you want, sweetie. Are you hungry?" (offering a source of nourishment, then when that does nothing for the distress, sniffing) "No, okay not a stinky diaper. Okay, maybe you just need me to hold you. Let's go for a little walk while I sing to you" (draping baby over shoulder or in baby-carrying device, singing favorite alt-rock song slightly off-key to baby thereby creating a permanent association between love and Smashing Pumpkins). If that caregiver becomes depleted, as any caregiver of an infant inevitably will, in a good-enough situation that caregiver has others on whom to call for support. In the good-enough family the caregiver can safely hand off the infant to another trusted adult and get a chance to replenish their resources.

It's hard and frequently sleep-deprived work to be the caregiver of small humans. Small humans don't communicate clearly. Their emotions are entirely unregulated. They poop their pants. They get on an airplane with us and wail loudly throughout the entire 10-hour flight. This may be why, prior to the isolating effects of industrialization on the family, humans, like our primate relatives, mostly raised their young in groups where care was shared among many adults. It's become a cliché to say that it takes a village to raise a child. Yet that's how humans best support caregivers to give quality connections to our young.

In such moments when the needs of infants, while met neither perfectly nor instantly, are treated with love, respect, and reasonable calm, infants learn about attachment and relationships. They begin to grow the neural networks of good-enough attachment that make emotionally-meaningful relationships easier later in their lives. Infants learn that the caregiver is not "me," because their needs aren't met perfectly. They learn that their needs do matter. Babies also learn an equally important lesson: that the differences between infant and caregiver don't undermine safety or take away the chance of eventually having its needs met well-enough. The caregiver is striving to be relatively calm (not perfectly!) as much of the time as possible, and continues to explore ways to meet the baby's needs until a resolution is achieved and everyone feels somewhat better (or falls asleep, exhausted).

Good-enough caregivers also model regulation of their own distressed states, and create emotional attunements with infants that are wordlessly reassuring and centering. Infants, as noted above, feel less pain when being held by their caregivers. Babies do better getting their immunization shots if one of the adults who loves them is holding them. The infant feels the adult feeling calm-enough, which is calming to the infant, which calms the adult, which calms the infant, round and round in a lovely synergy.

Your Love Will Shelter Me

Attachment research tells us that even children born with anxious, reactive, or fearful temperaments will develop a sense of themselves and the world as safe and secure when their caretakers are as attuned and responsive as possible to their needs. These caretakers are able to convey, through emotional resonance, that despite the distress of this moment all will be well with the world. For children, this experience—"The world is safe, I am good, and people are predictable"—is what is referred to as "secure attachment."

Secure attachment allows a child to learn that being apart from the caregiver doesn't destroy safety or connection, and that connection and safety will return. Children who are securely attached eventually internalize that belief so strongly that the actual presence of the caregiver gradually ceases to be necessary for the child to feel safe. We notice toddlers making this move to internalization of the good-enough caregiver through the "transitional objects" that they begin to carry through the world—an old blanket or a well loved, worn-out stuffed animal. These objects symbolize the caregiver. Their arrival in a toddler's life signals the onset of the capacity for symbolic thinking, the ability to understand that one thing can stand in for another. Transitional objects are material representations of being loved that children can take away from the actual connection and use to effectively self-soothe.

As they internalize care, securely attached children develop what psychologists call "object constancy." That's a fancy way of saying that babies come to believe that their caregivers will remain pretty much who they are and be constant in their love and connection, no matter what. They trust that any bobbles and missteps in the dance of relationship will be replaced with reliable love, care, and connection. Caregivers don't have to be robotically consistent. All they need to do is be consistent enough, present enough, and able enough to repair the ruptures in relationship that are increasingly inevitable as infants get older and are more able to directly articulate their needs. Normal child development creates more opportunities both for missed communication and also for mismatches between what the child wants and what adults will offer or allow.

The statement, "No you cannot have that bag of candy" may lead a small person to melt into sobs of "I hate you! You're so mean!" But the securely attached caregiver-child pair will recover from that and other similar adventures in learning the meaning of the word "no" and still feel mutual love. The child comes to trust that "no" is neither arbitrary nor punitive, but is simply part of life. It's not a cut-off or abandonment. It's a boundary (more about that later) that is tolerable even when no one exactly loves it.

A securely attached baby can grow into a toddler who can gleefully explore the world without fearing her caregiver will disappear. I watched one of these toddlers a few years ago while I was on a walk. A woman, who was later identified as her mom, was half a block behind her on the edge of a park, talking with another adult and pushing an infant carriage. Ms. Securely Attached, who appeared to be between the ages of two and three, was heading gleefully down into the park with her toy. About 40 yards out from her mother she turned and yelled, "Mommy, mommy!" A response and a wave from her mother sent the little girl back to her world of play.

This kiddo knew that her mom was there, and she was comfortable with her explorations of this safe-enough space on the Montlake play field. She also knew that when she needed to return to reconnect, as she did a few minutes later, she would be welcomed with open arms by her mom. She wasn't going to be yelled at for running off and making mom uncomfortable or anxious. Caregivers who engender secure attachment teach their children that the world is safe enough to allow normal development of autonomy. They are there, close enough and watching carefully, to ensure that things are indeed sufficiently safe for their child to spread their wings. In secure attachment, children practice going and coming and going and coming again, rehearsing greater levels of autonomy while still receiving adequate support.

Securely attached children grow into tweens and teens who are free to be tossed in the hormonal and social storms of adolescent development and explore ever greater levels of autonomy. They know that although their parents have limits to what is acceptable, they will still be loved and cherished even when they are pushing limits. The experience of being a parent who loses 50 IQ points and all of your cool and street cred as your child approaches middle school is normal; it becomes something that you can both can look back laugh about when your kids mature and apologize for their normative adolescent snark and arrogance. Parents who created secure attachment in their infants also are often the ones who don't take their adolescent offspring's apparent disrespect and tendency to grunt and roll eyes too seriously, while at the same time don't allow that adolescent to push them around.

So when 15-year-old Zeke's parents found cocaine in his dresser while they were putting away his laundry, they were able to manage their upset and fear. Carmen and Art immediately sought professional support for their entire family: "If Zeke is using cocaine, then we're missing something as his parents." Zeke was not defined as the problem by his parents. Their narrative was that Zeke and the family had a problem that was going to be solved together. They made their bottom line clear to Zeke. He could not use this drug, not because they were against all substances. They drank occasionally and as adults in a state where recreational marijuana is legal, they also had a toke or two when together with other adult friends.

Their bottom lines for Zeke were three-fold. First, his brain was still developing and deserved to do so free of interference from substances. Second, this drug was terribly addictive and could sabotage his life. And third, this drug was illegal, and obtaining it put him into contact with dangerous people. They loved him too much to let any of those bad things happen, they told him, both in and out of the chemical dependency counselor's office. They expressed their curiosity about what was missing for Zeke that he made this choice, as well as their desire to work together with him and professionals to help him fill that gap in his life. On the advice of their chemical dependency specialist, they also insisted that he have random urinalysis for the subsequent two years so that he did not need to lie to or deceive his parents any longer. "We know that if you have to be dishonest with us, that'll be destructive to you and to how you relate to us." The family figured out that Zeke had been struggling with low-grade depression for which the cocaine was self-medication. His parents enrolled him in a class on how to manage his mood. Together as a family Zeke, his parents, and his younger sister worked to change the family's diet to support his brain health.

Securely attached teens know that they can become angry, disagree with their parents' values, and generally act like an adolescent without ever risking love and connection, even when the parents are unhappy or apply consequences for the teen's actions. Those teens also know that they can still crawl into their parents' arms for hugs and soothing when there's a broken heart, a disappointing loss, a challenging day in the world. When they lose a cell phone, get their money stolen while on a gap year trip to Thailand, get a horrible neck tattoo, take up with a new friend who then makes off with a beloved guitar, get fired from a job, fail a class, or otherwise stumble in the world, they know that their parents will not say some version of, "You made your bed, now lie in it." Instead, those parents will do their utmost to prioritize safety and soothing before giving a lecture about how to avoid this experience in the future. Love before consequences, and learning, not punishment, are goals of parents who create secure attachment for their offspring.

Infants who are securely attached are then more likely than not to grow into adults who have a clear sense of self, knowing that they have their own feelings and needs, and that they are safe-enough in the world—even when those needs and feelings are in conflict with those of others. They understand that when a person they relate to isn't feeling well or calm, this mood state is temporary and that the person will return to be her or his predictable self at some point. They understand that they have a right to be loved and to be safe-enough in their relationships. They understand that they can make errors in relationships but that those errors can be repaired because people who are securely attached know that they are wanted as much as they want others.

Securely attached children also have been able to internalize the effective soothing behaviors utilized by their caregivers. As infants and small children, with unfinished brains and central nervous systems, we cannot soothe ourselves. The wiring for soothing simply hasn't developed yet. We thus depend on our caregivers to soothe us, and with time we become increasingly able to do this for ourselves. The neural networks of the orbital prefrontal cortex grow, and by the time a child is ready for preschool, we can watch her or him practice self-soothing, or soothe others. The tearful three-year-old who pats herself on the cheek and the five-year-old who hugs his friend when there's a skinned knee become adults who, when cut off in traffic, are able to take deep breaths and not leap out of their cars in a fit of road rage, or who, when sexually aroused by a co-worker, are able to remind themselves that simply because one has a desire, one need not act on it. These adults' capacities to regulate emotions and soothe themselves effectively without completely shutting down and numbing themselves are a direct result of the secure attachment experiences that they had as children.

As survivors reading about a securely attached life, you may be thinking that this is a fairy tale that I'm telling you. It's not. I've had the good fortune to observe a lot of good-enough parents—family members in my generation, my friends, people who've seen me for therapy—so I know that this is what it looks like.

> *When my friend Natalie's daughter was arrested for her work as a social justice activist, she and her wife Rachel were completely present and available for their daughter even though Natalie was terrified of what was happening. The moms paid for the lawyer, visited Abby in jail where she was being held without bond, and never once blamed their daughter for having lived the ideals with which they had raised her. Abby is securely attached. She knew that she could follow her values, even into a prison cell like her hero Gandhi, because her mothers' love and support would always be there. This didn't mean that at some point the moms avoided sitting down with their daughter to discuss the possibility of other less frightening ways of pursuing social justice once the charges were dropped and Abby was safely back in the free world.*

Falling, I Am Falling

Sadly, secure attachment wasn't your experience if you've been paying the price of admission to relationships. Almost by definition, being a survivor means that there was an absence of secure attachment experiences. Instead you had something not secure that ranged from somewhat problematic to overpoweringly so. When an infant is met with other-than-adequate or even truly-terrible parenting, attachment is always affected. A child's sense of self becomes distorted in ways that reverberate throughout many, if not all, of their emotionally-meaningful relationships.

These problematic attachment experiences taught you that relationships had heavy prices. Caregivers who, for whatever reason, are not consistently able to tolerate the normal needs of an infant and respond by being emotionally unavailable or disconnect from the child by withdrawing or withholding affection, or force the child to be silent through intrusive, insensitive engagement that is meant to soothe the adult's distress rather than the infants create children who themselves can only poorly tolerate connection with others. These caregivers' anxiety overwhelms infants and permeates the baby's emotional experiences. Connection with other humans quickly becomes painful for these children. Because those babies still crave connection, they are put in terrible double binds. Self-concept and contact with other people are marked by anxiety and feelings of being cut off, rather than by calm and connection. This attachment pattern is variously referred to as fearful, avoidant, or dismissive.

Adults who consistently treat infants as dangerous threats to the grownup's safety and sense of competency in the world create infants who are fearful of the new, yet miserable with the familiar. Such infants' growing sense of self is contaminated by a feeling that they are somehow dangerous or bad, largely because they are treated as such by their caregivers. This wounded self-construct makes connection with other people anxiety-provoking. Being close to someone is thus an opportunity for shame, as relationships evoke the experience of feeling bad at the core. This pattern of attachment is variously known as anxious, ambivalent, or preoccupied.

Anxious and avoidant attachment styles are common for survivors who grew up in less-than-adequate but not completely chaotic or dangerous families. Depressed parents, for example, will struggle to interact with their babies because of the effects of depression. One of the reasons that mental health professionals have developed interventions for depressed caregivers of infants is because depression undermines even the best parents' desires to attach to their infants. Infants will do their utmost to connect with their caregivers. They flirt, they coo, they blow bubbles, but they cannot keep it up indefinitely without eventually getting some kind of response in kind from the grownup.

Interventions for depressed parents teach them to respond to their infants, even if by rote, even if not feeling motivated to do so, because of the profoundly positive effects that this has both on their infants and, as it turns out, the parents themselves. Without interventions, however, babies finally give up. Infants turn away their faces, withdraw, and shut down. A baby tries again to convey its love and engagement, and once again gives up, shuts down, turns away. And tries again, and again, until at some point the baby just gives up. This kind of problematic relational dance, repeated endlessly, creates beliefs about one's self and one's relationships. Those beliefs yield powerful unconscious information to the survivor about how the relational world works. It's an inner voice saying, "You must try hard to connect, but in the end you'll fail." It's a message that says, "Your love will never be reciprocated." You become someone who is shut down emotionally, detached from feelings of love and unable, most of the time, to be vulnerable with other people because the pain of losing connection was too great for you to bear.

If you grew up this way, you entered adulthood believing that your ability to love is impaired. You're wrong. Please do not believe that you are incapable of love. Your capacity to love is neither broken nor gone. It's simply hidden from you so that you don't keep feeling the broken heart of having love unreciprocated, an expectation that was hammered into place before you had words.

You can watch a poignant and powerful example of what happens to small humans when their caregiver fails to respond in an online video, available at https://www.youtube.com/watch?v=apzXGEbZht0. Watching this can be painful for a survivor. But it might help you understand what it was like for you when you were little, thus giving you empathy and compassion for yourself once you get past how bad it feels to watch it. In this video, called the *Still Face* experiment, psychology researcher Edward Tronick Ph.D., the director of the University of Massachusetts Infant-Parent Mental Health Program, directs a mother to first engage normally with her baby, and then turn away and return to look at the child with her own face completely immobile and non-responsive.

Observe the baby, who does its very best to engage its mother when she presents with an immobile, unresponsive face. The baby smiles, burbles, reaches out, communicates interest in and love to the mother, tries so hard—and finally collapses into despair and turns away, sobbing. At this point the mother shows back up as her real self and comforts the child.

Too many of you reading this lived in that experiment for years. Your parent rarely noticed your distress or disconnection. You didn't have your love and attempts to connect reciprocated. For whatever reason, they didn't have the capacity to engage with you emotionally. You were that baby, and not for a few moments in a research lab that were repaired by your caregiver's immediate return to caring connection with you. That long painful minute in the video lasted for years of your childhood. A good, loving, smiling face did not return quickly, if it was ever there at all.

Each of these kinds of problematic attachment experiences is common in the lives of survivors. Such awkward dances of relationship create the foundation for many interpersonal difficulties throughout life. These experiences color a developing human's unconscious beliefs and expectations about what happens when trying to be close to others. Think of the adult caregiver as a mirror for the infant. If what is reflected to an infant is that she or he is difficult, demanding, frightening, or too much, if love is met with silence, or if nothing is reflected at all, then that is the self that the infant sees and comes to believe in. Such pictures of self, formed before there are words and encoded in the neural networks of the attachment system, are then often reinforced in abusive family environments with words and behaviors telling that child that she or he is in fact ugly, selfish, mean, too needy, or evil. Or the parent continues to withdraw, or to treat everything the child does as being about the parent, not as autonomous expressions of the child's self. Any of those responses encodes connection as dangerous, and makes connection a cue for bad feelings about yourself.

Even Wolves Raise Their Pups Better

When very early life has been marked by extremes of chaos, abuse, neglect, and other overt maltreatment, infants have the most problematic sort of attachment experiences. This generates an attachment style called disorganized. Someone I know refers to this as being "raised by wolves," although honestly wolf parents in the wild do a way better job with their pups. While traditionally this topic is discussed in terms of a child who has taken on the attachment style, my preference is to put the locus of responsibility where it belongs, and speak of "disorganizing caregivers."

A child's attachment system gets disorganized by caregivers who are often criminally dangerous. These children know that the world is completely unpredictable, and that caregivers can be both comforting and terrifying. Comfort is frequently closely associated with terror, leaving the child bereft of consolation. The child who had a disorganizing caregiver also knows that you can never tell when one thing or the other will be true, or for how long one state will persist in a caregiver until another one appears. The disorganizing parent turns on a dime from happiness to rage, from calm to chaotic, and is unpredictable. The child, blown in the winds of the dangerous disorganizing parent's emotional storms, struggles frantically to make sense of what's happening. These kids are constantly scrambling to find signs indicating that the next enormous change is about to take place so that they can seek some sort of shelter, however temporary or ineffective it might be.

Sometimes disorganizing caregivers are not dangerous themselves. Instead, they are so disengaged and uninterested in the child that they expose the child to danger from others. Being repeatedly unprotected from violence or sexual abuse that's perpetrated by people outside your family because your caregiver simply doesn't care or notice is another form of disorganizing experience. Abuse of this kind affects your attachment and self-regulation capacities every bit as much as if the perpetrator had been a family member. Predators identified these ignored kids and exploited your normal need to attach in order to get close enough to violate and exploit you sexually; they sensed that there were no adults in your life noticing what was going on. Horrifically, these extremely disengaged disorganizing caregivers sometimes hand their children over to predators simply to get rid of the responsibility of caring for their children. Nathan heard the refrain, "Don't bother me, go play with Uncle Owen," the countless times that his parents went off to their oh-so-interesting volunteer activities, leaving him in the hands of a man who made explicit images of Nathan being sexually assaulted.

Children's attempts to attach to disorganizing caregivers leave them feeling uncertain of who they are. These kids know in their guts that they are bad, wrong, selfish, intolerable, dangerous, and shameful because that's the version of self that was reflected to them in the mirror of their disorganizing caregivers. These children are left extremely vulnerable to relationships in which that narrative of self-as-worthless is reprised. A relationship in which bad things happen feels familiar, and bizarrely comforting.

Disorganizing caregivers also undermine children's capacities to develop their own goals, values, and desires, particularly if the caregiver is somehow threatened by them. Doing well in school? Not an option, because the primary caregiver struggled academically. Bad at sports? Never, because the primary caregiver was a star athlete in high school. The disorganizing caregiver's denial of a child's separate self is an outgrowth of the blurring of boundaries between children and disorganizing caregivers. Children caught in these relational traps are driven to over-attune to their disorganizing parents in attempts to achieve some brief modicum of occasional and temporary safety. Children with a disorganizing caregiver cannot afford to know what they want, need, think, or feel. Knowing these scraps of personal identity and selfhood puts whatever little connectedness might be available at terrible risk. And as one of my friends said of her family, "Forget attachment. I just wanted to live to see another day. I would do anything, anything at all, to survive."

Children living in these dangerous circumstances (which are not infrequently taking place inside of nice middle-class homes in a suburb somewhere) learn to read cues, even very subtle ones, emanating from disorganizing caregivers. The problem is that the adult interprets those cues to the child in confusing and sometimes downright contradictory ways. The child senses anger, but is told, "How can you possibly think that about me? You are a very nasty little person, thinking that about me. I am a kind and loving person." We'll discuss the lingering effects of that confusion of interpretation in a later chapter about detecting dishonesty and danger in relationships.

Children with a disorganizing caregiver must constantly change in order to ride the turbulent waves of connection to that person. Flexibility is a good thing, but this is not flexibility. This is a degree of protean chameleon-hood that damages the survivor's capacities to define a self. This is the child being required to have no values, no opinions, no accomplishments, nothing with permanence or clarity because the caregiver may respond dangerously to these expressions of self. The child has no choice but to continue to seek attachment, because human children are hardwired for this. Children need adults to be there while their brains are growing. So the child persists. Like B.F. Skinner's famous pigeons, who learned to peck for food based on the random stimuli that were present the last time the food pellet showed up, that child searches for clues as to what to do or not do in order to get it "right."

The terrible dilemma for the child with a disorganizing caregiver is that there *is* no right. What worked to create a moment of calm and safety yesterday stops working with no warning and for no apparent reason today. One day it's okay to cry when you're sad. The next moment your parent is screaming at you to "shut up and stop crying before I give you something to cry about." One minute it's okay to cuddle in your parent's lap. The next moment there are adult hands on your genitals, or into them, or worse. One minute it's a good thing to get good grades, in fact a necessary thing so that you don't get screamed at for being a stupid idiot. The next moment that straight-A report card has turned into a beating at the hands of a parent who's screaming at you, "Who do you think you are; you're no better than me." It can be large things or small—the color of your pants the religion you follow. It doesn't matter—it's all in flux, and you're going to be punished for not having predicted the next set of twists and turns.

Astonishingly, many people who had disorganizing caregivers grow up into decent, loving, and caring adults. They work hard to find a code of personal ethics by which to live and treat others. They find ways to deal with the pain of their childhood wounds. But they struggle to sleep nights, to calm the terror that lives inside of them. They experience the entire world as unsafe and unpredictable. And in a relationship they live with foreboding, with the sense that not only is there another shoe, but that it will drop at just the moment when they have finally taken a deep breath and relaxed their clenched emotional jaws a little bit.

One of the hard things that happens to people who've had disorganizing attachment experiences is that they are more vulnerable as kids to bad things happening. This in turn creates more vulnerabilities for more bad things. "Can't win for loosing" was how one survivor of my acquaintance put it after the third time someone without insurance drove into her car and left her with huge repair and medical bills that she could not afford to pay. "Could not afford" was because she was under-employed, a common state of affairs for people who've had disorganizing experiences in their childhood. Then she was put on probation at work because she missed so much time due to her injuries. Then her cat died. Her beliefs about herself kicked in hard. "I must be doing something wrong," she concluded, rather than, "I'm having a long run of crappy luck."

Your Inner Relationship Operating System

Attachment experiences of every kind generate what is known in attachment theory as an "internal working model" for relationships. This psychic structure is a non-conscious yet powerful paradigm through which developing humans make sense of themselves in relationships to self and others. You can think of the internal work model as humans' operating system (like Windows, Mac OS, or Android) about who we are and how we should relate to others. It delineates what you can expect in your dealings with others. As you might imagine, many survivors' internal working models are, as computer folks would say, "buggy." Your internal working models are riddled with distortions about who you are and about what to do with your own needs and feelings. Maltreatment tips the normal relationship between children and caregivers on its head, with children wrongly assigned to soothe and meet the needs of adults. This upside down paradigm teaches a child that soothing and meeting the needs of others is the price of admission to *all* relationships. Maltreatment pairs connection with the absence of safety. If you are only safe when you're alone, you learn that safety only comes at the price of losing relationships. A terrible dilemma—be connected (which is human) and feel terrified, or be safe and isolated.

The internal working model of children who grew up with fear-inducing or anxiety-provoking or disorganizing caregivers—and that would be you, dear reader—informs those children that they are there to soothe, meet the needs of, and generally take care of other people when in an emotionally-meaningful relationship. Your internal working model teaches you that other people have little or no mutual emotional responsibility to you. That model instructs you that you can never truly be safe if you want to be connected to any member of your own species.

"But," you might protest, "They fed me, they clothed me, they made sure I did my homework." True, they did those things. Some emotionally devastating caregivers are able to do enough of the basics of life that they don't appear on the radar screen of child welfare services. And some parents who try to be good enough—but are impaired in some way—offer what they can, which is often what can be done by rote, with little emotional heavy lifting. That's not the same as showing up emotionally for a child. Ultimately, children need secure attachment more than they need the most fashionable athletic shoes, a new video game, or getting their homework in on time, and almost as much as they need water and nourishment.

A survivor's internal working model is neither of relational mutuality, nor of relational predictability. It's certainly not a picture of relational safety. Instead, it is some version of a lopsided paradigm in which the survivor must give more than half the energy in a relationship in order to simply be attached and connected. As a survivor, you're that baby in the *Still Face* video, smiling, clapping, reaching out, doing your best, while your caregiver stares at you blankly. And that's if you were one of the luckier ones who didn't have a caregiver who screamed at you, hit you, or worse. Love and care in return, reciprocity and equality of commitment, the expectation of safety and protection from the other person, are all frequently absent from this internal representation of the relational world.

Compassion for Yourself

Before we move on to discuss some common relationship dilemmas faced by survivors, and strategies for changing those dynamics, a first but not last word about compassion. Compassion for yourself is going to be necessary as you read this book. There are so many places in the pages to come where your emotional parts (remember the EPs?) are going to be activated; I'll wager that there have probably already been several emerging per page. The EPs that are cruelly critical of you in a confused attempt at self-protection are going to be yelling at you as you read. This is because they embody the belief that you can only be somewhat safe if you hate and are mean to yourself, a stance with which I'm going to be disagreeing frequently and forcefully. Learning to think about yourself and your humanity without hating yourself is essential for this book to be useful. So please don't skip this section because the very notion of compassion for yourself makes your stomach hurt. Read this, please.

What is compassion? This term has gotten a lot of press due to the infusion of Buddhist mindfulness meditation practices into North American psychology since the 1990s. Compassion, called *Karuna* in the original Sanskrit, is a central construct of Buddhist thought. One thing it's *not* is pity, although those two words are sometimes used interchangeably in English. You don't want or need pity, which is ultimately disempowering and feels demeaning.

Compassion as I'm using the term is the practice of observing oneself or others mindfully in the moment *without negative or critical judgment.* This is vitally important to the process of learning that you can have relationships that do not exact undue prices. All of us do other than wonderful, and sometimes really crappy things from time to time in our emotionally-meaningful relationships. I, for example, tend to disappear into a book or a computer or tablet screen with great regularity, dropping a connection with another person like the worst cell phone. The most securely attached and mentally healthy people will speak thoughtlessly, be lazy in their commitments, act in ways that are violations of their values. We're human—remember the not-perfect thing?

For Yom Kippur, the Jewish Day of Atonement, there is an expectation that we will make an amends, known as "Tshuvah," to others for our missing the mark of our commitments in the previous year. Here's the Tshuvah I wrote to my friends and family in 2015. I share it because I think it illustrates precisely what I'm talking about with regard to self-compassion:

> It's that time of year when Jews look in the mirror and see our humanity and our flaws as clearly as we are able and offer amends. The word "Tshuvah" mans, at its root, "return," in this case, a return to a state of more honest and connected relationships with the people in our lives. It's not "repentance," which is the lousy English translation that shows up in the prayer books. It's about

reconnection to that which is best within us so that we may offer that in our dealings with others.

It's the time when we say, "I have not been the person I wish I could be. I've offended you. I've stepped on your metaphorical toes. I've been obtuse. I've been insensitive. I've looked away when someone else was disrespectful to you. I've been slippery in my honesty, foggy with my integrity. I've hidden in a book instead of calling and talking to you."

In short, I've been a human. For this, and all of the ways that I have not met my goal of having the best possible relationships with everyone for whom I care, I offer my commitment to do better in the coming year. And to everyone who was human with me, here's my heartfelt desire that we engage in mutual compassion for our missed marks so that we can support one another in being closer to who we want to be.

Survivors, when being fully human in these and many other ways, rarely see your behaviors as manifestations of yourself being simply human. You think, "If I say something like what Laura wrote there, all of my friends will agree about what an ass I've been." You don't yet understand that being fully and visibly human with others creates a space where you can be and feel more genuinely loved. You don't understand yet that you'll feel more safely connected because you've been transparent about your humanity. Instead it's more usual for you to go to a self-critical place inside of yourself and feel shame, self-hate, and despair.

Glenna says to herself, "Here I go again," as she realizes with dismay that she forgot to bring home the prescription that she promised to pick up for her roommate, who is also her best friend. An EP chimes in, "I'm screwing it up again." And when Dot asks, "Oh, did you get my prescription?" Glenna, in a fit of shame, evokes another EP and barks at Dot about what a hard day she had and how could she possibly remember that task. Glenna hates herself for not having been perfect, and her self-hatred transforms into defensiveness and being difficult for Dot to relate to. She's doing what her parents did to her when they blamed and shamed her for their failures, and she's unconsciously trying to pass her shame along to someone else.

Compassion for self gives Glenna a better choice. In that alternate scenario she breathes, hauls herself back into the present, notices that she is human and allowed to make mistakes. She remembers to practice self-compassion. She soothes her anxiety, speaks lovingly to herself, reminds herself that Dot has never even once reacted badly when Glenna was imperfect at this scale.

Instead she tells Dot, "Oh shoot, I forgot that prescription, I'm sorry. Do you need me to run back out and pick it up?" In Glenna's mind the narrative is now, "I am a caring friend and roommate. I am allowed to be imperfect. Dot will not hate me or think I'm selfish and stupid because I forgot to pick up her prescription. I am worthy of being treated fairly. I am a good, decent, and not selfish person. Now say that to myself again."

Glenna is practicing self-compassion, slowly, laboriously, somewhat by rote, and with great courage. This not only leaves her feeling less terrible (and possibly even better), she is also not drowning in shame and self-criticism. Her self-compassion allows her to be good to Dot and to remain connected to her, rather than trying to make the other shoe of rejection drop through defensive and blaming reactions. The young places of self-hatred and fear, long frozen inside, begin to be melted and transformed by the warmth of self-compassion and connection in the present.

Self-compassion is a powerful tool for healing from the crappy gift that's kept on giving, your avoidant, anxiety-provoking, or disorganizing attachment experiences. Observing yourself in the present without negative judgment, putting your human foibles—including those you believe to be your worst ones—into the framework of your courageous efforts to remain connected and human will all be vitally important as we next explore common relationship dynamics for survivors. We'll discuss developing self-compassion skills at greater length later in this book when we review how to improve your capacities for being in healthy relationships in the present.

None of this means that you get to act however you want or abandon self-awareness. Compassion isn't license to act without care for others. Rather, self-compassion means that you can truly, effectively observe yourself when you act as you wish you wouldn't. Self-compassion improves your capacities for engaging the power of personal change. It's an ironic truth. The more we hate ourselves—which used to feel self-protective—the less able we are to change, which in turn creates more risk and less safety in the present. Humans learn poorly when we are too anxious. Conversely, the more we accept that we are who we are in this moment, the more able we are to choose differently—should we wish—in the next. We can learn from our errors when our anxiety level is lowered by the practice of self-compassion. The capacity to observe ourselves and change is key to having the emotionally-meaningful relationships that we want, where we don't pay crazy prices for connection.

CHAPTER 4
Can't Buy Me Love

Adults whose relationship is for the most part uncolored by problematic attachment dynamics know that everyone is there by choice. Friends, romantic partners, people collaborating on work projects—all of them are making a series of continuing choices, sometimes consciously, usually not, to remain in association with the other person. Each of them has an internal sense of what is acceptable, what is marginal, and what violates their norms for safety, integrity, and comfort, in their interactions with other people.

Each of these folks knows—both from early attachment and subsequent experiences—that relationships of all kinds require attention, intention, and engagement. Relationships are full of moments of genuine connection, and also of hurt, misunderstanding, and confusion. In moments of difficult dialogues, the parties involved trust each other to be operating in good faith, possessed of a mutual desire to relate. They also trust that if things are chronically bad over time, then one or both parties will, after making efforts at repair, decide to create more distance, or even end the connection.

We are motivated to do a good job of repairing ruptures because we know the consequences of not making repairs, and we accept offers of repair because we value connection. As I'll discuss later, rupture repair is in fact one of the foundations of healthy, emotionally-meaningful relationships. Humans accept the possibility of a bad fit emerging from a connection that once felt familiar and comfortable. We know that change is inevitable, and that change doesn't always occur in hoped-for directions. Closeness waxes and wanes; it's not a fixed phenomenon. Well-enough-loved folks don't interpret temporary changes in closeness as evidence of anything other than the tides and rhythms of life. Each person is free to inquire, "What's happening?" when and if disruptions occur. Well-enough-loved people believe that it's okay to be honest and speak their minds because they've learned that honesty brings greater closeness over time.

This is the paradigm for emotionally-meaningful relationships that we're working toward in this book. It's the model Sue Johnson writes of so eloquently in *Hold Me Tight*. It's doable. It's worth hoping and working for. Yet it's unlikely that you've experienced much of this in your life. If you had anxiety-provoking or disorganizing caregivers in your childhood, you learned pretty much the opposite of this model of relating. Time to change that up.

Sacrificing the Self

One of the terrible backwards lessons your family probably taught you was that your safety and emotional well-being were at best secondary, and at worst negligible, when compared with the needs of the adults in your lives. Those adults were failing at the task of caring for the child you were and in the process giving you misinformation about how to be in a relationship with any other human being. You were told a lie then, explicitly or implicitly, that your safety did not matter. It's still a lie.

Here's the truth about healthy relationships: **You need to pay careful and close attention to what you feel, what you want, what you need, and what you know. You need to check carefully to ensure that an EP isn't filtering that information or trying to distract you and focus your attention entirely on the other person. You need to be as fully in the present as you are able to be. You need to know that paying attention to yourself first is the right thing, not the selfish thing. And then you need to build your emotionally-meaningful relationships on the framework of that knowledge of your own feelings, needs, and desires.**

These are probably shocking propositions for you. You were taught to pay the price for relationships and connections with humans by sacrificing yourself and by being loyal to people who were willing to use or hurt you. You mitigated some of the pain of those experiences by not knowing what you felt, thought, or knew. It wasn't safe in those moments to know how scared or angry or sad you were. You taught yourself to be whoever the adults required you to be, and to change when their requirements changed. As Carly Simon once sang, "I'm not necessarily the girl you think you see, whoever you want is exactly who I'm more than willing to be." That was the strategy you adopted for survival.

But that was then. This is now. Today, losing yourself is not an acceptable price to pay for love, connection, and attachment. Loyalty to yourself is essential. Loyalty to someone who hurt you, who has broken a relational contract, or who betrayed you while refusing to make a repair, is a contradiction in terms. When someone who is chronically unkind or unfair expects you to live up to your commitments to them no matter what, they're insisting that you pay a price for relating to them. That's not how humans do healthy relationships. It's how it was done with your less-than-adequate caregiver, but it's not really how humans make connection happen when we're all simply having to be good-enough.

Being loyal to yourself is a foundational component of making choices about being in relationships. The great Jewish sage Hillel, who was renowned for his compassion, famously said, "If I am not for myself, who will be for me? If I am only for myself, what am I? If not now, when?" As with most survivors, you are expert at being for others, but you are a rank beginner at being for yourself. You don't know that healthy relationships grow and expand us, rather than take from and deplete us. This is true even when a healthy relationship goes through a hard time, because a healthy hard time is a bit like a Pilates class for the soul, not meaningless torture.

Oh, You Gotta Have Friends

It is not, as you may have been taught, selfish or immoral to include yourself in the equation as you make decisions about what your bottom lines are in relationships. In fact, it is ultimately more moral and caring to ensure that there is mutuality in your chosen relationships with others, and clarity of motive on your own side of things. When you are loyal to yourself, you may stop offering others opportunities to engage in actions that harm you, and are morally harmful to them. As we'll discuss later in this chapter, a decent person (that would be you) doesn't want to be handed the opportunity to behave in exploitative, abusive, or unloving ways. A decent person wants to repair ruptures that have occurred through her or his own carelessness or inattention, not rationalize them or brush the hurt aside. The relationships you want are ones that nourish decency for all parties. Enough with you being the only decent person in the room. It's well past time for everyone to show up with decency.

Zan and Corinne have had this kind of good-enough, emotionally close, and sometimes rocky relationship since they met in ninth-grade band class at an all-girl private school. They are markedly different on the surface. Zan is an extrovert from a fourth generation upper middle class Greek Orthodox family. Corrine, introverted, is a working class Euro-American woman, the daughter of Lithuanian immigrants who was at the school on scholarship. They'll tell you that they each knew the day they met that they would be fast friends. In their forties now, their relationship has weathered the storms of each of them moving away from home to college, and the conflict that arose when Corrine, to Zan's surprise, did not follow her but instead went to the school of her own choosing.

It has survived Corrine's first marriage to a man who became competitive with Zan and tried to freeze her out of Corinne's life. It made it through Zan moving to Greece for two years to explore her cultural heritage. Today it's alive and well even in the face of their growing political differences. They have agreed not to discuss healthcare policy (Zan is an entrepreneur who's against all government programs and tax hikes; Corrine is a family practice doctor who'd like to see universal healthcare) or religion (Zan has become increasingly involved in her church; Corrine has become a stalwart member of a local secular humanist organization).

They have spent some years barely in touch; they have had some heated verbal exchanges. And each of them know that their relationship can contain their differences, that they will heal from difficult dialogues because each of them will do her part to repair ruptures, and that neither of them will blame the other or make it only the other one's problem. Two securely attached women, they can tolerate, and at times embrace their differences. Each of them enjoys jokingly introducing the other to the rest of their social circles as "My Tea Party/ Socialist friend, can you believe that?"

This is not a picture of an ideal, perfect friendship. It has had rough spots and difficulties and will again. They speak little and more superficially during presidential election years. There is no lifetime guarantee in what they have built, only an unspoken shared commitment to honest, caring, connection to the degree that's possible for both of them. It is simply the product of two securely attached people being able to use their capacities to continuously evaluate whether it's a nourishing experience for each of them.

Their friendship is a connection in which mutuality exists, and a relationship in which each person has clear yet flexible boundaries, and expresses her love for her friend. When Zan became vegan to keep her cholesterol down, Corrine, who generally hates to cook, found a recipe and prepared vegan moussaka for Zan's next visit, knowing that her friend would be particularly missing that cholesterol-laden childhood comfort food. When Corinne sold her parents' home after their deaths, Zan helped her grieve the loss of her childhood home and invest the proceeds of the sale her own trusted financial advisor.

Loss of boundaries is one of the prices you've been raised to believe you must pay simply to have relationships. If either Zan or Corinne had not been securely attached people, their relationship would have foundered long ago on the shoals of their differences. Instead, it has supported both of them to grow and stretch while negotiating these dilemmas of difference.

Absence of mutuality is another relational price often paid by survivors. In a relationship where one person believes her or himself to be essentially unlovable and undesirable in either an emotional or sexual sense, mutuality is absent. The survivor believes it's necessary to pay for the presence of the other person, literally or symbolically. But boundaries and mutuality, which seem like unicorns to many survivors, are hallmarks of healthy relationships. Let's explore what each of these means, and where the challenges lie for survivors in attaining them.

Boundaries—How to Not Buy Love

Boundaries are the places where you begin and I end, both emotionally and physically. We are all born boundary-less, having spent the nine months of our gestation firmly a part of the mother who is bearing us. We pass our first year with only a fuzzy and emerging awareness of the distinctions between those things that are "me" and those that are "not me." We learn through initial attachment relationships with caregivers whether we are allowed to have boundaries in relationships or whether the price of connection is the loss or violation of boundaries. Boundaries are a form of connection. They are the psychological equivalent of feeling my hand on your hand while you feel your hand on my hand. If you do that exercise with someone you'll notice that you both know you're connected, and you both know that you're separate as well. Separate, yes, but not distanced or disconnected.

Why are boundaries important? Because our bottom lines, our non-negotiables, our sense of what behaviors on the part of another person represent going too far to allow for continued connection, all of that reside in our boundaries. To be able to say "yes" to someone, we need to be able to count on our ability to also tell them "no" without the fear that "no" will make life painful or dangerous, or lead to permanent loss of connection. If you can't safely tell someone "no" because they will do something to you that endangers your welfare, then that person is probably not safe to have in your life. Saying "no" feels so emotionally unsafe for many of you that you assume it's never okay with other people and just don't say it. Where your emotionally-meaningful relationships are concerned, "no" simply isn't in your vocabulary.

The belief that you don't have a right to your boundaries is a common price of admission to relationships. Some people go entirely to the other side of the continuum and fear that any flexibility of a boundary will mean losing yourself. Your fear of losing a grip on your own perspective can sometimes result in rigidity. You become unable to flex when flexing is the emotionally wise thing to do. Survivors have EPs who experience having boundaries as a problem. Those EPs were taught that you have to pay for love, sometimes in the currency of your well-being, sometimes in other more material ways. Or you have EPs whose credo is, "Give 'em an inch and they'll take a mile—so give nothing, no matter what." A healthy, flexible, and yet clear set of boundaries prevents you from selling yourself out while still supporting you to maintain connection. Healthy boundaries nourish both parties' capacity to meet one another where they are.

Good Boundaries Make Good Relationships

The romantic ideal of love and connection is that there is no emotional space between lover and beloved. Love song after love song celebrates this notion. But the truth is that the best relationships occur when people have a clear sense of what they think, feel, want, and need in their interactions with others. Having clear personal boundaries is one effect of secure attachment. It's a foundation stone for good quality friendships, work relationships, and romantic connections.

Zan and Corrine each have good-enough boundaries from their good-enough attachment experiences. They can handle their differences, agree to disagree, and have clear bottom lines for their continued friendship. If, for example, Zan insisted on disrespectfully haranguing Corrine about the horrors of government-subsidized healthcare programs, Corrine would let Zan know that haranguing is not acceptable. It's okay with Corrine for Zan to express her discomfort with the whole idea of universal healthcare, but it's not okay with Corrine for Zan to do so by impugning the patriotism of people like herself who support those programs.

Corrine doesn't silence Zan; she simply doesn't tolerate being denigrated.

Similarly, while Corrine's opinions of people who believe in a divine being can be acerbic at times, she behaves respectfully toward Zan's own deepening embrace of faith. She expresses her own beliefs without putting Zan down. When she gets lazy and makes a less-than-pleasant remark about believers, she gracefully accepts Zan's expression of hurt feelings. She makes a repair of the rupture. Corrine remains curious and open-minded to learning about what religion means for Zan, trusting that her own values are solid. She knows that she won't adopt beliefs that are different from her own to please Zan or anyone else. In their conflicts, each woman trusts herself to have the integrity of her own beliefs, and neither fears being overpowered by the other's perspective. When one of them crosses a boundary by being disrespectful, the other person knows that she is free to protest. Each of these two securely attached people knows that she need not give up her values, her voice, and her safety in order to have a connection with the other.

I'd Do Anything to Keep You—Anything

Zan and Corrine's experiences sound like an impossible fiction for many of you. The idea that you can have boundaries in a relationship seems like an unrealistic fantasy. It's no surprise that survivors struggle with boundaries because to have them—to have a clear, felt, and expressed sense of what you feel, what you know, and what you want, and to have bottom lines and things are that non-negotiable—feels impossible if you want to keep someone connected to you. Integrity battles with the desire for connection and rarely wins.

> You want me to change my hair color? My politics? Okay, sure, whatever you want—just please, please, don't leave me. What do I want for dinner—oh I don't know, whatever you want. You don't like it when I'm not happy with you coming home drunk? I'm sorry, I'll stop complaining. You want to be able to call me names when you're angry? Okay, you have the right to express yourself however you'd like. But please, don't leave. I'm sorry for upsetting you. Really sorry. Please forgive me for not praising you, for not complying with you. You don't want to have a day job because it interferes with your creative process? Okay, I'll work a second job to pay your bills. Just please, please stay. Don't go.

Nancy, the character in the musical *Oliver!* who sings "I'll Do Anything" is a survivor of childhood attachment trauma. She's desperate for love, and expresses it by offering up all boundaries as a sacrifice. "I'll be anyone" is the price she offers to pay for what was a dangerous connection with Sykes, who kills her in the end. "I'll do anything, for you dear anything...I know that I'd go anywhere...I'd risk anything." And so she did. She risked and lost her life.

Sounds familiar to some of you, doesn't it? As a child you learned that connection, much less love, comes at a price. Love was contingent on silencing yourself, on becoming who and whatever your caregivers needed at that moment. Integrity—expressing what you feel, what you know, and what you want—was framed as being oppositional, resistant, unloving, bad, worthy of rejection, cut-off, abuse. When you were a child, you learned to apologize profusely at the precise times when you were yourself owed an apology because your boundaries had been violated.

> *I'm sorry I made you angry so that you had to hit me. I'm sorry that you got so upset by my B– in math that you had to go out and get drunk and not pick me up from school that afternoon. I'm sorry that you feel bad about molesting me; I'm not trying to make you feel guilty, really I'm not.*

In your adult relationships the words are different but the melody is the same.

> *I'm sorry you feel emasculated because I make too much money; I understand that you had to have an affair and buy your lover lots of gifts with my credit card to get your sense of manhood back. Of course I'll pay those bills. Of course I'll take you back. It was my fault. I'm sorry that you feel bad about forgetting my birthday. It's hard to remember dates, I know. Why don't we take you out to your favorite restaurant so you'll feel better and you know it was no big deal. I'm sorry. Very sorry.*

Feeling that you have no right to your boundaries in a relationship is a profoundly disempowering dynamic. Your experience that boundaries and personal integrity are forces that threaten connection has conveyed a message that relationships always come at the price of being untrue to yourself. The anxious, avoidant, or disorganized attachment patterns that follow you into adult life can make it very difficult for a survivor to navigate relationships. Even with a loving, caring friend or partner, many survivors constantly fear being precipitously dumped or unpredictably and arbitrarily punished for sins they didn't know they were committing until those alleged sins, and the person committing them, were labeled unforgivable. Never mind that a genuinely loving and caring person probably won't act like that toward you today. Forget that it's not unusual that other people are as—or even more—interested than you are in having a relationship. Ignore the reality that decent people will usually be forgiving even if you have seriously missed the mark because they have no investment in defining you as the bad guy.

Today doesn't feel real. Your EPs take you back in time, where you're waiting for the other shoe to drop. You wouldn't say it this way, and you think that other people are barely tolerating your presence no matter what they say. You believe that other people will never be fully committed to you. So to keep someone in your life you keep on paying what hasn't been asked. You are unable, yet, to know that this person is relating to you *because* you are you, not because you are paying them a price for sticking around.

Your internal working model leads you to expect other people in your emotionally-meaningful relationships to have requirements similar to those of the adults who raised you. Your EPs, which carry this working model around, believe that you are unlovable. The EP perspective is that you're the less-desired and less-desirable party in every relationship. Those EPs don't quite get that people might want to choose to relate to you because you are precisely the person with whom they want to be friends, partners, or co-workers. The pain of your past sends a loud message through your EPs. "Pay the cost of connection, whatever it may be. Emotional, financial, spiritual, do what it takes, because it takes more for you, oh unlovable creature, than it does for other humans, to find and keep connections." And you're not always sure that you're actually human anyhow, given how you were treated when you were little.

A common result of these long-standing non-conscious beliefs about what to expect in relationships is a pattern of frantic attempts to please, placate, and go along with whoever you are attempting to connect with, and to obscure or destroy your own boundaries. You offer to sacrifice your integrity, your money, your safety, anything that the other person might potentially require of you, just so they'll stay. Mind you, the person to whom you're making these offers may have no idea that you are doing this, nor any interest in you paying this price to relate to them. They might even have a genuine desire to relate to you simply because you're you, a being whose presence they cherish.

Ironically, your offers of sacrifice can ultimately become so off-putting to someone who's decent and caring that your actions lead to growing distance, and sometimes, sadly, end the relationship. This outcome feels confusing and completely terrifying. You were giving everything to this person. How could this person walk away? It must not have been enough, you think. You must not have been enough, again.

Wrong. Here's what's happened: This person in your life didn't want your everything. This person doesn't want to be, or be seen as, someone who would use or exploit you. This person is *not* one of the adults who raised you to pay prices for relationships. This person *wants* you to have boundaries. They find your absence of boundaries unattractive and off-putting, not a requirement for relationship. This person wants you to have a self. It's that self that was attractive in the first place. That's the self who could peek through the layers of attachment wounds when the other person didn't matter enough to you to turn on your wounded attachment patterns. And that's the self that you quickly put away as soon as the relationship started to mean something. Once someone matters your EPs start paying the price of connection.

This outcome of paying and losing no matter how much you've paid can be painfully confusing to survivors. You were trying as hard as you could to do what pleased the other person. You could neither notice nor understand that someone decent and good and caring doesn't want to be pleased by you at any cost.

The people who genuinely want connection with you today? They're emphatically *not* the adults who raised you. Today's people want mutuality. They want you, your opinions, your feelings, your integrity. You treat them like they want to silence, exploit, or punish you. And that's not who they want to be. The mirror you hold up to them by your continuing insistence on paying unasked for prices reflects someone they have no desire to be, with you or anyone else.

The internal working model that grew inside of you as a result of less-than-adequate attachment experiences has made it difficult for you to hear that, in fact, what the other person wants is simple. They want you to be you, not to spend all your energy trying to ferret out what they want and give it to them, no matter the cost to you. You feel so confused by this new scenario. You've worked so hard to give them what they asked for when what they're asking for is that you not give them everything they ask for. What does it mean that they're thinking about leaving because what they want is a genuine relationship with you, not with the version of you that's trying to please them all the time?

Your EPs may respond to this course of events with another round of self-hatred and self-blame because you did sort of push the other person away. But you didn't push them away because you were unlovable. It's not because you needed too much, or asked for things that were unreasonable. It's not any of that—it's not the rules of the EP that were forged in the flames of your being given less-than-adequate attachment. Have compassion for yourself here, please, because you were just following the rules, not realizing that someone else might not want to follow them.

A Chasm Is Not a Boundary

When you're first experimenting with having boundaries it's not unusual to confuse a boundary with a cut-off. "I won't speak to Jordan any more; she never respects or validates me!" Anica says triumphantly to her therapist. "I'm finally getting some boundaries." That's not a boundary. That's a cut-off, which is another way of having connection with someone that comes with a price. Cut-offs seem to work fine, in that they rid you of the particular problematic relationship. Then they don't work at all, because they prevent you from developing the skill of having a boundary and staying connected at the same time. It's easy to meditate in a cave; it's much harder to do so in a room full of distractions. The skills for having emotionally healthy relationships can only develop in the contact sport of a relationship itself.

It may sometimes be necessary for survivors who've not had much by way of boundaries to swing far to the other side of the continuum. You might find that you need to temporarily become harsh and rigid in your bottom lines. People frequently need to experience both sides of a continuum to develop a middle ground.

There are also some situations where a cut-off is the only wise choice. Complete disconnection from people makes sense when someone is actually dangerous to you (something we'll discuss at greater length later in this book). That's a decision that is sometimes, with some people, the least worst you can make out of a collection of lousy choices. You also don't have to keep trying endlessly. There are some connections that turn out to be too toxic or destructive to be given another chance. But if we insist that people be perfect in order to relate to us, then we are paying a new sort of price in relationships. This version has you reenacting the problematic relational dynamics that were imposed on you by parents who exiled you emotionally for not meeting their needs and expectations. Boundaries are about saying, "Here are the lines I want to color inside of," not "You're a bad person for sometimes coloring outside my lines."

No Fights, Please

Because you were taught to believe that connections were fragile and that you were expendable, it can feel almost intolerable to be in conflict with someone you care about. Standing up for what you want, feel, or know feels threatening to connection. You would rather have no boundaries than no relationship. Boundaries can be a place where conflicts happen, though. If your childhood included verbal, emotional, and/or physical violence—either against you or in your presence— conflict may frighten you and activate EPs that freeze in terror when a voice is raised because you expect that violence is about to occur.

Consequently, many survivors will either be highly compliant and/or engage in emotional cut-offs as ways of shutting down conflict in their current relationships. You will pay the price of having your opinions and desires made invisible, like burnt offerings on the altar of keeping what looks like a connection but becomes decreasingly so as you get more lost. It's not unusual for survivors to keep the peace at any price and avoid conflict no matter what, even if it means violating their own boundaries. Many of you go to extremes to make yourself invisible. "Whatever you want, it's not worth arguing about" or "Okay, fine, have it your way. My opinion isn't really important." This creates fusion, not connection. There's no connection if there's no one to be connected to. As we'll discuss later, having skillful conflicts is an essential component of genuine intimacy, so your fear of conflicts can become a barrier to getting the closeness you crave.

Why do you avoid conflict? For some people, it's because of the terror evoked by that anything resembling the violence of your childhood. You don't truly know that people can be angry in reasonably respectful, non-violent ways. You simply don't believe that a raised voice will not always be full of contempt and insult. You have no faith that conflict or anger will not shortly be accompanied by blows or destruction of property.

But even if there was no violence in your childhood, you experienced connection to your caregivers as tenuous. You learned—and your EPs carry around—the belief that if there are problems in a relationship, you are always to blame. Your EPs carry the corollary belief that you are the one who is always and only responsible for fixing those problems no matter any evidence to the contrary. Thus conflict can provoke shame and the sense that you've failed.

Shame often plays a big role in conflict avoidance. You take yourself out of the picture and tamp down any discussion of differences. You make yourself small the minute you sense distress on the other person's part. You do the magic trick of disappearing in place rather than have to stick around to hear what you expect to be told. You know in your gut that none of it will be good. You (actually, your EPs) know that you'll find out that once again you've been a terrible failure as a human being—disappointing, selfish, difficult.

So you simply get out of the way before you have to listen to what you are sure will be the story of another failure. You try to bypass another opportunity to drown in shame. Making yourself disappear like this forecloses the option that perhaps all you'll hear is that the other person isn't happy with this particular thing, not that you're a failure. You might even hear that they care about you and want to figure out how to work it out. You might learn that the other person is certain that this thing, which is annoying to them, is something that can be negotiated.

But you don't find out that things are different now. Because you have a pattern of "leave them before they leave you," it can be difficult to give yourself a chance to disrupt this model of self-in-relationship. Sometimes you are able to leave while you're still in the same room—you shut down, you make yourself small, you time travel. You're going to have to learn to be in the present, have compassion for yourself, and breathe to be able to stick around and change your internal set of rules.

Play It Again

Sometimes survivors find relationships with people who are decent, loving, and kind. These people are also human and flawed. These people don't want you to pay the price of admission. All they want is for you to be loving and decent and kind with them. They'll consequently be confused and sometimes pained by your attempts to turn them into the trolls exacting a toll at the bridge into connection. Yet sometimes you find yourself in old, familiar relational territories, ones that feel awful and yet well-known to you. How do you stop paying a price for relationship when your psyche seems to be whooshing through the worm-hole of time even though your body is firmly planted in the 21st century?

Many survivors unconsciously and repeatedly find relationships in adulthood that mirror the problematic attachment dynamics existing in your difficult families of origin. This phenomenon of playing the painful relationship card one more time is known as a *trauma reenactment.* Reenactments are achingly common in the lives of people given less-than-adequate attachment experiences. Most survivors have had some reenactments in life. Sometimes, without knowing it, you'll attempt to shove an otherwise okay relationship into the parameters of a reenactment. That way you don't feel lost and confused—only miserable, frightened, and despairing, which feels like normal relational life. Compassion for yourself is critically important at such junctures. Compassion allows you to observe yourself, to have insight rather than shame. Insight lets you learn. Shame stops learning in its tracks. One of the most effective and powerful strategies available to you is to be able to identify and step out of trauma reenactments. No one can make this kind of transformation without self-compassion.

A reenactment can be best understood as the replay of old familiar attachment patterns, in which the roles of victim, persecutor, rescuer, or bystander become reinstated in the dynamics of today's life. It only takes two people to get all four roles to play out. Being able to identify those roles and learn what you're feeling when you're in them is an important part of getting a refund on the price you've been paying for relationships.

Let's start with the role of the rescuer. A rescuer usually becomes a martyr when the person you're rescuing acts badly and you feel like a victim. Rescuers position themselves against the alleged persecutor (an ex-partner, your bad boss, your snarky kids) in order to save the victim. They will sacrifice themselves in order to accomplish that goal. In a common trauma reenactment scenario, the survivor portrays whoever they're relating to as the victim of the survivor's horribleness (survivor as persecutor, e.g., I'm hard to live with, I'm high-maintenance, I ask for too much). Then you must rescue the other person (survivor becomes rescuer) by sacrificing boundaries, self, desires, etc. (survivor becomes martyr). Makes you dizzy, huh?

Depending on how the script plays out, the rescuer/martyr may then move to occupy the position of victim: You've been giving and doing, and this is the thanks you get?! You feel persecuted by the other person and insist that they must step in and rescue you. Sounds familiar?

The bystander role in a reenactment is a position of helplessness or passivity. If one of your caregivers stood by and failed to protect you or intervene while other people harmed you, then this role is familiar to you. So, for example, the survivor as bystander feels terrible about how they are being treated, and says nothing for a long time. You don't stand up for yourself. Then, apparently out of the blue, you move into the role of victim/martyr and inform the other person that their behavior is intolerable and has to stop NOW! Since the other person has been going along doing whatever she or he was doing without corrective feedback, that person may feel (and perhaps have been) blindsided. They might then move into the role of either victim or persecutor. If everyone agrees that they're your victim, you return to the role rescuer/martyr, apologizing like mad as you go. If the other person steps into the role of persecutor, you may resume tolerating less-than-optimal or even bad treatment from them, because at this point the shame-carrying EP has kicked in and you're collapsing and scurrying to apologize.

So, for example, a man who was emotionally abused by his father finds himself working at jobs where his bosses are bullies. When he quits everyone is surprised, because he never once complained. A woman who was sexually abused by her stepfather has partners who end up being unfaithful to her. Her friends wonder how she cannot notice the cues. The child of a depressed parent marries people who are depressed. Trauma reenactments occur without conscious knowledge or intention on your part. They're the work of your EPs who are unrolling the script of how to be in relationships that was written by the less-than-adequate caregivers of your childhood. Adult Children of Alcoholics is a 12-Step program which is entirely about dealing with trauma reenactments engendered by having a substance-abusing parent.

You need both consciousness and mindfulness to detect a reenactment early enough to step out of the soap opera before you get too wet. Reenactments aren't completely avoidable. All of us walk into them some of the time, no matter how hard we've worked to become aware of what they look and feel like. I take the first few steps into them frequently. You don't have to keep paying the price by staying there. Reenactments can be ended or transformed.

Think of reenactments as a runaway truck heading in your direction in the form of a problematic relationship. For a moment you feel frozen in place, unable to avoid the truck. Your EPs are activated. You may feel that you have to sacrifice yourself to stop the truck, or just let it roll over you and accept the inevitable. But you have a better choice today. You can get out of the way of the truck. You can even jump in, start to drive it in a new direction and have it take you where you'd like to go.

Being fully committed to living in the present means that you learn to soothe your EPs. You have to remind them that nothing is inevitable except changes in the weather, death, and taxes. Your job today is different. It's not to learn to live with being run over. It's to learn to step out of the way of the truck. Today you get to be safe enough. You might have a rip in your sleeve from the truck coming too close. You might have a close call. And you are allowed to move—to step away—to not pay these prices. You do not have to pay the price of being run over in order to be in a relationship with someone. Your integrity, your boundaries, and your physical, emotional, and spiritual safety are neither necessary nor acceptable costs for you to pay to have connection and love in your life.

Reenactments feel right in a strange way. They're seductively familiar ways of relating and being related to. When you hear yourself thinking, "Here we go again," or, "This feels familiar," or "I know how this will end," you're signaling the presence of a reenactment to yourself. You think you know the outcome, but not because you're really prescient. It's because you're being time traveled—in an EP—to interpersonal patterns stemming from your painful attachment experiences of childhood. If you are a survivor of traumatic experience of abuse and betrayal, you may also be feeling the kind of hopelessness about the future that trauma exposure bestows on its victims. This is the symptom of post traumatic stress disorder (PTSD) called "sense of a foreshortened future," the one that makes bad outcomes feel as if they are inevitable.

Strumming Your Life

There also are neurobiological aspects of an adult survivor's difficulties with having and maintaining boundaries and staying out of reenactments. *A General Theory of Love,* by Lewis, Amini, and Lannon, is a book that was personally very helpful when I was navigating the murky waters of being in a new relationship with a person who was uninterested in doing a reenactment with me. Its authors were among the first to propose the notion that children with problematic attachment experiences develop what they call a "limbic resonance" to disordered dynamics of attachment.

Their term refers to the limbic system of the brain, the place where emotions are experienced and integrated into thoughts and memories. This is the part of the brain where the attachment is active when you're too little to know that you're separate from your caregivers. Think of the limbic system as the silicon chip in our brain's processor that has all the equations for understanding emotion and danger. Our limbic system helps us interpret emotional experiences, alerts us to danger, and makes us aware of difference. It's the place in the brain where emotional memories are integrated into narratives.

The authors of *A General Theory of Love* note that our limbic system provides the mechanisms by which infants become attuned to their caregivers, occurring through a reciprocal process in which each person in a pair transmits information to the other. Remember what I said earlier about adults controlling infants' brains? That's what's happening here. There's a reciprocal regulation of a variety of neurological and hormonal functions. The limbic system gets us vibrating on the same frequency as the person with whom we're attaching. If you've ever tuned a guitar using harmonics, you'll recognize this phenomenon.

Through limbic resonance we become accustomed to certain patterns of emotional and physical arousal. This includes the arousal patterns created by abusive or neglectful early relationships. We learn, in these less-than-okay and less-than-adequate attachment experiences, to resonate to the vibrations of withdrawal, rejection, and shame. When we enter a relationship later in life that has a similar set of dynamics, it feels right to our nervous system, even if and when we can intellectually see that something is very wrong. Being scared or hurt or angry is what a relationship feels like through limbic resonance.

The authors wrote, "A child enveloped in a particular style of relatedness learns its special intricacies and particular rhythms…and arrives at an intuitive knowledge of love that forever evades consciousness." Being involved in a relationship today that mirrors the dynamics of your childhood attachment experiences may stimulate these limbic resonances to the degree that, although you consciously feel horrible about being in this relationship because you're feeling sacred or mad or sad so much of the time, your brain is responding as if all is right with the world. Conversely, when you break out of familiar patterns and refuse the pay the prices of admission imposed upon you by your failed or impaired caregivers, things feel odd, wrong, and out of place.

A friend of mine recalled waking up one morning, early into her relationship with her now beloved husband, thinking, "What am I doing here?" She was missing her abusive ex, who had dumped her for not scrambling hard enough to meet his needs. She knew there was something bizarre about this. She told me that she felt lost. The new guy seemed lovely, sober, hard-working, decent—something was missing, something had to be wrong. What was missing and wrong, of course, was that there were no limbic resonances to her childhood experiences of disorganizing attachment. She had to talk herself by rote through the initial experiences of feeling wrong in relationship. She had to keep reality testing and contradicting problematic past messages inside of herself and get to a place where she could notice that this man truly loved her—no price tag attached—and that he wasn't going to leave because she had gained some weight or made a mistake balancing their joint checkbook.

Harville Hendrix, the author of many popular books about couple relationships, said something very similar in his Imago theory. He argued that in our most intimate relationships we unconsciously pick people who have characteristics—both good and difficult—of the people who raised us. He posited that difficulties in intimate relationships arise from how intimacy stimulates old wounds. What's familiar feels right even when it hurts. The bottom line—what we learned about love in our early attachments keeps steering us as adults. If what we learned was that a price must be paid, we'll keep offering prices whether people want them or not.

I'm Gonna Wash That Person Right Outta My Hair

The EPs running relationships choices of people employ two common strategies for soothing the anxiety generated by problematic attachment experiences. Each strategy is implicated in boundary problems. As we discussed earlier, one is to simply cut off contact with the source of anxiety and try to forget about that person. Although that looks like a boundary, it's not. Many adult survivors have done just that. They have minimal or sometimes no interactions as adults with the family members who did them harm. This does solve the immediate problem of dealing with an abusive person. It does nothing for working through the wounds to self, or for learning how to create boundaries that include connection. Cut-offs work fine until they don't. The minute a survivor gets back in contact with a problematic person from the past, all of the old dynamics are likely to activate as if no time has passed since the last contact. Cutting-off means that you're buying into the rule that you can have integrity or connection, but not both, and that you have to trade one for the other.

In present-day relationships, survivors who struggle to have integrity may employ cut-offs as an early strategy for not having their boundaries violated. Because of having little-to-no experience with having a healthy bottom line in relationships, survivors may set the bar for other people's behavior in such as way as to make it almost impossible for other people to stay in connection.

Carl was raised by parents who had no respect for his privacy and felt free to intrude on him at any time to demand his attention. He told his friend Janine that she was never to call him before 5:00 p.m. on a weekday, as he worked at home and needed to have a clear boundary around his work time. One afternoon Janine was in a car accident at 4:45 and called him for help. He was furious at her, accused her of having no respect for his boundaries, and told her that he needed to take a break from her for a month before he would be willing to see her again.

When they finally did reconnect, he was shocked to hear Janine tell him that she wasn't sure she was willing to be friends with someone whose boundaries were so rigid that they could not flex for a genuine emergency. "I really respect the work you're doing to try to have boundaries," she told Carl, "but this wasn't fair. I have to know that I can count on friends when something bad happens. It feels crappy being shut out of your life because I wanted help when something bad was happening."

Carl was confused. "I want to be there for you, but I need to have my boundaries respected. You're right. I think I overreacted. But I need to have my boundaries respected. I do. This is so important to me, Janine. You know how hard it's been for me to get here." "So let's negotiate, Carl. We agree that under normal circumstances, 5:00 p.m. is the boundary. I promise to respect that. And we

also agree that each of us will feel free to call on the other one for support if it's
an emergency, and that we'll trust one another not to abuse that idea. And that
you'll call on me, too," she added, gently reminding Carl that when he broke his
leg the previous year she hadn't known about it until after he had already called
a cab to get himself home from the emergency room so as "not to bother" her.

Getting Lost in You

Fusion is another boundary-blurring strategy used for psychic survival by some survivors. Rather than distancing yourself from someone who is treating you badly, you fuse with them. How this looks is that you stay as close as possible, making yourself meet as many of the caregiver's needs as you can, practicing self-abnegation, soothing the other person like crazy, being compliant. This strategy often has its roots in a relationship with an early caregiver who could not tolerate your developing a differentiated sense of self. These caregivers were punitive or withdrew affection whenever you exposed their imperfections. These children were the "good" babies who supposedly never cried, and who learned to walk, talk, feed themselves, and be potty trained by the age of one—all feats that are neurologically difficult for an infant to accomplish, but which some children do. This is not because you were brilliant, but because this is the price you were required to pay for attachment. Later on you learned to be quiet and not bother your caregivers. You asked for little, and you paid careful attention to who your caregivers required you to be.

In this scenario you may have no wants, needs, or feelings that are not those of the other person. You don't ever intentionally behave in ways that might create discomfort for the other person. Your goal is to surround the other person with ease, to remove obstacles and irritants. You check in frequently: "How are you? Are you hungry? Would you like to change the channel? Can I get you a blanket?" This isn't simply you being loving, because you're driven to this by your fear of what will happen if you don't give endlessly. Your caregivers taught you that relationships depend on you being the best possible servant to others. You attempt to anticipate peoples' needs, to breathe at their rate, to adopt their values, their style of dressing, even their use of language. You are a chameleon who, like the lizard of that name, changes color in order to blend in and feel safe. You check in as frequently as possible to ensure that you haven't missed something.

If the object of all of this care is not a decent and caring human being, and instead interprets your actions as license to use, abuse, and exploit you, then you start to see the problems with this coping strategy. If and when you begin to develop boundaries while you're relating to someone who's not decent and caring, you may be accused of changing the rules of the relationship and be threatened with disconnection.

All your self-sacrifice and being nice has not made a deposit in the emotional credit bank, You haven't guaranteed yourself a connection. There's no permanent record of your good deeds. It's like Snapchat or one of the other texting apps for smart phones where the message disappears right after it's been read. If you're in a reenactment, you might be with someone whose response to you fusing with her or him is to toss you aside at the point when you've been used up.

If the person is a well-enough attached decent human being, you might have the opposite effect and drive them crazy with your constant intrusions into their inner space. One evening after Jan had gone through her usual checklist of "How're you doing?" Larry shouted at her, "Enough already! I'm fine. If I want something I'll tell you! Leave me alone." Jan crept away, feeling bad and ashamed and confused because, "I only wanted to make sure that you were okay." It took several months of similar painful exchanges before Jan learned that Larry wasn't waiting for her to make everything perfect and that he would take initiative to get what was important. He didn't want Jan to be his servant. He wasn't her step-mom, who would whine endlessly to Jan's dad about how selfish Jan had been, even though she'd never asked Jan for anything. Jan's step-mom required Jan to read her mind. Larry wasn't interested in that. He knew she was human, not Betazoid. (And if you're not sure what this is, search "Counselor Troi." Then you'll see why you can't read minds.)

Bad Girls

Issues of culture and gender come into play here. Ideologies of femininity in many cultures tell many women that a "real" woman should have no wants or needs of her own. In some cultural contexts people get messages that they are expected to privilege the wants and needs of others over their own, no matter how unfair those demands might be. The truth is that in every culture there are people who use and exploit its rules and norms to exact a price of admission from survivors. In every culture there are also decent caring people who don't use that sort of excuse—and I believe that the decent ones are in the majority.

If someone attempts to coerce you into paying relational prices by telling you that you are failing as a woman or a member of your cultural group, this is a red flag about being in reenactment where your boundaries are being disrespected and violated under the guise of encouraging conformity with the world around you. Your EPs may feel as if this other person is right, partly because there are enough cultural cues that seem to support what you're being told. Your EPs will initiate a round of self-criticism that can lend power to this kind of coercive relational price tag. When someone plays the "You're not a good (fill in the blank)" card, that's the time to get into the present and remind yourself that you aren't required to pay this price. A good (fill in the blank) of any gender, culture, social class, sexual orientation, religion, or nationality is a decent human being. A good-enough human of any shape, size, background, or color is full of imperfections. All you have to do to be adequate is to show up and be compassionate. Adequate is just fine. Having boundaries isn't a luxury or something only other people's groups do. It's about not paying the price for a relationship.

All I Need Is a Little Respect

We've discussed the types of problems that arise when you haven't learned yet that you have the right to your own boundaries. For some of you the problem isn't simply that you don't know that you have a right to your boundaries. Sometimes you also experience difficulties with recognizing and respecting the boundaries of others.

If you were raised with a disorganizing attachment figure, that person may have had difficulties with her or his own boundaries. That caregiver might have permitted incursions of their boundaries by you when you were too little to understand that a boundary might have been there to cross over. More frequently, disorganizing caregivers engaged in persistent violations of your boundaries. They taught you to believe that even though what they were doing felt weird or icky or scary or painful, it was something you had to accept and treat as okay "Because I'm your parent" or "Because I love you."

However you got here, your internal working model for relationships doesn't include the idea that there is basic human right to say, "No, not that," or "No, that's enough," or "Ouch, that hurts, stop!" or "No, not now, no, don't do that." If you have this internal paradigm for connection, you've been told that to say "no" is to not love. Consequently, it feels like someone saying "no" to you must not love you, either. The model your caregiver gave you included no boundaries for you, and few boundaries for them. Boundaries, when they did make appearances, were imposed on you as controls and used as a means of punishment. A boundary or a limit was coded as evidence of love and care being withheld. Your caregiver's emotions and impulses had to be indulged immediately unless you wanted to risk being labeled unloving, selfish, or bad.

If you've had this variety of disorganizing attachment experience, you've entered the realm of adult relationships with skewed and distorted emotional information about boundaries. You know that you've had too many encounters with people who've labeled you disrespectful or impulsive or "too much." Too many times you have felt crippling shame because you can see yourself treating others very much like your disorganizing attachment figure dealt with you. You feel really terrible because that was something you promised yourself you would never do.

And still you don't quite get it. If someone truly loves you, says an EP, how can that person say "no" to you? If you're upset or unhappy, how can someone who says they love you not drop everything and be immediately available for whatever you want? If you're lonely, why can't that person just stop what they're doing to be with you and soothe you? Why doesn't that person play by the rules you play by? After all, you tell yourself, you'd be there in a heartbeat if the situation was reversed.

For those of you who recognize this pattern, your ability to understand other people's boundaries has been terribly undermined by your early attachment experience. Not only do you not know that you are allowed to have boundaries, you don't know that other people can have them, either. They're simply not a factor in how you understand relationships. When the adults in your life made anything resembling care contingent on their right to freely and repeatedly violate your boundaries, they modeled a price of admission to relationships of tolerating violation. In this confused paradigm, love means never having to ask permission, never having to say, "Please, is that okay with you?," "Sorry, I'll wait until you're ready/willing," "Okay, I understand that you don't want to do that, and I won't nudge you about it." Love means taking what you want, when you want it, and having that be okay with the other person. That was, after all, what your attachment figure did to you. That person took whatever she or he wanted. They told you that this was how you knew that this person loved you. That caregiver withdrew from you or harmed you in more direct ways if you protested.

When you've lived your whole life without good boundaries, it can be hard to learn to love and connect while both having and respecting boundaries. Learning that you can feel loved and cared for in the presence of someone's clear boundaries is challenging. It can be terrifying if your attachment figures were disorganizing. Problems of self-soothing and containment of your own emotions often go hand in hand with disorganizing attachment experiences that denied or violated boundaries. Your capacities to calm your own distress when you encounter a non-punitive boundary in a relationship may not yet be particularly well developed. If this is you, it can be extremely anxiety provoking to learn to respect the boundaries of others. You have to work hard to calm EPs who are certain—completely certain— that what's happening as boundaries are being asserted and respected is the prelude being dumped, rather than evidence that you're having a relationship with someone who is able to have her or his own boundaries.

You may initially feel that someone who requests that you respect their boundaries is rigid. You might feel controlled by them. As often as not this is the perspective through which an EP is viewing and interpreting those boundaries. If you were labeled as mean or withholding or accused of intending to hurt when you tried to have a boundary with your caregiver, or if your boundaries were interpreted to you as evidence of your selfishness/coldness/uncaring, that's how you've coded boundaries. If you lived in chaos where the rare instances in which a caregiver said "no" were your caregiver's attempts to punish or retaliate against you, it's hard at first (and second, and third, and tenth) glance to believe that a boundary in the present is simply the relationship equivalent of good fences making good neighbors. Talk about the absence of limbic resonances!

As we'll discuss in a subsequent chapter, survivors can learn ways of overcoming their limbic resonances. You can learn how to identify people and qualities of connection that are safe-enough and good-enough and don't exact a toll. You don't have to give up the right to your feelings, your preferences, and your opinions to be in an emotionally-meaningful relationship. In fact, you must have your feelings, preferences, and opinions to be in the healthy relationships that you hope for and deserve. Mutuality of boundaries—we are all allowed have them; all of our boundaries are flexible when appropriate; we all negotiate boundaries in the context of our connections with one another—is a hallmark of attachments where no unhealthy, unreasonable prices are being paid.

CHAPTER 5

Your Cheatin' Heart

"Faithless love, like a river flows."
J.D. Souther

In addition to neoteny and the attachment system, another thing that evolutionary psychologists think is hardwired into humans is the ability to know when we are being tricked or lied to. This cognitive mechanism is known as a "cheater detector." It was essential for early hominids and humans to know who or what could or could not be trusted. Life and survival in the savannas of Africa where humans first emerged depended on our ability to make such assessments relatively quickly and without engaging in much thought or deliberation. All of us are the descendants of hominids who did that well enough not to get eaten by a mega-fauna.

A frequent casualty of less-than-adequate attachment is the loss of the ability to utilize our cheater detectors. There's a good reason why this happens. If we were safe to know that something bad was happening with our adult caregiver, it would have been nearly impossible for us to stay attached. Remember, we go to our caregivers when we're in danger. Our brains' attachment systems weren't built for the situation you grew up in, where danger and attachment were contained in the same person. Plus, you had to stay attached, because, as you may recall, it was necessary for survival. The child you were found yourself in an intolerable dilemma of choosing between knowing the truth of what was happening and being attached so as to survive long enough to figure out that something had gone very wrong.

Faithless Love

In the early 1990s, a cognitive scientist named Jennifer Freyd set out to understand why some children who were sexually abused by a family member became unable to remember that trauma until much later in life. As a student of human cognition, she was curious whether there might be a cognitive mechanism that would make sense of this phenomenon.

What she discovered occurs at the intersection between our need to survive and attach and our need to know the truth about what is happening in a relationship. If you're free to know that you're being betrayed, then you'll probably figure out that's what's happening. But if the choice you have is between knowing that you're being betrayed versus having some kind of attachment, attachment almost always trumps awareness of betrayal. Freyd used an analogy of a person who goes cross-country skiing and breaks a leg. If the person is alone on the trail when this happens, the most important thing is to get back to where help is available. In such instances the skier manages to return to civilization, ignoring or perhaps even not feeling pain in the broken leg until safely with others. Survival trumps knowing the pain, even though the skier will likely compound the damage of the broken bone by getting to safety. If the skier is out with others, though, the attachment and support to get to help are there. One of the companions skis back to call for help, and the others keep the injured skier company. That skier immediately feels the pain of the broken leg, but won't have to do any additional damage to get to safety and have the injury treated.

Freyd's theory helps explain why some sexually abused children don't remember what had been done to them until much later in life. Attachment to the caregiver who was abusing them was necessary for survival. The ability to remember and think about and know that they were being betrayed had much less survival value compared to the need to be attached. The knowledge of betrayal was only useful once that early relationship was no longer necessary for survival

One striking exception to the timing of when people begin to remember sexual abuse turns out to be if someone that the survivor cares about and was responsible for was at risk. For instance, if an abused child had a much younger sibling, that person might remember the abuse early enough to try to protect the sibling. It turns out that many of these delayed recalls of childhood sexual abuse occurred later in life when the survivor had a child who needed to be protected from an abuser in the family.

Freyd's subsequent research has found that the closer the relationship between the abuser and the survivor, the more likely it was that memory for abuse was affected. Attachment, which equals survival for a child, almost always trumps knowing the truth about betrayal. When the truth finally became knowable the experience of remembering the betrayal is traumatic and disruptive to the relationship. The disruption is now tolerable because the relationship is no longer necessary for survival. Freyd named her paradigm Betrayal Trauma Theory (BTT). It is now one of the well-accepted scientific models for understanding the relationship between early trauma and the ways in which memory for those experiences is affected.

As it turns out, sexual abuse is not the only betrayal by a caregiver that survivors have learned to un-know in order to maintain attachment. Lots of other below-standard experiences at the hands of caregivers get forgotten, misremembered, or downplayed. Less-than-adequate attachment experiences are an invitation to large-scale dissociation of the knowledge of how one has been betrayed by a caregiver. The child knows emotionally that something is not right—even if no pain is involved—because caregivers who harm children usually know that they're committing a crime and exude disturbing emotional states, all of which are aversive for a child to remain in contact with. The kid wants to leave the situation as quickly as possible.

But leaving physically is just not possible for children. Infants, children, and very young teens cannot pack their bags and head out the door. At these ages the brain isn't developed enough. Kids don't have the skills and tools for navigating the world, much less the money. Kids can't file for divorce and child support from problematic caregivers. The best a teen can do is get involved in sports or music or the school paper and have a legitimate excuse for being away from the parent for as long as possible during the day—but that teen must still return at night to the scene of pain. It's very hard to legally emancipate and be freed from dangerous caregivers, even for an older teen. For infants and very young children staying attached is not optional, but neither is leaving.

So infants in less-than-adequate, anxiety-provoking, or disorganizing attachment relationships with caregivers begin to learn how to dissociate. This means that you become unable to remember, unable to feel, unable to think thoughts about the painful relationship and what's being done to you. You proceed to un-know what you're feeling. You silence your cheater detectors no matter how loudly they are blaring in an effort to let yourself know just how profoundly unworthy of trust this adult is.

Betrayal is a form of cheating. It's generally to our advantage to know when we're being betrayed so that we can end our association with the person who is betraying us or insist on a return to honesty and loyalty. This is unless, of course, you're a young human and the people betraying their responsibilities to you are the adults you're dependent on for care. Then it's directly to your evolutionary *dis*advantage to know that you're being betrayed, because attachment to those who are supposed to care for us trumps everything else. Attachment is our only path to survival when we are young.

As part of finessing this very tricky piece of cognitive magic, children begin to switch out responsibility for what is happening to them and make it their fault. This process of blaming the victim (yourself) is facilitated by the fact that very young children have a normal tendency towards omnipotence. Omnipotence goes something like, "Everything that happens is happening because of me." In the good-enough family, this is a fine state of mind to have. Good things are happening, and it's because of me, because I'm good. This is an excellent way to start life, because you're experiencing both the love of your adult caregivers, who perceive you to be good, and you also believe that you're having positive effects on others and the world around you. When you encounter difficulties later in life, you won't assume by default that they're happening because you're other than a good and lovable person.

In the families you came from, though, this normal developmental phenomenon of feeling responsible for everything becomes a source of vulnerability to self-blame and self-hatred. You internalized the words that were thrown at you. Your grownup was unhappy and it was your fault. Your grownup hit you. Of course you made them do it. Your grownup told you that you were a little piece of crap. If you hadn't left the blocks out where they stumbled over them when they came home wasted, they wouldn't have tripped and broken their nose. It's your fault, your bad; you're the monarch of darkness, the horribly powerful creature who can get people 10 times your size and age to behave badly. The spotlight was turned on you to make it easier to single you out and punish you for existing. Sometimes your caregiver did that directly, hurling insults at you. Sometimes you had to figure it out for yourself by reading between the lines and watching the patterns. Either way, you got the message. You learned that you were the problem. That way you were able to maintain the belief that the adult was good and loving and safe. This Alice in Wonderland, upside down reasoning allowed you to remain attached.

Children in less-than-adequate, anxiety-inducing, and disorganizing attachment relationships with caregivers are offered a devil's bargain that returns with a vengeance in the context of adult relationships. Know that you are betrayed and lose connection. Lost connection means a risk of death. Un-know betrayal, maintain connection, then continue to be subjected to betrayal and harm. Continued connection means danger, shame, suffering, self-hatred, and the development of a belief in paying prices to be in relationships.

People living with betrayal trauma also manifest a range of forms of psychological distress. If you've been betrayed, you are more likely than people who weren't to struggle with chronic illness, or with depression, anxiety, and other forms of psychological distress. Many addictive and compulsive behaviors also occur in the intersection between biological predispositions to addiction and the need to silence knowing with more powerful means than the brain can generate on its own. It's not surprising that when people get sober from substances or abstain from compulsive behaviors, they often begin to remember and know things that the addiction or compulsion helped to keep silenced and unavailable to consciousness.

Betrayal Blindness

Imagine for a moment that you live in a house where all of the smoke detectors have been disabled. You've been convinced to do this because your spouse has told you that the noise they make when the batteries are running out is painfully unpleasant to her/his sensitive ears. Your spouse reminds you that s/he has a great nose and will likely smell smoke, if there is any to smell, about as quickly as a smoke detector would sense it. You want to be a good, flexible spouse, and besides, how likely is it that a fire will break out in your house? Not very likely, you think. Neither of you smokes, you don't have a fireplace, the wiring is new. So you agree to disable the smoke detectors.

Two weeks later you smell smoke. You search the house and find your spouse pouring water on something. "Did you smell smoke?" you ask. "Oh no," comes the response, "You must have been mistaken." Two weeks later you smell smoke again. The response this time is, "There must have been someone walking by an open window with a lit cigarette." And then you hear, "Honey, maybe you should get yourself checked out by a neurologist. I'm worried about you smelling things that aren't there." The smoke detectors are all disabled, so you have to rely on your spouse's validation—or absence thereof—to make sense of what you're smelling. And then your spouse burns down the house. You barely escape, burned in more ways than physically.

If your cheater detectors have been disabled by the effects of less-than-adequate attachment experiences, you've become the person with the pyromaniac spouse in the house with disabled smoke detectors. You have become systemically *blind to betrayal*. Freyd and her co-author, Pamela Birrell in their book *Blind to Betrayal*, show that betrayal trauma theory is pertinent to relationships between adults as well. They found that when people have their cheater detectors turned off because they believe that dissociation of betrayal is the price of admission to a relationship, people become impaired in their capacity to know that betrayal is occurring. Not until the metaphorical house of the relationship is in flames does it become possible to know that betrayal has occurred.

People with histories of less-than-adequate attachment often develop betrayal blindness as the price of admission. Consciously or not, you sense that if you know the truth about how you are being betrayed, the relationship you're paying for will end and you will be blamed. "Why," you will be asked by the traitor, "Why oh why could you not have let sleeping dogs lie? Why did you have to poke your nose into things? Why did you have to stir things up?"

In this version of things for which you are blamed, there are two important ideas that are both wrong and are both lies. First, by the time you are able to know and speak the truth about being betrayed, the relationship is already damaged, sometimes beyond repair. You didn't screw things up by noticing that the house was on fire. The traitor is the one who has wounded the relationship, possibly fatally.

The fact that the traitor's body is still around and in proximity to you is irrelevant. The connection, the attachment, any pretense of emotional intimacy and transparency, is already long on its way to smoldering embers that are being hauled away to the dump. You sensed what was happening as the relationship got worse. Worsening conditions may have even helped you to bring your cheater detectors back online. But sometimes you sensed nothing at all until the entire force of the betrayal was made known to you and you were escaping from a burning building. You telling the truth, you paying attention to a clue, you confronting the traitor—none of that was the problem. That whole backwards thinking reflects a rule from your less-than-adequate attachment experience. The rule that telling the truth is a bad thing turns out to be as false today as it was when you were little.

Second, your desire to connect isn't what made all of this happen. You weren't so needy that the person had to betray you. You weren't the one who committed infidelity—and by infidelity I don't mean only sexual infidelity. There are many other ways for a person to be unfaithful to a relational commitment. Abuse is a form of infidelity to a relationship. Abuse violates a commitment to make the other person's welfare equal to your own. Workaholism can be a form of infidelity to a relationship, too. Simply because the "other person" in your relationship is an 80-hour work week and not someone your spouse is having sex with doesn't make the infidelity to the relationship any less. Unilaterally withdrawing from sex and refusing to address that when you're in a monogamous commitment is another form of infidelity. You didn't commit to celibacy when you committed to being faithful.

It's essentially important to remember that you didn't make this person betray you. They did it all by themselves. No one is so needy, so difficult, so boring, so distracted, that they deserve to be betrayed. Feedback—yes, requests for change— yes, betrayal—uh-uh, no way.

The paradigm of infant omnipotence in which roles were switched and you were to blame for everything not-okay that the adults did to you is as inaccurate today as it was then. The traitor broke a commitment to you, just as, decades earlier, your less-than-adequate caregiver broke the human contract for care. Your betrayal blindness from childhood created vulnerability to betrayal in the present. It didn't cause it. Even if the traitor was responding to a problematic dynamic in the relationship with you, the traitor always had choices for solving the problem that did not include betraying you.

Was Blind, But Now I See

Betrayal blindness and disabled cheater detectors should never be prices of admission to relationship, connection, and love. We need to be able to smell smoke and know that there's a fire before our house burns down. We need to be empowered to notice that something in a relationship isn't right before we are harmed. A relationship that requires you to shut off your cheater detectors and dissociate your discomfort about what's happening is not the attachment, love, and connection that you deserve. It's psychologically damaging and a reenactment of how you were required to un-know the ways your caregiver betrayed you when you were small.

Learning to turn the voice of your cheater detectors back on requires that you develop trust in your assessment of others. This is a very different perspective on trust than most people have. Because much of my work as a therapist is with people who have had experiences of betrayal and have had to turn off their cheater detectors in order to stay in relationships, I begin most therapies by telling people that I do not expect them to trust me. I expect, rather, that it is my task to behave in a trustworthy manner, and my job to empower them to learn to trust their assessment of other people, including me.

This shocks people who've spent much of their lives being told, "Trust me," or being asked, "Why can't you trust me?" They come to therapy, as to other relationships, with the belief that the burden is on them to assume my good intentions and to be vulnerable to me without having any evidence of how I will respond to that transparency in them. The idea that it is on the other person in a relationship to demonstrate worthiness of trust is foreign.

Earning trust is, of course, the scenario in good-enough attachment. The caregiver behaves in a trustworthy manner with the child, who is then free to develop cheater detectors. Those children can confidently tell caregivers that they don't like their preschool teacher with the expectation that their caregivers will be curious about why that's the case, rather than try to silence them or shame them for having and expressing opinions.

Developing and trusting your own evaluative skills is a necessary step toward being able to see clearly in the interpersonal realm. Learning this skill takes quite a bit of work, especially because many survivors have two modes when it comes to evaluating other people. You either trust too much with no data to support that or you're suspicious, again in the absence of data. These two interpersonal phenomena tend to co-occur, with people going back and forth between the poles.

Who Can You Trust?

Let's start developing your assessment capacities with an experiment. Think of several people you have known in your life whose actions toward you and/or others were primarily honorable, good, and decent—a teacher, a librarian, perhaps a friend, maybe a co-worker, or someone you've observed or heard of. If you can't come up with anyone you actually know, think of a fictional character that exemplifies these characteristics. Your example person doesn't have to be perfect. In fact, it's best if you know something about what they do when they're not being their best selves.

Try to think of at least two such people, even if that's hard to do, so that you have more than one person's idiosyncratic ways of expressing trustworthiness. Now consider what they did and said that exemplified their decency, honorableness, and worthiness of trust. Some things they might have had in common include:

- These people said what they were going to do and did it. They were transparent and kept commitments. No smoke and mirrors.

- Those people took responsibility for their own actions. They made few if any excuses, and when they did, the excuse was reasonable and called for by unusual circumstances (e.g., late to a meeting because there was an accident on the highway).

- When they screwed up and were less than decent and honorable, they said so, and took initiative to repair the breach. You don't hear them say, "You made me do that."

- These people were relatively consistent. They weren't rigid, but you could predict with some degree of certainty how they would act.

- These people had pretty good mastery of their emotions in most circumstances. They didn't yell or explode at others as a matter of course, and they weren't shut down. You didn't have to guess at what was going on with them, but they didn't over-share either.

- These people were genuinely curious about others. They listened without any predetermined assumptions about what they would hear, and they responded to what was being said, not to whatever monologue was happening in their own heads.

- These people never, ever used violence to solve problems. No matter how angry or upset they were, they never resorted to violence—verbal, emotional, or physical. They didn't call anyone names, put anyone down, or use sarcasm or contempt to silence others.

- These people used authority in a collaborative and, where possible, empowering manner. They weren't authoritarian.

- These people had insight into themselves. They did their best to understand who they were and what motivated them. They were as transparent as they knew how to be.

There are probably many other characteristics that you can think of. Keep an ongoing list of characteristics of trustworthy people, written down somewhere that you have easy access to. If you, like me, live in the electronic world, put your list in an easy-to-reach electronic storage cloud. If you're old-school, write it on a piece of paper and keep it in your wallet, purse, or backpack—anywhere you'll have easy access. Continue to edit the list, adding to it, modifying it, pruning it. It's going to become your master list for the "What makes people trustworthy" algorithm that you're developing. It's your version of the checklists that psychologists and other mental health professionals use for assessing people. In fact, it's kind of the reverse of the one we use to figure out if someone is a sociopath.

Now start to assess people you know. You may need some time to know how a person scores on your list. People can be challenging to read. Very few of us, even folks like me who make our living assessing other human beings, are especially good at quickly determining how a person measures up. My own tendencies to betrayal blindness means that I've been terribly—one time dangerously—fooled by people who meant me no good. Survivors, especially those of you who grew up in dangerous families, are often very good at reading the cues for danger in others, but not very good at reading the cues that signal trustworthiness. You might misread someone's behavior because it confuses you or doesn't fit into your pre-existing paradigms for people. That's okay. This is an experiment, a learning process.

Neither ignore nor give undue weight to your initial impressions. Humans like to make snap judgments and rely on stereotype and minimal information; it's cognitively more efficient. Please resist that urge, even though holding the ambiguity and continuing the assessment process will probably evoke some anxiety for you. People can grow on you, demonstrating their trustworthiness over time. That's what often happens in my therapy office. I keep showing up, behaving in what I hope is a trustworthy manner, encouraging people to keep assessing me, and never assume that I've done enough, but rather know that trust is something that I must earn daily. I offer repair of ruptures. I take responsibility for when my own stuff leaks.

People can also grow *off* you, showing you that, as time goes on, they are less willing to deal with you and others in an honest and decent manner. It can be instructive to see what someone does when they're under stress. Can they be more their usual self than not, or do they give themselves a free pass to behave badly when life is going poorly? Those are very important pieces of data.

If you don't feel that your list or your own assessment skills are adequate, there are several resources available to assist you in honing your skills. For starters you can study the work of Paul Ekman, a social psychologist who carefully researched what truth and lies look like on human faces. Over many years, he has developed a system for coding people's facial expressions. If you think that your own skills at detecting deceit are too affected by years of having had your cheater detectors turned off, reading his work can give you a leg up on restoring your capacities. You could even develop better-than-average skills at detecting deception by reading his research findings. There's a link to his work in the Resources section of this book.

I also suggest reading Gavin de Becker's classic book, *The Gift of Fear*. De Becker is a survivor of a childhood from hell. He's a lot like you, dear reader. For some reason he didn't turn off his cheater detectors, probably because he had a younger sibling to protect. He was somehow able to learn how to be effective in his relationships with others, and to parlay his skills at detecting danger into a lucrative career as a threat evaluator for celebrities.

His book is about how to turn on and listen to your cheater detectors. He does a masterful job of describing ways in which people invite you to turn your detectors off as well. De Becker says, clearly and directly, that if you are afraid of someone— not afraid of connection, not afraid of being seen or known, not afraid of being vulnerable, but afraid of that other person—then you should pay attention to that signal from inside. He has a useful algorithm he calls pre-incident indicators, or PINs for learning what the early danger signals are. The PINs are:

- *Forced Teaming.* This is when a person implies that he or she has something in common with the chosen victim, acting as if they have a shared predicament when that isn't really true. Speaking in "we" terms is a mark of this. For example, "We don't need to talk outside... Let's go in."

- *Charm and Niceness.* This is being more polite and friendly to a chosen victim than the situation calls for in order to manipulate him or her by disarming their mistrust.

- *Too Many Details.* People who are lying will usually add excessive details to make themselves sound more credible to their chosen victim.

- *Typecasting.* An insult is used to get a chosen victim who would otherwise ignore the insult, to engage in conversation to counteract the insult. For example: "Oh, I bet you're too stuck-up to talk to a guy like me." The tendency is for the chosen victim to want to prove the insult untrue, and to engage with the dangerous person.

- *Loan Sharking.* This involves giving unsolicited help to the chosen victim and anticipating that they'll feel obliged to extend some reciprocal openness in return.

- *The Unsolicited Promise.* This is a promise to do (or not do) something when no such promise is asked for, which usually means that such a promise will be broken. For example, an unsolicited, "I promise I'll leave you alone after this," usually means the chosen victim will not be left alone. Similarly, an unsolicited, "I promise I won't hurt you" usually means the person intends to hurt the chosen victim.

- *Discounting the Word "No."* Refusing to accept rejection and a clear boundary. "No means yes" to someone who's not worthy of your trust.

Notice how many of these behaviors remind you of one or more of the less-than-adequate adults who raised you? You can see how vulnerable you are when you're in a relationship with someone who has unclean motives. Those folks sound familiar. The other person is tapping into familiar attachment patterns, strumming the strings of your limbic resonances.

For people who had to turn their cheater detectors off in dangerous families, the PINs model cuts through years of trial and error to offer a solid and well-tested methodology for making the first cut when assessing other people. If someone is dangerous to you, don't stick around to find out if that person might someday, somehow be worthy of your trust. You can already know that this person is unworthy and unsafe. PINs also do a good job of differentiating between scary—as in, humans and connection and attachment feel scary—and dangerous—as in, run, do not walk, away from this person.

Another useful resource for people working to turn their cheater detectors back on is Martha Stout's *The Sociopath Next Door*. I find it helpful because it makes sociopathy understandable and its assessment accessible. This book isn't about scary mass murderers (most of whom aren't sociopaths anyhow, despite what TV crime shows would like you to believe). It's about people in daily life whose damage from less-than-adequate attachment manifests in an absence of empathy for others and a willingness to use other people to achieve their ends. Most people who are not worthy of trust are also *not* sociopaths. But if you're trying to get your cheater detectors working after decades of having them turned off, it can be helpful to have information about what extreme untrustworthiness looks like.

Many of you believe, as a result of having to turn off your cheater detectors, that betrayal blindness is the price of admission to relationships. Wrong, wrong, wrong. The relationships you deserve never require you to systemically ignore that something is wrong or dissociate from your discomfort. If you insist on honesty, transparency, and integrity from people with whom you have relationships, you will not be alone in the world forever. The stark reality is that when you are in what looks like a relationship where you are being betrayed, you're already alone.

Don't Hit Me Baby One More Time

One of the worst kinds of relational betrayal is abuse. If you believe yourself to be unworthy of love, particularly if you were the target of abuse from a caregiver when you were young, you may have come to believe that being abused in some way is a necessary price to pay for being in relationship. This is a lie. Abuse is never, ever a price that anyone should pay for connection. It was wrong when you were little. It's no less wrong now.

Abuse in a relationship can take many forms. The hallmark of any form of abuse is the presence of *coercion and control*. You don't have to be hit or kicked to be abused. A person may also be physically violent one time without being abusive. Although violence is never acceptable, it doesn't turn into abuse until it becomes a means of coercion and control. You can assume that when physical violence occurs more than once, it's entered the realm of abuse.

Many forms of abuse do not involve physical violence, and many of the targets of the non-physical kinds of abuse say that these are harder to identify because the parameters of the abuse are less obvious than when someone is hitting, kicking, throwing things at you, or destroying your property. So look for the elements of coercion and control. Those are the indicators that you're in an abusive dynamic with someone else.

Verbal abuse turns out to be alarmingly common in romantic relationships. If the other party uses threat, denigration, gaslighting, or other forms of emotional manipulation to force you into behaviors that feel like a violation of your values as a condition of being in connection or that confuse you repeatedly about what's real, that's abuse. Extreme jealousy in which one party interferes with the other's associations is abuse. If your best friend tells you that you must join her or his religious organization in order to remain in the relationship, that's abuse. Consistent undermining of your free choices, and punitive responses to your bids for autonomy, are evidence of coercion and control.

Financial exploitation can also constitute abuse. If a person stays in your life contingent on you paying for everything, then that's not a relationship—that's abuse and exploitation. A price of admission in dollars and cents is even more costly because some other form of undermining or disrespect almost always accompanies it. If a spouse or partner confiscates your paycheck and will not allow you to know how the money is being spent, no matter how badly you balance your checkbook or how late you pay your bills, that's coercion and control. That's abusive.

Bryce was raised in a family where his father beat his mother, and took her paycheck to buy himself "toys" like snowmobiles and ATVs. His father verbally abused and demeaned him, telling him, "You're a little shit, just like your mother, ugly as sin." Bryce internalized his father's epithets, and he lived with a burden of self-hate and a belief that he would be extremely lucky to ever have anyone want him. Bryce vowed that should he ever be lucky enough to find someone willing to marry him, he would be loving and generous with his wife, and always be grateful that she was willing to have his worthless self. When he met Elspeth and fell head over heels in love, he immediately began a campaign of buying her affection. He purchased expensive jewelry for her for every date. He went into debt to take her to concerts of her favorite artists, whose music he did not enjoy. Most worrisome to friends with whom he talked endlessly about her, he repeatedly tolerated her telling him about all of the other men she was dating. She flirted with other men in front of Bryce, and upbraided him when he squirmed, telling him that if he couldn't handle her being so attractive to other men, then he should find someone plainer.

When they married after a whirlwind six-month courtship that left Bryce in serious credit card debt, things deteriorated. Elspeth quit her job so that she could pursue her dream of becoming a massage therapist. Of course, Bryce was going to pay the tuition for massage school. Of course, he would pay all of the bills when Elspeth was in school. When she graduated and got her license, Bryce looked forward to sharing some of the expenses, only to find that Elspeth had decided that she could only do one treatment a day because, "It's not good for my body to do more, dear." Bryce started to volunteer for overtime at his job to meet the growing number of bills. Elspeth kept her tiny income for herself. She also began to complain loudly that Bryce was never home. "If you're not around, why should I stick around the house?" She began to go out most nights with friends, frequently returning home well after Bryce had staggered in exhausted from his second shift. Their sex life had disappeared long ago.

Bryce hit a wall when Elspeth began to talk about going back to school again to get a certification in sports massage. "Darn it, Els, when are you going to start contributing financially to this family?" he muttered. And that was the end of Elspeth. She became enraged at Bryce, accusing him of being a cheapskate who had lied to her about wanting her to have a comfortable life. "How dare you expect me to make money!" she yelled at him.

Two days later Elspeth moved in with a friend, who turned out to be the man with whom she had been having an affair since she was in massage school. She filed for divorce and requested maintenance on the grounds that she had been essentially out of the workforce since marrying Bryce. She also sued for half of everything he owned, and half of his future earnings. All of this was devastating to Bryce. The only conclusion he was able to draw was that his father had been right. He was an ugly little piece of shit, and the only way any woman would want him would be for him to pay the freight for everything, always. "The mistake I made was to ask her to contribute financially," he told his divorce lawyer. "If I'd just kept my stupid mouth shut, I'd at least still have her."

Bryce's story is a painful classic in the annals of survivors in relationships. He entered a reenactment with Elspeth, who was configured a lot like his father. The limbic resonances between them were strong. It felt right, even though he knew it was wrong, to be denigrated, devalued, and used financially. He had turned off his cheater detectors long before he met Elspeth. Thus, his ability to code her withdrawal from the marriage or the financial exploitation as betrayal was impaired. He blamed himself for what happened.

Elspeth never hit Bryce. She didn't yell at him until the very end. She didn't verbally put him down and call him names. But her infidelity to him began well before her affair. It extended far past her flirtations with other men. Bryce was betrayed by her willingness to use him financially, and to exploit his vulnerability about his attractiveness and lovability.

No one, and I mean *no one*, ever, ever deserves to be abused in any way in a relationship. No one. I don't care how difficult you've been, or how badly you've screwed things up, **you do not deserve to be abused**. Abuse is never an acceptable price of admission to relationship. Never. When someone tells you that you're lucky that he or she put up with you and implies that the price of that tolerance is abuse, that person is telling you a big fat lie.

If you have actually been a difficult person, if you've been unfaithful to your commitments, or if you've violated boundaries, you do deserve nonabusive consequences. You owe amends and you need to make a repair. You owe a willingness to hear the other person out as he or she tells you their feelings about your effect on them. If you're the one committing betrayal, you've put the connection at risk. The model of 12-Step programs is a good one for how to act when you've done something that's genuinely not okay versus being a little (or a lot) too human.

So you make a "searching and fearless moral inventory." You "admit...to the nature of your wrongs." You exhibit willingness to change. You initiate the process of making amends to people you've harmed, unless doing so would harm them or others. You behave with responsibility toward the person you have wronged in some way. You don't expect that person to stick around or to absolve you if you've genuinely behaved badly and made no gestures in the direction of amends. Something you might not know is that this entire process is also something you're doing for yourself, so that you can be a person of more integrity, so that you can repair yourself and prepare for being a better person with whom to relate.

Notice that in none of this is the statement, "You must tolerate being screamed at, called names, berated endlessly, made to feel worthless," or the assertion, "You must redouble your efforts to pay a price of admission to a relationship," or the notion, "You must abase yourself in shame at your bad behavior." Abuse is not a reasonable consequence for you having missed the mark, even if you've behaved pretty badly. Abuse is a betrayal of human connection that no one deserves.

Turning on your cheater detectors will assist you in identifying abusive dynamics in a relationship more quickly. Why is speed important? First, the emotional and physical health prices of being in abusive relationships are very high. Depression, anxiety, post-traumatic stress, cardiovascular problems, and other diseases that are caused or worsened by systemic inflammation are common in people living in chronically abusive circumstances. Second, many people who behave abusively in nonviolent ways and use coercion and control are themselves wounded in attachment. An abusive person in your life today may be amenable to psychotherapy and open to the possibility of change in ways that the adults who raised you were not. Going to therapy is not a panacea, and there are no reliably effective treatments for people who engage in violent abusive behaviors. Couples therapy is contraindicated for people who are in violently abusive relationships, and no good couples therapist should be willing to see you and a partner if one of you is being physically violent with the other. But if physical violence is absent, therapy might be helpful. It's better for all parties that you interrupt a destructive pattern early by being clear that you do not deserve to be abused, ever.

Be cautious and self-protective. Abuse that escalates to physical violence is dangerous. Women in violent relationships are at risk of death and serious injury. There isn't any accurate data yet about risks of serious injury or death for men in violent relationships. No man deserves to be abused even if we don't have enough data yet about lethal risks to men from their partners' violence. Violent relationships are hard to leave because of their debilitating effects. Leaving doesn't necessarily feel safe, and often isn't. More women who had been in physically violent relationships were killed at the point of leaving than at any other time.

If the severity and intensity of the violence increases, if the violent person escalates the potential lethality of his or her tactics, or if that person is threatening to kill you or the kids or him or herself, please take this very seriously. These are known red flags that predict a lethal outcome for one or both people. Stay alive. Get to safety. Go somewhere that the violent person can't have access to you and the kids. Restraining orders have not been shown to protect people from violent partners. Don't make filing one your first step. Don't wait to take steps to protect yourself until it's at the point where you think that one of you is going to die. I've testified in too many trials for battered women who had to kill in self-defense. These women's cheater detectors often didn't come online until the last minute when they realized that they or their kids were about to end up dead if they didn't act. **Being at risk of dying or spending the rest of your life in prison is too high a price to pay.**

If you're not sure about the level of danger you're in from a violent person and you need outside validation for your cheater detectors, you can use Dr. Jacqueline Campbell's Danger Assessment checklist. It's available online and is in the Resources section of this book. There are several red flag behaviors—strangling you, threats to kill you, threats to kill children, and suicide threats—that mean that someone is very likely to end up dead if you don't get away to safety as soon as possible. This is a research-based tool that's collected data from hundreds of intimate partner violence situations, including those in which one or both parties (or their children) were killed. There are versions in several languages as well as a version for women in same-sex relationships.

If you score anywhere past the middle on this scale, it's past time to get out and to safety. Do not blame yourself for the violence. Do not think that staying will make things get better. It won't. You could die. The other person could die. Your kids could die. Get to safety, and do it now. Put this book down and get to safety now, please. You can always read this book later, when you're safe. You can't read it if you're dead.

We Won't be Fooled Again

Turning on your cheater detectors can at first seem to make life more difficult. You may feel raw, bombarded by information that you're not yet sure what to do with. Resist the urge to shut this information down. Like an arm that's fallen asleep because you've been lying on it for too long, the painful sensations you're feeling are neither permanent nor evidence that something is going wrong with you. They're new information arriving as you become more fully alive and attuned to knowing what's happening with other people. Take a deep breath again. Use your assessment checklist. Know that being deceived and betrayed is never the price of admission you must pay for an emotionally-meaningful relationship.

CHAPTER 6
Alone Again, Naturally

Human beings truly exist only in relationship to one another. One of the founders of attachment theory, the psychoanalyst and pediatrician Donald Winnicott, famously said that caregiver and infant invent one another. Mothers and fathers only become parents when there is an infant. Our development as individuals occurs in the context of attachment. Despite having the presence of another person with us from the moment of conception, one of the common emotional experiences for survivors is of being alone in the world, deeply lonely, unable to call upon others for support. Often this belief is accompanied by a complementary one saying that the survivor's job in the world is to be of use to others. The price of relationship, connection, and love: Be of use and support to others, and know that you won't, and perhaps shouldn't, get support when you need it. You accompany others. They don't accompany you.

This imbalanced view of relationships derives from particular kinds of experiences that you've had with your caregivers. Some of these experiences were not intended to affect you in this way, but they did. Your caregiver may have been depleted in some way—emotionally or materially—not only during your infancy but also throughout other times in your childhood. Depleted adults are not intentionally withholding care from children. They're usually barely keeping themselves afloat. A profoundly depressed caregiver or one who is working too many minimum wage hours to make sure that there is food on the table and a dry place to sleep, is living in the lower reaches of psychologist Abraham Maslow's famous hierarchy of needs. It's taking every ounce of this person's energy to ensure that you have the basics of survival available.

If you were an eldest or close to eldest child in that family, you likely began very early to pitch in and take over whatever components of caring for younger siblings that you could. Otherwise good-enough parents who are struggling with poverty, low-wage and long-hour jobs, and effects of systemic discrimination are often among these depleted caregivers. These adults deserve compassion and social policies that support their capacity to parent.

Although outside of the U.S. almost all countries in the industrialized world have excellent social safety net systems that support parents with low-cost, high-quality childcare, lengthy paid parental leave, and subsidies for all families with young children, these systemic supports for parents are absent in the U.S. You can get these things if you have enough money, but many people I know pour almost all of the second parent's income into the cost of childcare. As a result, depleted parents in America frequently have nowhere to turn for support that would allow them to be emotionally good-enough for their children.

Children in depleted families learn early that expressing needs for emotional care and support from parents usually ends in disappointment. If you're sick and someone has to stay home with you, it costs your parents money if they're working one those low-paying jobs that have no sick leave. This teaches you that the cost of you needing to stay home from school with the flu is that there's less food on the table at the end of the month. So you hide your illness and go to school aching with fever. If you've been bullied at school for wearing hand-me-downs and your parents don't have the emotional energy or time off from jobs to advocate for you with school administrators or teachers, you don't tell them. You learn how to handle it on your own. You might shoplift clothes in order to fit in. You learn that you're alone with life's problems, so you solve them as best as you are able with your not-yet-developed brain. Your parents don't want you to adopt this view of the life, but they're too alone themselves to be able to really help you out.

Children have a hard time understanding that their caregivers would be there for them if they could. That requires a level of insight that most kids don't have. You won't be able to see and understand the difficult choices your depleted parents make until you're older. Children are concrete and arrive at the conclusion that what you see is what you get. A child raised by depleted caregivers expects the not-very-much that those exhausted parents have available. Kids from these families are likely to internalize a version of the world in which needing something is burdensome to others. If that's your story, you've developed strategies for being hyper-autonomous and needing no one. You've created a personal ideology of "independence." You decide that you should never allow yourself to know how much you might want to lean on someone when you're hurting.

If your needs for support are particularly strong and shame-inducing for you, you may project that shame onto others to defend yourself against what you're feeling. You might label people who ask for or accept help as "weak" or "users." This is how people who grew up poor but found ways to be financially secure in adulthood end up being contemptuous toward people, including their own family members, whose financial struggles might require food stamps or state-provided healthcare.

If you are the child of depleted parents, you may believe that the price of admission to relationships is to need nothing from anyone, ever. You might have a pattern of encounters with other people that are brief, superficial, and focused on meeting a particular limited need for the shortest possible period of time. You try not to have emotionally-meaningful relationships so as not to risk that your mask of needing no one might crack a little in the face of genuine care.

Fiction is full of this kind of so-called "strong silent" character. Jack Reacher and James Bond are two of the better-known versions of this archetype. They ride into town, deal with a bad guy, have a brief sexual encounter with someone, commit violence in the name of dealing with the bad guy, and then leave. They have no permanent connections. Jack Reacher doesn't even own a second set of clothing.

Or one can be more academic about this and pronounce oneself an existentialist of the nihilistic variety. Morbid existentialism can seem appealing for a survivor. The notion that we are alone in the world and that there is no inherent meaning can feel like a validation of one's experiences of emptiness and meaninglessness. Nihilism and its intellectualized rationale for disconnecting from other humans can be soothing for a time. "L'enfer c'ést les autres—Hell is other people," the famous closing line from Sartre's play *No Exit,* appeals to people who have been raised in a hell created by their caregivers.

This strategy of avoiding anything that might pull away the mask of invulnerability is frequently woven into narratives of masculinities. This is likely because such narratives over-emphasize hyper-autonomy, "standing on your own two feet," and other themes of not being in relationship. What psychologist Ron Levant calls "normative male alexithymia" is the difficulty that many men have with knowing what they feel and expressing those feelings, especially when the feelings in question are tender and vulnerable. This phenomenon is a component of some men's patterns of paying prices for the relationships they allow themselves to have. In this world view, feelings are coded as a luxury, vulnerability as a weakness, humanness as a flaw.

This is not to say that women don't also adopt this position of being entirely for others and avoiding emotions and connections altogether by not allowing reciprocity. Rather, it is to notice that vulnerability to adopting this belief is particularly high for people affected by a rule saying that a real man needs no one, but must make himself available to be leaned on when others have a need. This "sturdy oak" narrative of masculinity was first named in the 1970s by psychologist Robert Brannon. But it's not about being a man. It's about protecting yourself from knowing how much you do need to connect with other people.

The belief that if you have relationships you must pay the price of needing nothing is related to another belief. That's the one saying that other people require that you give to them or do things for them if you want to have connection with them. It's the price of being someone who's of use, who's handy and helpful. Cyrano de Bergerac exemplifies this price—he's a good friend to all who allows himself to be used to compose a paean of love to Roxanne, the woman of his dreams. But he's writing it for someone else because he believes himself too ugly to love. He's willing to be used just to get a little closer to his beloved. If this is your narrative of the price you have to pay, you believe that you must buy your way to having relationships by ensuring that the other person is always getting good value for having deigned to relate to you.

This isn't anything like healthy reciprocity. In relationships where there is mutuality and reciprocity between the parties, people invest in an exchange of care and support that may be imbalanced at times. It is, however, marked by the inherent assumption that each party is free to ask for, and is eligible to receive, support when needed. This is the model derived from the good-enough relationship between a child and her/his caregivers. The caregiver has sufficient resources to care for the child, and as the child matures and has capacities to contribute in some way to the general welfare, the child is encouraged to do so. This is not to repay parents; it's part of learning how to be a contributing member of the human family. A kid in a good-enough family isn't doing laundry to earn her or his keep, but because everyone in the family contributes according to their abilities. The child's participation is developmentally appropriate, and not the price of the child being loved or cared for.

So a good-enough parent of a three-year-old will make a game of working together with the child to see who can pick up the most blocks in two minutes, and praise the child for being helpful. Contrast this with a depleted parent who angrily gives a child the task of cleaning up the blocks alone because the parent has too much else to do, offering no praise or acknowledgement for the child's participation, or with an abusive parent who lets kids know that they are barely welcome, and requires them to earn their food and shelter by being their parents' servants.

For survivors from depleted families, getting support from others isn't frightening the way it might be for people who were overtly abused. It doesn't feel risky. It simply feels completely unavailable. If you've worked hard to defend against your desires for care, you may actually disown the need, and stake your claim to being a highly autonomous loner. Your EPs have dissociated the need for care from others so completely as to have little to no access to it.

Help, I Need Somebody

The problem with an equation in which the price of admission is to need nothing is that human beings are not able, no matter how capable we are, to meet all of our own needs. If we have the financial wherewithal, we might be able to cover up our needs by paying people money to meet them. This strategy allows us to bring needs in through the back door and pretend that they're not emotionally important by having the price of admission be cash. But when we are ill, or hurt physically, our dissociated emotional needs may show up in ways that we are unable to fob off on paid help. Yes, you can pay someone to clean your house when you're too sick from chemotherapy to do it yourself. But being able to discuss your fears of death and disfigurement when you have a serious illness requires being seen and known as having human needs. That's hard to do with a stranger brought in to perform a service.

A belief that the price of admission to relationships is silencing your needs has the corollary that your having needs, whether they're met or not, is a problem. You further assume that the only way to proceed is to take care of others. Notice that you're not defining the needs of people you're trying to relate to as problems, since you've constructed the relationship on the model that you'll meet their needs. You need them to have needs that you can meet. You may in fact be someone who is highly skilled at exquisitely meeting the needs of others, and may end up having a number of relationships in which your entire function is meeting the other person's needs in some way.

Many people in the helping professions fall into this dynamic. The safest relationships are our professional ones where our needs (except to make a living) *must* not be met, except accidentally, and it's all about meeting the needs of others. It's easy for you as a professional to seem calm, regulated, and emotionally present with people in relationships where no one expects you to be transparent or vulnerable. You kind of meet your needs for human connection of some sort when you're a professional helper. The price you pay is that you are never completely known, because the structure of the relationship is that you're focused on your patients or clients. Your apparently intuitive ability to understand their needs is in part because their needs are yours—you know what you're missing, so you know what they want, too. You can even vicariously experience being someone who gets her or his needs met by meeting those of your clients, or by supporting them in becoming people who are able to ask for what they want and not pay prices in relationships.

Everyone is endangered when a helping professional avoids directly meeting her or his basic human needs for love, care, and nurturance. Research indicates that sexual boundary violations by helping professionals are more likely to occur when the helper is practicing an extreme version of the need-nothing strategy and then comes to an especially low or hard place in life. Going through a hard time is not an excuse for a professional to violate sexual boundaries. No helping professional should ever have sex with her or his patients or clients, not ever, in this or any other lifetime or galaxy. Many of those who do are far more likely to have been denying their own needs in the rest of their life for way too long.

This pattern of paying the price by having no relationship rather than having needs—or only having relationships where you're of use—is toxic. If your caregiver was not simply depleted, but was rather actively punitive in response to your normative dependency needs, this dynamic can be even more malignant and shame-inducing. If your caregiver got angry at or endangered you when you expressed your needs, if you were shamed or humiliated simply for having developmentally normal needs, you were left feeling that you're in danger when you express a need in a relationship today.

Noel's parents had conceived her entirely by accident, due to a failure of birth control. "If abortion had been legal, then you wouldn't have shown up and ruined our lives," was a statement that she began to hear early in her life. She asked her therapist, "How many kids know the meaning of abortion before they can read? Me, because my parents told me they should have had one." Her parents lacked the capacity to welcome Noel into the world, and punished her for existing from the moment they discovered the pregnancy. Noel's mother regales her with stories of pounding on her own belly, hoping to dislodge Noel from the womb. Her father referred to her as "it." "Why won't it stop crying?" Noel has very early memories of her mother holding Noel's nose pinched closed to stop her from crying, and can recall the panicked feeling of being unable to breathe.

Because her parents were also highly educated, upper middle class people with plenty of money, as well as pathological levels of narcissism, Noel's job was not simply to have no needs. It was also to be a source of narcissistic nourishment for her parents as her penance for having been born. She had to look good, do well in school, be a star in sports, and shine precociously at social gatherings. Failure on these and any other dimensions was punished with beatings in places that showed no bruises, withholding of food, and in one particularly painful instance, giving away her cat, the only creature in her family who wasn't cruel to her. By the time she entered kindergarten, already reading at third-grade level, playing piano, and charmingly serving the guests at her parents' parties, Noel had the price of admission to relationships completely figured out. She would be the best little girl in the world, and eventually, she would get her parents to love her and be nice to her.

School was the best thing that ever happened to Noel. There, when she was perfect and giving and hard-working, no one hit her or sneered at her or took away things that mattered to her. There were double benefits. Her parents could brag to their friends about their daughter's stellar academic performance, and Noel could befriend her teachers, who were mostly decent, caring people. Some of them noticed that this child took every opportunity to stay after school and help out until she had a lesson or a sporting event to attend. Because Noel's internal working model so strongly informed her that all relationships with others were contingent on her performance, it wasn't until she was an adult and in therapy that she realized that many of her teachers wouldn't have cared if she stopped being their little helper. "They just liked me, didn't they? Because if I had a kid like me I would be so grateful, and like her so much."

Noel crossed the path of a predator when she was 14. Her swim coach first groomed her emotionally, sensing her extreme vulnerability and emotional neediness, and recognized that she had no protective parent around. Her parents didn't mind when Mr. Jackson began to pick her up for meets and let her spend the night at his house when there was an especially early morning practice. They told Noel that she was lucky that someone was willing to go out of his way for her, and they reminded her that she'd better repay him by winning races. When repayment became sexual demands, Noel was swept away by feelings of love and relieved that someone was touching her pleasurably, not painfully. Only when she was an adult and in therapy did she stop saying that this was an "affair" and to reappraise what had happened to her as abuse and exploitation.

This adolescent experience started a pattern of Noel being sexually used by older mentors. "Coach first," she said, "then thesis advisor, then mentor at my job, then two bosses. I was always just so grateful that someone was paying attention to me and being nice to me that I figured the least I could do was put out." Two of these relationships involved sexual sadism, and even though those activities terrified and hurt her, Noel was unable to say "no." She described spending much of her time in these encounters waiting for the men to grow tired of the game and rid themselves of her. "I knew that I was worthless at the core, and once the novelty of fucking me wore off, I expected to be discarded."

Despite her stellar academic and work performance, Noel found herself rarely doing as well as others around her. Some of this was because so much of her energy was being consumed by servicing a powerful man in the environment. While she was occasionally given so-called favors by these men such as co-authoring a paper with her advisor when she was in graduate school, the favors were decidedly one way. "I wrote the paper, then he added a few lines and got first authorship," she recalled. "He told me I was lucky to be publishing with him, which I was, by the way. He's pretty well known in the field, and it was good for me to have my name linked to his." But peers who wrote their own papers and got first authorships got better job offers.

Some of this was because Noel was emotionally isolated from other people. She had developed a version of her "to be used" relationship paradigm in which the only relationships she could have were those where the price of admission was sexual availability. She couldn't risk trying to have relationships with her peers, as the men who were having sex with her were in positions of power and could punish both her and the peer. Because she couldn't offer sex to her peers, she believed she had nothing to offer them. When projects were assigned, she did the work but never participated in the less formal, team-and-relationship-building activities that helped people move up in her profession. So when someone thought of whom to promote, or when there was a great job opening at another organization, no one thought of Noel.

There was also the kind of cost she paid for being read—correctly—as the sexual partner of the (usually married) older and powerful man in the workplace. Her peers rarely trusted by her. They thought that her loyalties lay with the man she was having sex with. In fact, several of these powerful men did pressure Noel to be a source of information about her peers—another way that she was made to be of use.

This entire strategy fell apart when Noel went to work for a genuinely kind and caring man who was deeply religious, married and monogamously committed to his wife. Avi enjoyed mentoring and promoting women in male-dominated occupations because he had been raised with his mother's stories of career struggles. Noel quickly became overcome with anxiety. She would flirt with her boss, who would kindly remind her that although he liked her a lot, he had strong values about keeping his commitments. "Including my commitment to you, Noel, not to sexually harass you. I don't like our lawyers that much." His refusals felt like rejections to her. She would lie awake at night wondering what she had done wrong to make him angry at her. During the day she was unable to concentrate, worrying that she would be fired at any moment. Her productivity took a nosedive. When he found her sobbing at her desk late one night, her boss told her that he thought it might be a good idea to see a therapist. "I want you to succeed," he told her. "And I don't understand why you're struggling so much with tasks that I know you've done brilliantly in the past. So I want you to get some help."

To say that Noel was confused by this exchange is the understatement of the millennium. In her internal working model, Avi was supposed to do one of two things at this juncture: Have sex with her, or get rid of her. He wasn't supposed to both not have sex with her and not get rid of her, and instead tell her to see a therapist. Yet she needed her job so, confused or not, she went to therapy. She tried seducing her therapist, Julia, who gave her the "not in this lifetime, any other lifetime, on this planet, or in any other universe would I do something that I knew in advance would harm you" speech, which was additionally confusing to Noel. "Maybe you're not into women?" she asked the therapist. "And that would matter why?" Julia answered. "Well, then, it would be okay because you wouldn't want to have sex with me anyhow. I thought you were a lesbian." Julia responded, "And that meant I would have sex with you? Nope. You're my client. I would never do something that I knew would do you harm. So, not in this lifetime, etc."

Noel had such a powerful paradigm for her price of admission, one that was so deeply engrained in her internal working model, and so thoroughly soaked into the core of her EPs, that therapy with a therapist who was kind and caring and wouldn't take anything from her but the agreed-upon fee turned out to be excruciating—even more excruciating and confusing than working for a boss who also wouldn't have sex with her and remained supportive and encouraging. She could hardly stand having two emotionally important relationships in her life in which there was no horrific price to be paid, where all she had to do was show up and keep her basic commitments.

Noel's story isn't unusual. Her hardest—although not only—price was sexual availability. Other people pay a price by working an 80-hour week for 40 hours of pay, or by going to work no matter how sick they are, or springing for dinner to the point where people routinely come out to eat with them and are unprepared to pay. If this is you, you're the one in a household of two able-bodied-and-minded adults who does all of the cooking, cleaning, laundry, and grocery shopping so that the other adult is free to be creative and spend time with friends. Sometimes the price shows up when you don't know how you're going to ask someone to take you to a medical procedure where the clinic requires your escort to come with you and stay the entire time, not drop you off and then show up to take you home. So you just don't get important preventative care done at all. No matter that you've done this for three of your friends, and would gladly do so again if asked. You know that if they've started to rely on you doing things for them, they'll have a harder time getting rid of you. Yet you "know" that you're all on your own when you need help.

Believing that the only reason you are not alone is that you are paying such a heavy price for connection is a wound of attachment arising from abuse and neglect in childhood. If the only ways you were able to get your basic young human needs met was to perform and put out, you learned early that there was no relationship without price. Being alone as you grow older is one of your fears. Who, you wonder, will have anything to do with you if you can't offer your usual price to people for companionship or care?

Continuing to pay these prices because you fear being alone never allows you to test the hypothesis that some people might actually want to associate with you simply because you're you. Noel found this out about three years into therapy when she fell while hiking (alone) and spent a night, shivering with cold and pain, at the bottom of a ravine where there was no cell phone reception. When she wasn't at work the next morning, her boss—Avi—was sufficiently alarmed by this uncharacteristic behavior to call the police, and when they refused to do anything because 48 hours hadn't passed, he organized a search party of himself and three co-workers, all of whom recalled her mentioning something about plans for a hike the prior evening. They scanned her social media pages for mentions or photos of hiking spots and picked the two that came up most frequently. Noel was stuck and hurt about a mile down the trail at one of them.

When Avi and the team found Noel, she began to apologize profusely. "I was terrified about how angry he was going to be," she told Julia. "But he wasn't mad at all. He kept saying how blessed he was that he found me, how upset he'd have been if something terrible had happened to me." When the EMTs came he insisted on riding with them to the hospital, and held her hand while her broken leg and wrist were splinted.

"And now you're coming home with me," he told her. "I've already phoned Joyce—she's got the bed made up in the main floor guest room." "And I figured, aha, you're finally going to fuck me, just when I'm at my worst." Except he didn't. He and Joyce were just so nice to me and wouldn't let me do a thing." When Noel tried to get on her feet too soon to clean the room she was staying in, she experienced her only encounter with Avi's anger. "What kind of putz do you think I am who would want a person with two broken bones to get up and clean? Seriously, that's what you think of me?"

"I wasn't getting any work done, I wasn't helping out, I wasn't putting out. And it dawned on me—oh, this is the thing that we've been talking about, isn't it? That people aren't necessarily going to want to use me, right? And that it feels weird and scary and makes me want to run, right?" "Right," Julia said. "You've got it. This, that's what we're talking about."

You're Ain't Heavy, You're My Sibling

It doesn't have to take falling off either a real or a metaphoric cliff to notice that you don't have to be alone in the world. You don't have to almost die of being alone to learn that being accompanied in life need not come at a terrible price. Avi and Joyce were neither saints nor unusual. They were simply decent human beings who had the desire to have Noel in their lives, had resources of time and energy in abundance, and could express their care for Noel by assisting her when she needed it. This episode was the beginning of them becoming her "mom and dad of choice," the people whom she asked to walk her down the aisle five years later when she married a decent loving man who had been carefully screened by her new "parents" before she said "yes." Her biological parents had long ago cut her off because she had ceased to react to their efforts at emotional coercion and control. "So give the inheritance to the Sierra Club, fine," was her attitude. "No money can ever balance out how badly they've always treated me, and would continue to if I allowed it."

The concept of a family of choice began to show up in writings by lesbian, gay, bisexual, and transgendered people who were rejected by their families of origin due to their sexual or gender orientations. LGBT people found that they could have sisters and brothers, mothers and fathers, aunts and uncles, and be older siblings to other, younger LGBT people who were coming out and leaving unloving homes. If you've ever been to a Pride celebration, you've watched people dancing to the disco anthem *"We Are Family."* That's the theme song of families of choice. It resonates powerfully for many LGBT people who came out and left home before society became more able to see the humanity of everyone, regardless of how they loved or expressed gender.

Anyone can have a family of choice that stands by you in times of needs and celebrates with you in times of joy. Sometimes it includes members of your original family, but it is always a grouping of people who exemplify the good-enough family.

They are your good-enough emotional home, "the place where they have to take you in." Creating a family of choice powerfully disrupts internal working models that predict being alone and used by others. A family of choice can give your EPs repeated opportunities to practice noticing that you can have relationships that are toll-free and emotionally-meaningful, and have people in your life who care about you without using you.

In families of choice everyone gives and everyone gets. There are implicit agreements that people will do their best to be kind to one another and repair ruptures when they occur. The word "choice" is super important. You have chosen this family. They have chosen you. No one has assumed that a price must be paid; these are relationships that are voluntary, reciprocal, and mutual. Noel knows that Joyce might call her before Thanksgiving to see if she can join her biological kids in helping with the family dinner. Joyce knows that Noel might say "yes" or might say "no," depending on whether she can really do this, and Noel knows that if she says "no" she doesn't have to bring the equivalent of a doctor's note excusing her. She's still—and always—welcome for Thanksgiving. In your family of choice, founded on the rules of good-enough, safe-enough, and enough to go around, relationships aren't about paying prices.

You can't advertise for people to be in your family of choice on Craigslist, so how do you do this? Pay attention. Pay attention to the relationships you already have where there's no limbic resonance, no use, where even though it feels weird people are still hanging out with you. Notice people who are generous of spirit and yet have good boundaries, people who say "no" when they mean "no" and yet often say "yes" because to do so gives them pleasure. Notice who shows up for you before you ask for help because they're paying attention, and who seems to be pleased to be there for you, not because they're doing their version of paying the price of admission, but simply because they want to. They like you, they really like you. Notice those folks.

There's a Yiddish word—"nachas"—that roughly translates as, "the pleasure I get from you being happy and doing well." Look for people who have a high capacity for nachas. Give people a chance to show you that they simply like you, rather than like what they can use in you. My own family of choice, which includes biological family, in-laws, friends, an important mentor, and my spouse, is something I've built over more than 40 years. We aren't always happy with one another, and I have had times when things were strained and one or several of us were in a trauma reenactment. Not all of the people in my family of choice are in one another's, and some of them don't understand entirely why I am close to someone they're uncomfortable with. It's like any good-enough family.

Emotionally-meaningful relationships need not be romantic ones. A family of choice, filled with loving friends, will not meet your sexual needs. It will, though, help get you emotionally into the present. In a family of choice you can practice having emotionally-meaningful relationships that are reciprocal. Being a good member of the family you choose is not about being used, or having no needs of your own. It's about everyone having needs and knowing that there's enough love and care to go around.

CHAPTER 7

Hold On to Yourself

If it's not uncommon to find yourself defined as disrespectful or even abusive, or if you repeatedly allow others to disrespect and violate your boundaries, if your relationships are disruptive instead of nourishing, then you have some important pieces of personal work to do. You've been paying a price in damaged relationships for having been raised by an anxiety-provoking or disorganizing attachment figure. None of this was your fault. It's entirely unfair that you're the one paying for the errors and sins and crimes or simple inadequacy of your caregivers. You aren't the problem. You are the solution. The potential to turn things around rests in your willingness to make some changes to your insides. These are pieces of the puzzle that you can solve. These are small, powerful things you can do differently that can change your life.

You'll need to develop several new emotional capacities. These are skills that people with good-enough attachment experiences normally learn from their good-enough caregivers, and are capacities that all humans could benefit from improving. Maybe only the Dalai Lama, Thich Nhat Han, Pema Chodron, or other life-long meditators have mastered them. These great masters continue to practice such skills for hours every day. No one's ever going to be good enough at these skills to rest on their laurels.

Yes, your skill set is in need of some updating to reflect realities in the present day. No, you are not a failure to not have figured this out by yourself. Remember, I will never blame you for living with the consequences of someone's inability to give you the attachment experiences that all humans need. One small and very powerful thing to do here is to let yourself be a beginner. So let's take a deep breath, and now another, and another.

Compassion

And then another breath, in and out. Breathing is something that each of us does from the moment we exit the womb until we die. Unless you have struggled with asthma or another chronic lung disease, you pretty much take breathing for granted. You don't think about it. You just do it, which makes the breath a perfect place from which to build the skills of mindfulness and self-compassion.

The very old emotional technology of Vipassana—or mindfulness—meditation comes to the West courtesy of thousands of years of its development in Buddhist thought and teachings. It, in turn, rests on even more millennia of Hindu practices of meditation and yoga, which in its original form is an embodied form of mindfulness practice. At the philosophical core of mindfulness is the precept of *Karuna,* which is defined as active compassion for all living beings. This isn't only a Buddhist construct, just in case you're thinking, "Hmm, not for me. I'm a (fill-in-the-blank other spiritual tradition)." The notion that we should care for the vulnerable among us and not do unto others as we would not have them do to unto us are liberally sprinkled through Jewish, Christian, and Muslim holy scriptures as well, and is present in the values of secular humanism.

However, it is within Buddhist meditation traditions that the development of compassion has been transformed from a construct to a specific practice that has been integrated into Western models of mental health in the past three decades. Psychologist Marsha Linehan, who is now an ordained Buddhist roshi, or senior teacher, brought mindfulness meditation practices to scientific psychology as part of dialectical behavior therapy (more about DBT later in this chapter). Jon Kabat-Zinn, in *Full Catastrophe Living,* introduced Western readers to mindfulness meditation as a means of coping with illness and pain. Thanks to these and other teachers, more Westerners have access to these technologies of consciousness than ever before.

The charm and challenge of mindfulness meditation is that it is simply about attending to the breath. You notice yourself breathe in, and breathe out, and do that again for awhile. You might say, "in, out, in, out," to yourself. You might start with doing this for 30 seconds. Eventually you might advance to longer time periods. It takes a lot of time and practice to master the simple act of breathing mindfully for 45 minutes, which is what books and formal classes both recommend. Ignore them. You don't need to feel like a failure. Simply be willing to breathe and do as much of it mindfully as you can today.

When thoughts come to your mind, notice "a thought," and return to your breath. In, out. When a sensation from your body enters your awareness, you notice "a sensation" and return to your breath. In, out. When a judgment enters your mind, you notice "a judgment" and return to your breath. In, out. You notice, you breathe, you notice, you breathe. Simple, yet quite challenging. Simple, and—done over and over—extremely powerful. Mindfulness practice develops the capacity to observe, describe, and not be distracted entirely by the productions of our minds, particularly the critical, self-hating, self-blaming productions of our minds.

Compassion is an absence of negative judgment. It is the practice of observing and describing without evaluating. Self-hatred, self-criticism, shame, and mistrust are all productions of our minds. They are products of lenses that were put on our inner vision by less-than-adequate attachment experiences, by abuse, and by neglect. Observing ourselves with compassion requires developing the skill of noticing and then moving beyond the judgments that populate our mind, things we call thoughts but are in fact ruminations, which are productions of our EPs.

Not Poor Pitiful Me

Pity, unlike compassion, is a form of judgment. "Poor dear," is not "I notice this person struggling and in pain." We don't want to be pitied because we can feel the judgment inherent in pity. Because compassion is often used as a lazy synonym for pity in English, many of us recoil at first from the concept of compassion for ourselves.

Self-compassion is the opposite of pity. It's noticing ourselves and not judging, seeing ourselves clearly. It's telling yourself, "I notice that when I am in close relationships to others, I begin my narrative of inadequacy." It's not telling yourself, "How screwed up am I. Every time someone gets close to me I sabotage it by convincing him or her that I'm not good enough." Notice the feelings that emerge when you run the latter version of yourself in your head: anxiety, depression, despair. Notice what's possible when you speak to yourself through compassion. You can see your behavior, which then allows you to make choices about your behavior.

Inay described herself as "ferociously independent." Her parents were immigrants from the Philippines who were rarely home, working two jobs apiece to keep the family financially afloat. When they were home, they were exhausted and emotionally unavailable to Inay and her siblings. As the eldest, she was often the one who cared for her sisters and ensured the smooth running of the household. Her parents were too depleted to offer Inay good-enough attachment. She learned to depend on no one but herself. She went to school shaking with fever, taped up a finger she'd broken while trying to pry open a stuck window, and never once asked for help. She didn't want to add to her parents' burdens.

When she needed surgery that would require her to be on bed rest for two weeks and off work for another month, Inay began to panic. How would she feed herself, walk her dog, take care of the house? She knew that she couldn't ask her fiancé, Naz, for assistance because she believed that their relationship was built on her never asking him for help with anything while tirelessly and cheerfully assisting him with anything he wanted. She had the same beliefs about her friends. "I'll just have to figure this one out," she told herself. "Calm down, stop being a baby, and make this work."

Naz came home to find her looking at websites for renting wheelchairs and reaching devices and asked, "Umm, Inay, when were we going to discuss how to help you out during your recovery?" Inay noticed herself feeling the onset of panic again when Naz noticed out loud that maybe she couldn't do it all by herself. She told herself, "This is bad, very bad."

This was where her six months of mindfulness practice began to kick in. "Breathe in, breathe out, notice your judgments," she said silently to herself. "Observe, describe. Naz is offering help to you. Notice his tone of voice: warm, caring. Notice his facial expression: happy. Notice your judgments, breathe in, breathe out."

*Noticing without judging, and noticing the judging processes from her highly
activated EPs allowed Inay to move into the present. Naz was offering to help
her. He was not sounding annoyed, put off, or burdened. He was not her
parents who loved her, but simply had not had the energy during her childhood
to notice when she was ill or injured. She felt tears in her eyes, sadness for the
child she had been, and for her parents, who she knew would have offered help
when she was sick or hurt if they had had a molecule of energy left in their
bodies. She noticed her awareness that her family of origin had staggered under
the weight of racism and anti-immigrant sentiments, which had undermined
her parents' capacities to offer emotional care to their children.*

*All of this occurred within a minute or two of Naz's question. Inay used
her breathing and her practice of mindfully observing herself to move from
judgment to compassion. She allowed herself to notice that the offer of help was
both appealing and scary, and could tell that to Naz without judging herself.
She was particularly able to voice her concerns that by needing care for an
extended period of time, she would overload Naz's capacities, and thus was
able to challenge her beliefs about the absence of mutuality being a required
component of their relationship. Naz, who had been raised in an extended
family where his parents' care for him and his siblings had been supported by
a network of grandparents, aunts and uncles, and older cousins, turned out to
have a well-developed template for assisting someone who was sick based on his
family of origin's way of doing things.*

*Throughout her recovery from surgery Inay had to practice compassion for
herself multiple times daily. Each time someone showed up to help she used her
mindfulness practice to notice the emergence of her EPs with their judgments.
"You're being lazy, you could get up and do this, they're going to get sick and tired
of this, you're gonna owe them forever," etc., and notice, "There's a judgment."
Rather than treating the productions of her EPs as thoughts deserving of
attention, or adding an additional layer of judgment about having these EPs,
she became increasingly able to accept the help offered.*

Inay's story illustrates the centrality of compassion for self in disrupting the
dynamics of paying the price for connection. Her price tag had been marked, "Ask
for nothing ever." Any and all normal human dependency needs on her part had
become subject to judgment. They were sources of shame and anxiety. As she became
more proficient in applying her mindfulness practice and more able to observe her
judgments of herself, she also became more skillful at letting those judgments go
and noticing the present. Mindful compassion for self supports living as much
as possible in the present. As we've discussed earlier, this present-time living is a
foundational skill for giving up paying prices for love, attachment, and connection.

"But what about behaviors that deserve judgment?" some of you are asking.
"Does this mean that we should be compassionate about abuse of children and

violence and…?" Excellent question, dear reader. Nothing in this model excuses anyone from behavior that's dangerous or cruel to other living beings. Compassion isn't the same as letting someone off the hook. Compassion doesn't offer excuses for being cruel or dangerous to others. We can continue to have negative and positive judgments of another person based on the effects of their actions; a person who does harm to other creatures or the planet is both a fallible human (compassion) and violates basic norms of decency (judgment) and deserves a consequence (judgment).

Compassion for self doesn't mean that you don't hold yourself to an ethical standard. Rather, self-compassion is about how you observe and respond to yourself when you fall short of that standard. I can be unhappy with myself when I break my rule of "never be the subject of your barista's therapy session," which is my shorthand code for wanting to treat others with respect no matter what. If you shame yourself for violating your own values you're going to avoid contact with people altogether to avoid shame. You won't change the behavior; you'll simply add to your load of self-hatred.

If, instead, you observe yourself with compassion, you can learn how to keep faith with your values more effectively the next time. So let's look at me and my "be good to the barista" rule on a day when I'm stressed, rushed, have a cold, and the barista made me a caffeinated drink twice even though it clearly said decaf on the cup. I notice that I came into the store already running a narrative of what a terrible day it was turning out to be in my head, and when the drink came out wrong for the second time, I was snippy. Ugh.

What could I have done differently? Smiled, because I know that I cannot smile and be annoyed. This is called "opposite action." When you're heading down a path of behaving poorly, turn yourself around 180 degrees and do the opposite thing. I could have found myself or the situation funny, because laughter cannot co-exist with annoyance and anxiety. I could have taken a deep breath and reminded myself that if this is the worst thing that happens to me all day, I'm a lucky woman. I could have thanked the barista for taking the time to get it right, because gratitude interferes with unhealthy entitlement and the dynamic of treating the barista as if she were my personal servant. Oh, okay, I can do all those things. I can practice self-compassion, which allows me to observe my actions, notice them, notice my choices, and relax into change.

Compassion for self is the gateway through which the next set of skills enters. There are many ways to develop the ability to be compassionate with yourself. If you live in an area where there are mindfulness meditation classes, or courses in mindfulness-based stress reduction, you can attend such a class. Classes are helpful because they create a framework of showing up once a week and practicing with others. If classes aren't available where you live, or if you know that you don't do well with schedules and classes, there are places online where you can learn mindfulness skills. I'm partial to a site called Audio Dharma, which broadcasts teaching talks from the Redwood City California Insight Meditation Center, but there are many other places on the web where you can find instruction in mindfulness meditation. A link to that site, which allows you to download its contents as podcasts, is available in the Resources section of this book.

Holding On to Yourself

One essential emotional capacity for survivors is what psychologists call "distress tolerance." This simply means that you learn that painful emotions are not going to kill you or drive you crazy. If you can tolerate distress, you know that you can live through painful feelings without doing violence to yourself or others even if you feel like you want to scratch your skin off or punch a hole in a wall. Your anxiety-provoking or disorganizing caregiver didn't believe that about emotions. That caregiver's EPs taught your EPs to experience emotions—particularly painful ones—as dangerous things that must be silenced quickly, by whatever means necessary. What they frequently did to silence their distress was to do something harmful to your emotional or physical well-being.

What does distress tolerance look like? When your best friend tells you that s/he needs to be left alone for the next four days because s/he has a big project to finish, and your EPs start to flail in fear and tell you that s/he is lying, and really just wants you to go away, distress tolerance means reaching inside of yourself and saying the equivalent of "*There, there, now, now, it's going to be okay. S/he is not trying to get rid of you with an excuse. S/he really does have a big project to finish. S/he loves you and is your friend. And these icky feelings you're having are just icky feelings. You're not in any danger. You're not going to die. S/he'll be back and you can ask her/him about the project. You'll be okay and safe enough.*" Remember Glenna from earlier in the book? That's what she was doing when she was talking to herself. She was practicing her distress tolerance skills.

You'll have to practice these skills repeatedly to become fluid in their use. Think of it as learning a new emotional language. If you move to a country where you don't speak the language, you realize almost immediately that even little kids speak it better than you do. You don't feel shame about this. After all, if you're like most people living in the United States, you probably weren't raised to speak Czech or Croatian or Thai or Urdu. You understand that it's going to take time and that you're going to make audible and slightly embarrassing mistakes of grammar and vocabulary. For example, when I was an adolescent on my first trip to Israel I inverted two consonants as I proudly ordered "stone juice—meetz avaneem" instead of "grape juice—meetz anaveem" from the vendor in the market in Tel Aviv.

The vendor laughed, and so did I. I was clearly an American kid doing her best to communicate with the locals. I have only learned to speak my acquired language of Hebrew by opening my mouth and sounding like a four-year-old with a strangely advanced knowledge of grammar and a vocabulary full of holes. I have to re-experience this every single time I go to Israel and brush off my rusty Hebrew. I don't feel shame or humiliation, and the Israelis around me are appreciative of my attempts to engage with them in their native tongue, even though they all speak English just fine.

Learning distress tolerance as an adult instead of having it taught to you as a native emotional language by good-enough caregivers is a similar process. The biggest difference is how much survivors shame themselves for not having this as part of their native emotional language. Please don't call yourself stupid or berate yourself for not having learned this until you were a lot older than five years old. Your less-than-adequate caregivers never mastered this skill. If they had, you would have been given a more secure and adequate attachment experience. Instead of shaming yourself, treat yourself as that juice vendor in the market in Tel Aviv treated me. Have a sense of humor about it. Have the same patience with and compassion for yourself as you learn this new language as you would if you were trying to pick up a new spoken tongue or were trying to master programming in C#. You'll not get it the first 10, 20, or 50 times.

Know that you will stumble on the way to developing this skill. Little kids who are learning distress tolerance as a "native language" do. If you've raised children you know that there were times when your otherwise emotionally capable five- or 15-year-old hit overload and temporarily lost her/his emotional skills. Even people who have pretty good distress tolerance skills have limits in their ability to apply them when their load of life stressors exceeds their current coping capacities. Like an overloaded electrical circuit, all of us can blow sometimes.

Distress tolerance also requires overwriting all of the problematic neural networks that you grew due to your less-than-adequate attachment experience. This makes it harder to acquire distress tolerance as a survivor than as a little kid. Your old strategies for dealing with distress, many of which did not involve tolerating it, will call to you from your EPs. You'll find yourself wishing you could drink/smoke/eat ice cream/cut yourself/over-exercise/dissociate—all of the things that you've already done in your life that seemed to work to make distressing emotions go away.

If you're not in recovery from an addiction, you might still do one of those things. Getting better skills doesn't mean that you don't still have the ineffective ones stored somewhere in your emotional attic. But if you are in recovery, especially if it's a very new and fragile recovery, I strongly urge you to call your therapist or sponsor if you're teetering on the verge of a relapse. Get to a meeting if you're in 12-Step, do whatever it takes to support your precious gift of abstinence. "One day at a time" is actually an excellent distress tolerance skill. You can stand this, whatever this is, just for this minute. Just for the next minute. Meanwhile call your sponsor and go to a meeting, please. While relapse is normative, it's also preventable.

You may also really want to soothe yourself by dropping into the pay-for-connection relationship patterns that have been so much a part of your life. That's one of the ways you've managed distress. You might find yourself obsessing about what someone important to you might be thinking and feeling about you. You might start spinning a tale of rejection and abandonment in your head, which will ramp up your distress. So you'll spring into action doing things in relationship that sort of soothe you, but which re-up your payments on the connection.

You'll try to make yourself indispensable and violate your own boundaries. You'll cook a special, elaborate meal even though you have a huge project due. You'll buy tickets you can't afford to a comedy show you know s/he'll love. Even though the last thing you want is to be touched you'll put out sexually. You'll agree to do something sexual that scares or disgusts you because you think this will "prove" that the other person has to keep you. As sex columnist Dan Savage says, being "GGG—good, giving, and game" with a sexual partner is something you do because you want to, not because you're afraid that saying "no" to something is going to result in abandonment or punishment.

When you're struggling with tolerating distress, you might have problems with boundaries. If you've been asked to pay attention to respecting another person's boundary, you'll push on it anyhow. Your distress may grow into a crisis that'll feel like a legitimate reason to violate the other person's boundaries. Your distress will be coming from very young places inside of yourself. Your EPs, the source of the distress, will be broadcasting on all frequencies about how much danger you're in because of the boundary.

You'll do these things and risk feeling shame and humiliation. You'll feel as if you haven't sacrificed enough of yourself to protect the connection with this other person. You'll tell yourself that you failed to debase yourself sufficiently. You'll try to figure out how to get the other shoe to drop so that you can get the tension over with and move on with self-hatred.

If you can start to breathe mindfully, you may notice that shame and humiliation seem oddly more familiar and thus strangely more tolerable forms of distress than the distress of feeling scared or sad or mad. **Notice this phenomenon. Don't judge yourself, please.** Then do your very best to have compassion for yourself so that you can observe what happened inside of you. Breathe and send compassion to yourself so that you learn something about where you tipped past the point of being able to tolerate your distress. When you are able to observe yourself compassionately, you can walk back through the pattern of thoughts, feelings, and actions to the point where you can say, "Hmm, if I had done this differently, if I had said that to myself instead of the thing I did say, then I might have been able to choose not to pay a relational price."

Geoff and Adam were on the verge of having a nasty fight about where to spend their tax refund money. Adam got up from his seat and said, "I'm declaring a time out. I'm going to my study to cool down, because I love you and this topic is not worth fighting about. We're not going to figure this out if we're both feeling this upset." He got up and left the room. Geoff sat there, beginning to panic, tears coming to his eyes. "He hates me, I know he does," he began to mutter to himself. "We never should have gotten married. He's going to come out of his study and tell me he wants a divorce. How will I face my friends?" He began to hyperventilate in panic and was on the verge of walking to Adam's study and pounding on the door to insist that they resolve this issue RIGHT NOW when he stopped himself. He pulled hard on his wedding ring to get himself into the present, so that he could remind himself of the last time he let this line of self-talk get to this point. That was when he had last turned a manageable, albeit painful, conflict into a truly awful fight that took a week to recover from. He had pounded on Adam's door, yelling, "How dare you walk out on me," and in general acted like his worst self. When that fight had ended, he felt covered with despair, and yet calmer. Then Adam had barely spoken to him for two days.

So this time Geoff used what he had learned from his previous experience. He remembered that he habitually calmed himself in relationships by paying the price of losing, feeling unloved and disrespected. He reminded himself that he was often calmer when he was rejected and Adam was angry with him. He knew that he felt safer in a weird way when he had made the other shoe drop and was in familiar relational territory. He pulled on his wedding ring again, reminding himself that it was not 40 years ago when his parents would disappear for days on end. He hugged himself tightly, and whispered to himself to listen to what Adam had said five minutes earlier. "I love you and this topic is not worth fighting about." "Okay, Geoff. He loves you. He doesn't want to have a fight with you. He's not trying to get rid of you. You can live with the feeling of not knowing what is going to happen next. He took a timeout. That means he'll be back."

He didn't feel much better, but when Adam came out of his study five minutes later and enveloped him in a huge hug, Geoff's terrified EPs calmed down a little more. The distress, which had felt as if it was going to last forever, had been intense, but brief. Geoff used his skills to tolerate it, and got the outcome that he wanted in the present, which was better connection with his husband.

An important thing to consider at these points in your life is that survivors' painful emotional states frequently feel as if they go on forever. This is because they are coming from your EPs, the little kid parts of you. All emotional experiences, from wonderful to horrible, feel like forever to little kids, both actual ones and the ones inside of us. It can help to start looking at your time-keeping devices to see just how long these "forevers" last in the present. Armed with that information you can tell yourself the next time that this horrible feeling will probably last no longer than 15 minutes or so, which is not forever.

Geoff had tolerated it. He'd brought his younger emotional parts into the present by pulling on the ring that was the symbol of Adam's love and commitment in the present. He'd been able to remember what he had learned from having compassionately observed his stumbles during the previous round of conflict. He got the outcome he deserved, not the one his EPs feared yet expected. His attachment to Adam became more secure, more rooted in present time because his actions helped rewire his brain and his attachment system. We'll talk more about using this skill in relational conflicts at greater length later in this book.

Notice that a big part of distress tolerance is recruiting information for your EPs about being in the present time. Radically being in the present is a foundation of distress tolerance. Sensory methods work the best and most quickly to pull you out of the past and get your little inner time travelers to phone home. Smell, which is one of the most archaic senses and occurs in the old reptilian part of our brain that works even more quickly than our limbic systems, can be a good way to pull yourself into present time. You'll need to use a scent that's entirely associated with now and has no connections to your childhood. Touch is next. Geoff's wedding ring was a good example of this—an object that he could feel, that was always available, and that was clearly associated with the present. Touch is also a sense experienced in very old parts of our brains, so it will work quickly to assist in bringing you into the present. Petting the dog or cat or keeping something in your pocket you can rub on, like a rock or a crystal or a piece of nubby cloth, all represent good ways to bring yourself into the present with touch. You can add sound, which comes later in brain development, or visuals, which come last of all. Use anything sensory that you find helpful.

Another skill you'll need to master here, which is complementary to distress tolerance, is what we call "affect (or emotion) regulation." This translates as learning to turn down the internal volume of the distress, and getting your EPs out of the mix long enough for you to bring your brain's prefrontal cortex online again. Ironically, this also means actually knowing what you feel and not numbing yourself or dissociating from emotions. When you've had an anxiety-provoking or disorganizing attachment experience, part of it was that you weren't given the skills necessary to get your nervous system to learn how to calm down. Calming down isn't something we can just do; we have to learn how to do it. Some of you dealt with this challenge by simply shutting off. You fooled yourself into thinking that you're emotionally regulated. Numb is not the same as regulated, however. It's being shut off. When the shut-off valve fails and you don't yet know how to reach for the emotional rheostat, you won't have tools for shading yourself from the brightness of emotional intensity.

In good-enough attachment caregivers regulate infants, who eventually internalize that regulation and are able to effectively self-regulate as time goes on and the brain develops. In other forms of attachment, but particularly in the disorganizing kind, caregivers may themselves be very dysregulated. Those caregivers can't help the infant to self-regulate, and sometimes actually aggravate an infant's dysregulation. For example, if the caregiver's response to a crying infant is to cry and scream and yell at the baby to "shut up," this worsens the baby's feelings of being out of control and overwhelmed by emotions. If this was your experience, the baby you were didn't learn how to calm her/himself and turn down the volume on emotion from a "10" to a "2." If one of your parents dealt with their difficult mood state by riling you up at the end of the day and then getting angry with you because you didn't go to sleep at bedtime, your normal childhood challenge of learning to regulate your arousal were worsened by the addition of shame.

Even though you're an adult, your EPs experience emotion at high decibel levels, just as you did when you were a little person. Those parts of you become activated by what happens in relationships, particularly at those moments when it seems as if connection is somehow at risk, or when it feels like someone's getting in too close. You may have been perceived and labeled by others as emotionally uncontrolled or "too intense" when what was happening was that an EP had just arrived on the scene. As we discussed earlier, some of you have tried to solve this problem by dissociating from your emotions and shutting down completely. On the surface you've always appeared to be calm and emotionally regulated, while you were in fact cut off from emotion and poorly equipped to deal with your feelings when the cover was ripped off of them by life events. These young coping strategies aren't solutions that will work for helping you have the relationships you deserve. Learning emotion regulation so that you are able to have a Goldilocks experience of "just right" is an important skill for having the healthy relationships you deserve.

Emotions can be a powerful source of valuable information when you have them tuned to a frequency where they are information about the present, and not information about the past. Emotions are helpful when you have the ability to identify the emotion you're feeling right now. Knowing and naming your emotions empowers you to make better choices because you're receiving accurate information from your emotions about what's happening right now. Our emotions provide excellent data about the present if only we allow ourselves to have access to that information.

Feelings, Nothing More Than Feelings

Emotions are bodily experiences to which we have attached names. This is, once again, one of those things that children learn in good-enough attachment experiences. "You're angry right now, aren't you?" the adult says to the child. "Oh, look how happy you are!" The four basic emotional states—mad, sad, glad, scared—are all feelings that the well-enough-attached and adequately-cared-for human child learns to experience in the body and give names to. A securely attached person can tell the difference between irritation, annoyance, frustration, anger, fury, and rage—all names of bodily experiences on the continuum of "I don't like this and I want it to stop." Many survivors only know numbness or intense feeling, not the gradations in between.

To shore up your self-compassion around this task, think for a moment about how many aspects of your childhood got in the way of acquiring the basic skill of naming your emotions. Let's start with your body. For many of you a body was not a safe place to be. Bad things were done to your body, things that hurt or confused you, that overstimulated you or left you numb. Too many survivors I work with have medical problems that they ignored or denied or simply couldn't feel, illnesses that were not diagnosed until a very late stage. Some survivors dissociate far out of their bodies simply to not be taken down by the intolerable bodily sensations engendered by childhood abuse.

If this is you, then your first step toward emotion regulation is learning to become safe enough in your body that you can feel it responding to what's happening in the present. There are lots of ways to approach this task. Here are a few I know about. Some people find it helpful to engage a skilled body worker who will agree to touch only certain designated parts of you and will assist you in breathing and grounding as they do. Some of you would rather be charged by an angry rhinoceros than do that! Some people find it helpful to start by developing an awareness of sensation in a relatively neutral part of their body, like a big toe. For others of you, though, there are no neutral body parts.

Trauma therapies can help people process the painful experiences that led you to leave your body. There are some specifically body-oriented trauma therapies, such as somatic experiencing, sensorimotor psychotherapy, and generative somatics, that blend work in and with the body with processing trauma. These can be especially helpful to people whose response to trauma was to numb out of their bodies entirely. Bodywork with a trauma-informed professional can also be helpful. Bessel van der Kolk's book, *The Body Keeps the Score,* describes how this founder of the modern field of trauma treatment now incorporates yoga into his work with trauma survivors.

My own path back into my physical self came via taking up a martial art—aikido—just after my 50th birthday. Even harder than learning to perform the techniques was the part where I started feeling my body in ways I hadn't since I was three. It was terrifying and painful, and I humiliated myself for months until I figured out that I didn't have to numb out and be self-critical every time I couldn't understand what was happening. Now it's 13 years later. I'm working on getting my black belt, something that surprises me every single time I say it. So find your way back to your body, by whatever method you find doable and tolerable. Take the time you need to get there. It's going to be worth it.

Next, learn to describe what your body is experiencing without naming the emotion. Simply describe the sensations. For example, "My face is flushing." "My breathing is getting shallow." "I feel tightness in my jaw." "I'm shaking." When we begin to become emotionally aroused, our nervous system sends signals that lead to predictable bodily changes in breathing, blood flow to and from the skin and gut, and levels of tension in our muscles. When a good-enough caregiver is noticing and naming emotions to a child, that caregiver is seeing those physical cues and mirroring them back to the child with emotion names. You can do this for yourself. Again, remember that this is not your native language. It'll feel like you're doing it by rote, and at first you are. You'll screw up and feel foolish and maybe embarrassed along the way. With practice comes deepened knowledge of your bodily states, and greater fluidity and capacity to know what you're feeling, and name it effectively and accurately.

What you'll also begin to notice is the storyline that's developing in your head in response to these signals of arousal in your body—what psychologists call "self-talk." There may be several layers of narrative that you'll learn to identify. Emotion regulation will require you to become the editor of those narratives as well as the author of new ones that are self-compassionate, not self-hating or shaming. One layer of self-talk might be about what's apparently happening now in your relationship with another person. "Oh my goodness, that person is so unhappy. I wish I could help her/him feel better about her/himself." That's an experience in which you mindfully observe, describe what you've observed, and think kind thoughts about the other person. Securely attached people have that kind of experience.

The next layer of self-talk is where problems often begin for survivors. It's the layer run by EPs. This layer looks and sounds like you're thinking, but you're not. Instead, you're ruminating. Rumination is the process repeating a narrative of fear and danger, going around and around over the same uncomfortable spot, digging yourself further into misery. Rumination might sound something like, "Maybe I didn't do a good enough job cleaning up the kitchen last night. I know that's important to her/him. I'm just making things worse by being lazy and self-centered. I was in too much of a rush to get to my TV show. What kind of friend/roommate/spouse do I think I am? What an idiot!" This layer of self-talk taps fairly directly into attachment narratives. The other person is neither happy nor calm.

That feels unsafe for you. Your price of admission to relationship is to get people back to happy or calm no matter what. You failed to do that. You are bad, wrong, shameful…you know the drill.

Sometimes when you have had caregivers who were cruel or dangerous, another layer of self-talk is run by a particularly malignant internal construct known as an "introject." Think of an introject as an undigested representation of the adults who were cruel to you. It's not you, and it's not telling you the truth about you. It's loud, and it sounds authoritative, and it sounds like it's you talking to yourself, and it's as wrong and alien as it is loud. If you're a Star Trek: Deep Space Nine fan, remember the symbiont in Jadzia Dax? That's an introject.

This is one of the points where you can make a change in your emotional state. The ruminative self-talk about attachment and connection that was authored by your less-than-adequate caregiver simply causes you ever higher levels of emotional distress. That distress, in turn, activates other, even more problematic inner narratives in which your distress ramps up higher. "If I don't make this up to her/him, something really bad is going to happen. S/he'll realize that s/he needs to get rid of me. I'll be alone again. I hate myself." These are narratives of shame, self-loathing, and abandonment terror, and they activate those emotional states. It's EP land, and sometimes introject land. Those are not good places to live. They are not places in which emotionally-meaningful relationships can flourish.

When your problematic narratives have taken over the experience of being around someone who's feeling any unpleasant emotional state and your EPs get activated, you start dishing out payment for connection, big time. Someone else's distress leads you to believe that you're in a huge emotional debt that you've got to start paying down fast, before you get dropped, and you'll start doing whatever you can to rebalance the emotional account.

So you might become over-solicitous and apologize for not having done something perfectly. You might try to be the entertaining baby, telling a joke, or giving fistfuls of compliments—anything to allay the other person's unpleasant emotional state. You might be apologetic or overly grateful when someone is simply decent. You'll be in a reenactment. Or you might do a version of emotional dysregulation, going from the narrative of shame to the narrative of angry martyrdom: "Why doesn't s/he just get over her/himself? Damn it, I worked hard all day and then I had to come home and clean up the damn kitchen. Let her/him take care of her/his own crybaby self." These narratives of shame and anger are paths to shutdown and disengagement, not to regulation of emotions.

Compassionately noticing and interrupting your ruminative self-talk is a next step in emotion regulation. When you can change your narratives from those of shame and self-hatred to those of curiosity and open-mindedness, your emotional state will give you information about what's happening now. You'll stop traveling back in time to the relationship with your less-than-adequate caregivers. You'll probably notice that you have an EP or two masquerading as a prophet of doom. That EP was accurate about what was happening when you were the actual age of this emotional state. In the families where you grew up, something bad was definitely going to happen.

However, that EP's perspective is inaccurate about what's happening now. Its prophecies of doom are the ruminations that dysregulate you. Now is the time to thank your little soothsayer and award it with retirement. "Thanks for having helped me stay alert during my childhood when it really wasn't safe for me to relax my guard. I'm not around those people today. Let's come into the present together, and you can take a long-needed nap now." Someone I know has named his inner prophet of doom "George." He talks back to George when George puts on his prophesying robes and starts to preach doom and gloom and terrible relational outcomes. "George, please be quiet. The last 100 times you tried to predict the future you were wrong. When I listen to you I make mistakes and either I suffer or other people suffer. Look at the calendar, George! It's 2015, and you don't know about 2015."

When you learn to regulate your emotions more effectively, you'll notice that they're hovering somewhere between "1" and "4" on the infamous 10-point scale beloved of psychologists. You are having a bodily experience. You are able to describe it, and to have a narrative about it that does not raise its level above five, and may bring its level down below four. And you are able to name it. You'll know enough emotion to make good choices, taking on neither too little nor more than you can handle.

Naming—giving language to experience—is the step that moves emotions from indefinable feelings in the body to known and familiar phenomena. Naming links up your prefrontal cortex with your limbic system so that you experience emotions in the present and integrate them into the narrative of daily life. Feelings cease to be strange forces that emerge from your chest like the creature in *Aliens* and become familiar, even helpful. When I know what I'm feeling and have a name for it, I also have information about what I want to do in the interpersonal field. If I know that what I'm feeling is grief, then I have information that I've had a loss, and it's a big one. If I know that what I'm feeling is sadness, then I've had a loss, and it's not so large. If I'm exasperated, I don't like what someone else is doing, but it's not that big a deal and I may or may not do something to try to change things. If I'm outraged, I neither like nor am willing to tolerate what's happening, and I'm going to do what I can to get things to be different.

Take Your EPs to Emotional Intelligence Camp

There are many ways to get healthy distress tolerance and affect regulation skills. Again, like any other emotional competency, they are not things that humans come by intuitively, and those who have these skills were taught them, directly and indirectly, by caregivers who were good-enough. You're not a failure as a person if you struggle with these skills. Remember the "stone juice?" You'll be ordering a lot of stone juice, or scratching your head and hesitating for a moment before saying "Oh yeah, grape juice" long before you fluidly and without thinking know the words you want.

A great way for some people to get the entire package—which also comes with some wonderful skills in assertiveness, boundary-setting and creating, and a whole host of other interpersonal skills that you didn't get in childhood—is a psychological intervention called dialectical behavior therapy (DBT) skills training. I think of DBT skills as going to emotional intelligence camp in the best possible way. There are other campers, there are counselors (group leaders), there are slogans, and craft projects. There is also a highly effective, evidence-based collection of learning activities that can get rid of most of your prices of admission to relationship if you're willing to do the homework.

Don't be put off by the fact that when you go online to check it out, you'll see that all DBT books talk about treating borderline personality disorder (BPD). I know that's a label a lot of survivors have been given, and it's one that feels crappy because a lot of therapists get weird about people who've been given that label. Ignore that thing about BPD. DBT skills training is for anyone who wants to be more effective in their relationship with themselves and others. As they say in AA, "Take what you need and leave the rest," and in this case, take DBT skills training if you can and ignore the damn label.

Most of the people with whom DBT was developed were survivors of complex trauma being observed in a framework that wasn't particularly interested in or concerned about trauma. DBT skills are something every single one of us can benefit from. Even people who've had good-enough attachment experiences can benefit from deepening their capacities. DBT skills do that. There's a link to information about DBT in the Resources section of this book, including one to an excellent self-help website where you can find tools for teaching yourself these skills.

One caveat about DBT came to me from people I know who live with dissociative identity disorder (DID). DBT is apparently not always as helpful for people living with DID as it might be, particularly when there is not much co-consciousness or collaborative interaction among internal parts. Luckily, psychotherapists Suzette Boon, Kathy Steele, and Onno van der Hart have developed a modification of the skills training model especially for people living with trauma-related dissociation. Their book, *Coping With Trauma-Related Dissociation*, for which you'll find a link in the Resources section, comes highly recommended by my friends, colleagues, and clients who live with DID and other forms of trauma-related dissociation.

Another way you can give yourself a jump-start on improving your skills in emotion regulation and distress tolerance is via a therapy called eye movement desensitization reprocessing, or EMDR. EMDR was developed by Francine Shapiro in the late 1980s as a trauma treatment. It's especially helpful when you can't find words for what happened to you, as it involves very little talk and lots of following your therapist's fingers (or a light) moving back and forth. I know, it sounds pretty woo-woo, doesn't it? I thought so too, until about 1995 when I saw it be very helpful to someone I was working with at the time. It was so effective that I promptly learned how to do it and have used it ever since.

There's another thing that EMDR can help with, which is to strengthen or develop weak or missing personal capacities. This technique, created by master EMDR teacher Andrew Leeds, is called resource development installation. Resourcing assists people to have—or have more of—a valued personal characteristic. So, for instance, you can work with an EMDR practitioner to install the quality of self-compassion or the ability to tolerate ambiguity. If you'd like to find an EMDR practitioner, you can check out the EMDR International Association's website, which is in the Resources section at the end of this book.

There are a number of other evidence-based therapies you can use to build additional emotional capacities. The Association for Contextual Behavioral Therapies is an organization that has resources about acceptance and commitment therapy (ACT), a mindfulness-based treatment that helps you to deal more effectively with difficult thoughts and sensations. Functional analytic psychotherapy (FAP) teaches people how to be more effective in taking smart risks and being vulnerable in connection. Its mantra is, "Acceptance, Courage, Love." Websites for these two approaches to therapy, both of which are research-based, can also be found in the Resources section of this book. I integrate concepts and strategies from all of these approaches in my work with survivors.

Plain old talk therapy, done well, can also be a valuable place in which to learn about attachment. Research on what makes therapy works has shown that the relationship between therapist and client is more important than anything else that therapists do. A therapist who ascribes to a relational theory of therapy and yet cannot pull off the evidence-based skills of empathy, genuineness, and positive regard will be much less helpful for you than a therapist who practices cognitive-behavioral therapy, which isn't particularly interested in the relationship, yet does engage in these and similar evidence-based relationship-building behaviors. Research supporting the impact and effectiveness of evidence-based relationship variables in psychotherapy is as strong as—or stronger than—research supporting any specific technique. These variables account for a much bigger percentage of what makes therapy work than does any technique.

A therapist who demonstrates warmth, genuineness, positive regard, and the ability to repair ruptures with you will offer an experience that, while not substituting for good-enough childhood attachment, can open a window onto what that kind of attachment feels like in real time. That therapist can do just about any technique and be helpful to you. John Norcross's book, *Psychotherapy Relationships That Work*, summarizes this research. Read it so that you can assess whether the therapy you're getting is living up to the evidence about what makes it effective

Planning for Safety

Remember earlier in the book where we talked about making yourself a relationship safety plan? Another component of the process of learning not to pay the price of admission for emotionally-meaningful relationships involves getting yourself away from the edge and keeping yourself safe-enough. The concept of safe-enough in relationship to other humans seems odd and unattainable to many people who were raised by anxiety-provoking or disorganizing adults. No wonder. These adults didn't provide you with many—or any—experiences of being safe-enough. Notice again the "enough." Life is a risk, but life can be safe-enough, enough of the time. This is true for all humans. There are no guarantees. Yet there are things we can do to increase the quality and quantity of safety in our lives. You don't have to wait for the asteroid to hit you when you can see it coming from miles away. You can increase your safety with intention, purposefully, to get yourself closer to the quality of relationships that you deserve.

One of the ways you can be powerful on your own behalf is to make plans to stay relationally safe. This concept is an extension of what I do as a therapist when I'm working with people who are doing violence to themselves as a coping strategy. I don't ask them to just change and stop the behavior. Rather, I invite them to collaborate with me to understand the function of their dangerous activities, and to learn how they might increase or reduce their risk for using those less-desired coping strategies. The goal of this process is for people to become safer with themselves by understanding what invites episodes of self-inflicted violence and plan other things to do in those moments.

A first step in developing a personal safety plan is to be a scientist studying the amazing creature you are, and ask, "Hmm, Dr. Survivor, what is this person doing that might be endangering her or his safety in relationship to others? What are the functions of those less-than-safe relationship patterns? And what actions is this person taking to be safe enough?" You'll have lots of chances to use your self-compassion skills in this experiment. You'll both be looking at what has gone well in emotionally-meaningful relationships as well as examining in some detail what happened when things went haywire.

Remember Joe? He had learned that he blew up relationships when they threatened to get "too good" or "too close." He had entered adulthood with a belief, founded in his attachment experiences, that all good connections would end. He had a well-worn strategy of avoiding the more painful aspects of

relationship loss by taking the initiative to control loss by making it happen. He was "unsafe" from his pattern when in relationships. He was perpetually at risk of blowing things up, even when he knew he was most loved. This insight took time and lots of self-compassion, as well as much grieving those relationship losses that he realizes might have been self-inflicted.

His safety plan for himself began with work on self-compassion and distress tolerance, as well as work on self-shaming and self-blaming self-talk. He worked on his belief that it was better to be hurt by his own hand than to suffer the "inevitable" hurt caused by another's rejection of him. He challenged his preverbal belief that everyone would leave him.

Joe and his therapist discussed what his danger signals were, exploring what the narratives were that would begin to run in his mind when he was feeling too vulnerable, or telling himself that the other person was on the brink of realizing the so-called "truth" about him being worthless and unlovable. Together they developed another component of his safety plan, which involved telling new potential partners about his history: "I tend to get freaked out when things are good and do stuff to end the relationship." This way Joe accomplished several different safety goals. He made his old methods transparent, so that men he dated could call him on them when he began to enact them, and he began to recruit some help in disrupting his narrative from the man with whom things got serious.

Joe also began to identify circumstances that might activate his old pattern of paying the price for relationships by sabotaging them. He noticed, by being a careful investigator of his own history, that when he was otherwise stressed by life, he was more likely to expect rejection from a partner. He also noticed that if he had more than two glasses of wine or two beers or one shot in an evening, his narrative of being easy to reject would start to play loudly. So his safety plan included developing strategies for managing stress, which in Joe's case included puttering in the garden, no matter how much it was raining that day, as well as his daily mindfulness practice. He also committed to drinking no more than his limit on any given evening.

An effective relationship safety plan should have several goals. They should all be achievable and realistic for you. If you struggle to assess whether other people are trustworthy, your safety plan will probably include giving yourself sufficient time to gather the data necessary for accurate assessment. It will probably include strategies to reduce your betrayal blindness and increase your awareness of what you're feeling in the moment. If your old pay-the-price belief is that the only way someone will relate to you is if you give yourself away and have no boundaries, your safety plan will involve you noticing cues that activate your narratives of worthlessness, and will also include work on identifying and setting boundaries.

The goal of a safety plan is to help you stay out of reenactments or leave them as early as possible. Safety plans are usually more effective when you have someone—or several someones—collaborating with you in creating and maintaining them: a friend, a 12-Step sponsor, a therapist, a clergyperson. One woman I know who was working on her right to be loved started to blog about her safety plan. She told me, "Being accountable to my 200 subscribers is a highly-effective strategy for me. I get applause, and I get a lot of help." Remember that a safety plan is not something you're going to do perfectly. Each time you struggle with implementing it, go back into investigative scientist mode: "What was I doing/thinking/feeling/telling myself when this got to be too hard to do?" Ask this question with curiosity and compassion, not in a "What *was* I thinking, idiot" manner, please.

Walk yourself back to the point where you struggled with safety and ask yourself what you need to tweak in order to be able to be more effective in your safety plan. This walking-it-back strategy is called behavior chain analysis. If you do an internet search on that term, or on the term "relapse prevention," you'll find many different sites that offer step-by-step advice on how to do this if your own strategies aren't working as well as you'd like. A link to a trauma-informed behavior chain analysis site is in the Resources section of this book. There's also information about this skill in the DBT skills workbook.

Do Fence Yourself In

So how do you acquire boundaries if you've never had them? Because boundaries are outgrowths of what you feel, want, know, and think, many of you who had less-than-adequate attachment experiences don't do so well with this skill. But when you can have self-compassion, tolerate distress, and regulate your emotions, you have laid the foundation for noticing and protecting your boundaries.

Begin with the most simple and the most powerful of things—what do I feel, what do I think, what do I want, what do I like? Resist beginning with "What does this other person want me to like, want, and feel?" Instead, begin with "What do *I* want?" Not, "What will make someone like me?" Not, "What would my parents have wanted from me?" Not, "What do my adolescent children insist that I do for them?" Begin with "What do *I* want?"

These are excruciatingly hard questions for survivors to answer—harder than people who aren't survivors can begin to imagine. I sometimes send clients to the paint store for handfuls of color chips and ask them to sit with those kaleidoscopes of color until they know which ones they really like. Then they get to come back and tell me, a person whose color scheme is quite visible in my clothing and office décor, why they like those colors, including colors that they can easily intuit that I probably do not like very much (e.g., anything on the yellow, orange, brown, and red palettes. As I once told someone, "If you catch me wearing something orange you'll know I've had a personality transplant."). I remind them, as they leave, that they need to practice self-compassion while they do this experiment.

People leave my office thinking that this will be easy, and come back having struggled for hours with the task, if they were able to do it at all. This is why I start my clients off with self-compassion, so that they don't shame themselves about how hard it was to do this thought experiment. Sometimes they have figured out that they love orange and really hate purple, and then get to navigate telling me—a woman who wears a lot of dark purple, and no orange ever—their truth, which is often excruciating and scary for them. Having no boundaries with one's childhood caregivers has meant years of saying, "I'll have whatever you're having" or, "If you like it, I do, too." The tears that come when I respond by saying, "Tell me about orange. I want to know how it delights you, because that way I'll know you better," say volumes about how unusual or even dangerous it was for survivors to know what delighted them.

Good-enough attachment figures did just that with their child. They were curious about the child's experiences in the world. They reflected back the joy, delight, excitement, and interest that the child was experiencing. In this way the well-enough-attached child had her or his preferences mirrored accurately, and was able to own them. The good-enough attachment figure also encouraged choices— "Would you like one or two carrot sticks with your lunch?"—that were within the child's developmental capacities. Anxiety-provoking and disorganizing caregivers undermine or subvert this process of boundary development in the child in a myriad of ways. They say, "You won't like carrots; I think they're icky," or worse, "What do you mean you don't like it when I touch you like this?"

Developing boundaries starts with seemingly simple things: touch, taste, smell, color, sound. Become a researcher studying yourself once again, doing little experiments, noticing what you like, what you don't like, and why you feel the way you do about the sensory world. Start small, perhaps with "Kale or spinach, which do I like better or dislike the least?" Give yourself choices that allow you to compare and contrast. Notice if you feel mad, sad, glad, scared, or numb when you have this experience or are around this person. How can you tell which feeling it is you're feeling? Feelings are information about our boundaries. Practice giving the feeling a name. Make a list of feeling words to carry with you and try them on for size to see which feeling names fit.

Notice the sensations in your body, your face, your gut. This can feel frightening if you were sexually violated or physically abused; your body was not a safe place to be back then. Your EPs would prefer you not have or not feel your body. Soothe those feelings. Notice that you're here now, not then. Notice that the distress associated with being aware of your body is brief. Notice your face flushing. Notice the tightness of your jaw as you have an experience, or the softness in your hands. Breathe deeply into your belly (this may be scary). Breathe again, then repeat the questions. Do the Hokey Pokey, shake yourself about, breathe again, now ask the questions again. Notice where you are. Notice your body is safe-enough right now. You can apply your skills from emotion regulation to this task of learning how to have boundaries.

Do this again and again, exercising this muscle of self-knowledge. Do this when you're by yourself. Watch a video on YouTube or some other streaming video service and notice your responses to what you hear or see. Do it with someone you know will be kind and honest with you. Stay curious about yourself and your experience and be open to finding out something new.

This continuing exercise in gathering information about yourself is an excellent, albeit challenging, starting point for developing boundaries. Because, as the cliché goes, "There's no accounting for taste," it's usually a little easier to begin practicing boundaries by asserting your fondness for brown over beige, or the sound of Mahler versus the Grateful Dead. You can then work your way up to more challenging boundary statements such as, "I don't like it when you respond to my request for you to pick up your clothes by calling me OCD. I don't care if it's true or not. I want you to stop saying that to me. I experience that response as contemptuous and dismissive, and that's not okay with me." That's a black belt, advanced boundary skill—and you can get there. We'll talk about that more when we discuss the value of having healthy conflict in relationships.

As you continue in your practice of self-compassion, you may realize that as a survivor you are likely to find even these very simple assertions of self somewhat or very anxiety-provoking. Back in the 1970s when feminist therapists like me were doling out assertiveness training as if it were the cure to everything that ailed women, we noticed that people had the hardest time being assertive with the people who were closest. It turns out that this is not only an issue for women and survivors. It is more of an issue when you are fragile in your relationship to your boundaries, and when the very young places inside of you are louder than your present-day self.

This is quite a challenging skill, your newly developing capacity to give up the price of admission that required giving away your boundaries in exchange for relationship. Do yourself the courtesy of acknowledging how hard it is to practice this new set of behaviors. Don't expect yourself to master it quickly. Let yourself be a beginner, an advanced beginner, and then an intermediate student. Take longer than you first thought you would need. Be a tortoise. No need to be the hare. The more important someone is to you, and the more you want to stay connected to that person, the more difficult it may be to have your boundaries with her or him, to speak even banal truths about how you're not going to do what they want. You'll be surprised by how many of the people in your life are just fine with your boundaries.

So let it feel daunting to tell your spouse of 20 years that you actually have never liked action thrillers and really want to go see a comedy the next time the two of you go to the movies. That's okay. You're not a wimp, you're not avoiding conflict, and you're not inadequate and shame-worthy simply because this apparently easy request is so hard. Your self-critical/self-protective EPs need to take a rest here. Self-compassion needs to show up and take charge. You're practicing a new skill. As with any new skill, you're going to be a little shaky and uncertain the first nine thousand, nine hundred and ninety-nine times, whether it's having a boundary, playing golf, learning to play the clarinet, or performing *bo nikkyo* (the stick form in aikido that I was attempting to master around the time I was starting to write this book).

It's not unusual for people to have their boundaries challenged by others' intentional or inadvertent use of guilt- or-shame-inducing statements. Guilt and shame are invitations to give up boundaries. They bring EPs out in the blink of an eye. You might take some of these voyages into guilt or shame as you start to practice boundaries with someone you've known for a while. The other person might feel that you've been dishonest about your actual feelings and needs. They may think that you're changing the rules of the relationship in mid-course, and might imply—or even say directly—that this is a bad thing.

Time for self-compassion. They're a little bit right, but that's not the point, and neither is shame nor guilt. You really hadn't been able to be with them or yourself as you are now. You weren't as clear about what is and isn't acceptable to you. You might be changing up some of the unspoken agreements between the two of you. None of these changes are a reason for you to feel guilt or shame. You're not a bad person—neither a liar nor a deceiver. You're what all of us are: human and changing. In your case, you're also healing from wounds of less-than-adequate attachment and learning to stop paying prices for relationship. We do not promise others that we will never change when we enter into relationships with them. We do, explicitly or implicitly, promise to be as honest as we know how, to keep commitments as best we are able, to take responsibility for our errors, and to accept apologies with grace when others miss the mark. We do not promise that we will never, ever change.

You can refuse to accept the false belief that guilt or shame is a price you must pay for staying connected to someone when you start to have clearer and more accurate boundaries with them. You can offer empathy to them for how weird and unpleasant this whole thing is. "Yes, you're right. I am changing, and this is confusing for you," without fusing with the other person, losing yourself, and withdrawing your boundaries. You can be truthful, "Yes, I wasn't able to tell you this before. Of course you feel lied to. I wish I could have found my capacities to be honest with both of us a lot sooner" without being self-abnegating and falling over yourself apologizing for your existence.

And then you get to find out whether this relationship is one that requires unhealthy prices, or whether it will eventually flourish when you decide to stop paying them. Some relationships get better—even lots better—when there is more clarity of boundaries. Some people—friends, spouses, kids, work partners—feel better when they don't have to deal with the weird stuff that's evoked in relationships when people are paying an unasked-for price. And some people turn out to be absolutely committed to you paying that price, and unhappy that you're no longer paying it. It's a risk. I have a paragraph in my consent-to-therapy form that speaks to this kind of risk of change and healing, which says:

> *Therapy also has potential emotional risks. Approaching feelings or thoughts that you have tried not to think about for a long time may be painful. Making changes in your beliefs or behaviors can be scary and sometimes disruptive to the relationships you already have. You may find your relationship with me to be a source of strong feelings, some of them painful at times. It is important that you consider carefully whether these risks are worth the benefits to you of changing. Most people who take these risks find that therapy is helpful.*

This is all true any time you change, no matter what method you use. You don't have to be in therapy to incur the risks and benefits of change. Having boundaries in your relationships and refusing to pay the prices set by your less-than-adequate childhood caregivers carries risk. But there are lots of risks in not having boundaries, lots of costs to paying the price of admission. You've been living with those risks to your emotional, physical. and spiritual well-being your whole life without ever having consented to it. Why not take on new risks, those of your choosing—that include the benefit of giving up unhealthy prices for love, connection, and attachment?

CHAPTER 8

Rolling in the Deep:
Grief, Conflict, and Beyond

Something inside woke up and sang along the first time some of us heard Bonnie Raitt sing, "I can't make you love me if you don't," back in the 1990s. You recognized the narrator of the song, the person who crawls into bed with a near-stranger to try to silence the hateful voices inside their head, the person who tries to be brave and honest about the fact that this isn't love, this is just sex and the creature comfort of bodies touching. The song wasn't solely a hit because Bonnie Raitt is, in my opinion, one of the best singers of her generation or because the melody is powerful and haunting. It's because so many of you have lived in—or continue to live in—those lyrics: "And I will give up this fight, 'cause I can't make you love me if you don't."

That was my karaoke song. It felt true, right, and like my life. Being loved for myself, not settling for something less just to have something at all, seemed mythical and impossible. Good was too good to be true. Twenty years ago I was a believer in the notion that if I did not put up with and indulge the person I thought I was spending the rest of my life with, I would be alone forever. My shame at being in a less-than-optimal relationship, my fear that if I left I would risk being exposed to the world as a sap who would pay almost any price and who couldn't even come close to practicing what she preached, my shame at what I had allowed—all were imprisoning. My internal working model of attachment, one that was all about having to pay to be related to, was operating full force. I had buckled down for the long haul with this person, and reassured myself that I had great friends and a good career, so I would be okay.

Then some important things in my life went painfully sideways for a few years, and I became temporarily less able to give my former partner everything she expected from me. I had to ask her for help. I had to ask her to step up. I stopped being able to pay what I had been doling out. Within less than a year after I began to withdraw the payments, she left our relationship of nearly 20 years, thereby confirming my assessment that I was only being tolerated by her for what I was willing to give her and do for her.

She ripped off my betrayal blinders as she left. I was left blinking with fear at what I believed to be the truth that she scattered in her wake like so many bright and ugly monsters. I thought I was truly unworthy of love and here was the evidence to confirm my beliefs. Twenty years of giving on every possible dimension had earned me no sufferance, no patience, nothing except a letter from her attorney demanding half of what I would make for the rest of my life.

In the grief and shame of being left behind at the worst time of my adult life, I had an enormous, painful, and powerful awakening. I realized that I could not have ever made her love me, any more than I'd been able to make my parents love me once I grew a mind of my own. Being generous, giving, available, patient, putting up with things that I would never accept being done to anyone I cared about, none of that had worked. She couldn't tolerate my needing her to reciprocate what I had given for so long. She found herself a better golden goose who was even more indulgent with her than I had been and who asked nothing of her—a new version of who I'd been in 1979, not yet worn down.

She didn't leave me because I had failed; her leaving was inevitable. I had chosen, in my twenties, a reenactment of the attachment patterns of my childhood. A reenactment has a predictable end point, and ours had finally gotten there. She had played her part, as I had played mine.

Being the loyal and committed person I am, and being certain in my inner self that this relationship was as good as I would get even as it became less ideal over time, I had stuck it out. I had silenced the voice that, less than two years in, had said to me, "Laura, you've made a terrible mistake." I had allowed paying ever-larger prices of admission to erode my sense of being loveable, attractive, worthy of being faithful to. In the wake of her departure, I was finally able to see a better truth. It was not that I wasn't worth loving. It was that I had been doing a reenactment for a long time. I didn't have to agree to that ever again.

After the shock and the pain wore off, I realized that she had given me a powerful and wonderful gift—a bit like the one given to me by the thieves who stole my manuscript. It was the gift of an "aha" moment. I got it—finally—that I couldn't make someone love me, no matter what I did. Either someone loved me and wanted to be in a relationship with me—as a friend or romantic partner—or didn't. Chronic ambivalence and foot-out-the-door syndrome were something that felt familiar, and they weren't attachment and care. Spending years being some version of the baby of the *Still Face* video was futile.

I figured out that I deserved to be loved. Shocking, but true. I did not have to pay for it. I couldn't buy my way into connection with money, caring, performing, putting my own needs aside, cleaning the house, making no demands, or you name it from the list of things I had taken with me from my family of origin. I could have a romantic relationship that was like the ones I had with my friends, who were in my life because they wanted me in theirs, nothing more or less. I would have no more unspoken relationship agreements like the one I'd been having with my former partner.

Things that I had been saying as a therapist to other people for upwards of 20 years finally landed. (Okay, I'm a little slow to take my own advice sometimes.)

During the subsequent years I've been doing my best, quite imperfectly, to practice what I preach, learning with much struggle to transform my own internal working model of relationships and doing all of the hard, scary things that I've written about in this book—and then doing them again, and again, and again. The changes began with grief.

The Tracks of Our Tears

To get to the tears, to give up this fight and instead turn our energies to the real and worthwhile task of building nourishing relationships requires that we first grieve. This grief serves the function of clearing away scar tissue and emotional pus from your unhealed wounds. Marilyn McMahon, a poet and survivor of combat trauma stemming from service as a nurse in Vietnam, wrote of her own recovery from post traumatic stress disorder (PTSD), "Wounds heal from the inside out and the bottom up. They must be kept open, inspected, known." Most survivors have done with the wounds of their hearts what burn specialists call "premature temporary closure," growing an apparently healed skin over a gaping wound. You've done what you could not to be raw and in pain all of the time. Paying relational prices has been one of those strategies. If you paid prices you didn't touch the grief, pain, and anger of having been required to pay them by the people who raised you.

You're going to have to touch those wounds to have space to experience the kinds of connections you deserve. Grief, like a cleansing storm, shows up when you open yourself up to your inner experience. Singer-songwriter Cris Williamson wrote, "When you open up your life to the living, all things come spilling in on you." When you open up the possibility of connection without toxic prices, the grief comes spilling in. Don't fear it. Don't close up around it. Let it well up. It isn't dangerous to you, although it will hurt like hell for brief periods of time.

Earlier in this book, I referred to my work with someone who was furious at having to be the one who was responsible for her own welfare. I briefly mentioned then that before she was able to make the commitment to be responsible herself, she first had to grieve what she didn't get and never would get. So let's talk about that for a bit—your grief at never having good-enough attachments as a child, your grief for your younger, suffering self.

Good Grief

What do I mean by grief? This is an important question, as I have learned that so many survivors equate grief with despair and hopelessness. You avoid even touching your grief, much less going fully into it, because you are fearful of plunging into despair, fearful of becoming bereft of all hope, sensing how dangerous both of those emotions can be for you. You sense, correctly, that your grief will expose you to your pain, and you don't entirely trust your skills at handling that pain.

Grief is neither despair nor hopelessness. It is also not a predictable, step-wise process in which first you're angry, then you bargain, then you move on to acceptance. It's both more complicated than that—as in, it's not something that happens in a straight line—and it's much more simple, too. Grief is simply the bigger, more intense sibling of sadness, carrying with it emotional truth about what is absent and missing in present time. Grief is sadness that goes more deeply, that persists over time, because it's about losses and thefts and betrayals that are long-standing and not transient. Grief is large because it reflects the enormity of the loss being grieved. It is as safe as any other emotion when it is clean and free of guilt, shame, and self-admonishment. In other words, grief holds no inherent danger, despite its power and tempestuousness.

Grief can feel scary. It is not dangerous and it will not kill you. It also won't last forever, though it will sometimes feel very long—interminably so. Remember, earlier, when we talked about the timelessness of emotion when you're in an EP? Grief feels like that. Some of it will be the frozen sadness of EPs that was unsafe for you to know about when you were young. You needed to maintain attachment to the adults who were the sources of those losses and not confront them with the emotional truth that they were not really there. Today, here in the present, you are able to feel what it wasn't safe to feel then. It's a memory of what you felt then, even though you're experiencing it in this moment. This emotion will feel like it's lasting forever. I promise you it won't go on forever, although it probably will go on for quite a while.

Around the time that I was finishing this book, I was working with someone who was doing some incredibly courageous grief work. At one point that person asked me how long we'd been focused on that material. When I replied, "about four months," I got a look of incredulity. I was informed that it was feeling more like four years. You might have that experience.

Grief that allows you to fully embrace the hard work necessary to stop paying prices is just this simple, intense, deep thing. It's a lot like the tropical storm that washed through the Pacific as I sat and wrote these words while staying on the Big Island of Hawai'i. Intense and powerful, the storm moved through. There was sun sparkling on the waves that were, for a while, higher and more deeply aqua in color because the storm had come through. The rain and wind came back intensely, the ocean welled up to flood the road behind the house, and then subsided again. The rain pounded down, making the intensely green vegetation that covers the wet side of the island explode with growth. That's grief: intense, powerful, passing through in waves, cleansing, and ultimately nourishing of growth.

The Power of Love

When I wrote *Your Turn for Care*, I introduced the concept of the "death of hope." Clients and friends alike had shown me how common it is to be caught off guard by the intensity of grief that emerged when their abusive elders died. They had expected relief. Instead, grief poured in. They were surprised to discover that they had been holding out generally fruitless hope that the relationship with the abuser might heal right up until the time that person went into the grave. If you've experienced the death of an adult who harmed you, you'll probably recognize this phenomenon. That sort of enduring, rarely conscious hope for a healed relationship with your original attachment figure is remarkably common for people with attachment wounds. It makes perfect sense when placed in the context of anxiety-provoking, avoidance-inducing, or disorganizing attachment experiences like the ones you had.

Remember the baby in the *Still Face* video? Before going into despair and giving up, the baby behaved in a hopeful manner. The baby tried and tried and tried, as hard as possible, to reconnect with the mom. Infants are the original believers in the power of love. They love other humans in their lives unabashedly, full-on, unguardedly. They risk everything for love. They know no other way to be with people and neither did you. All of you offered this sort of fierce, persistent love to people before you had words, before trying too many times, before feeling discouraged, before starting to blame yourself for painful relational outcomes.

In the good-enough family, children are encouraged by adults' responses to them to believe that hope and love are possible because they are. Ruptures—when they happen, and they always do—get repaired because adults who can provide good-enough and secure attachment keep offering that kind of connection. When I hear my securely attached friends mourning the deaths of their beloved parents, they use words like, "My mom was my biggest fan," to describe the ways that their good-enough relationships with their parent continued to unfold. Even though some of these friends went through periods of conflict with their parents, they knew with certainty that love and attachment would eventually win out. One friend has talked about how she told her parents that they had to stop being critical of the man she was bringing home or they could plan to stop having a relationship with her. They loved her and they wanted that relationship more than they disapproved of the man. They changed their behavior and apologized to their daughter for having reacted so poorly to his being from a very different culture. They mended things with him as well, which turned out to be an even better choice, because he went on to become their son-in-law, one of the people who cared for them tenderly in their last years.

But as we've discussed earlier in this book, in families where the attachment offered is less-than-adequate, children come to believe that they make bad things happen. They also believe they could also make good things happen, like make the grown-up happy, if they would just do the right thing—whatever that is—which could have been the wrong thing just two hours ago. Those persistent attempts to do the alleged right thing—whatever it might be—are the embodiment of hope in its earliest form. "I, the kid, can make things better, yes I can, and I will keep trying, yes I will." We are problem solvers, we humans. Solving the problem of attachment to a disorganizing, fear-inducing, or anxiety-provoking adult is high on the list of things that children do when their families are not emotionally safe places.

Children consequently do all kinds of painful mental gymnastics to keep alive the hope of being adequately cared for. They twist themselves into pretzels to keep their hearts open, and offer love to their less-than-adequate caregivers. Think back to our earlier discussion of betrayal trauma theory, which shows us that children will even make themselves unable to know about or recall abuse they have suffered for many years, so that they can keep on having connection to and feel love for the abusive parent. Children famously fight their rescuers when they are being removed from abusive parents. Unlike child welfare authorities, they have not given up hope that their parents will become good-enough. Even though this kind of hope has no foundation in reality, it is frequently more potent and longer lasting than are realistic and data-based expectations.

Children who were not offered good-enough attachment grow up trying to remain loving and hopeful about the adults in their lives. They twist this way and that, trying to find the spot in their family's life where they are doing it just right and the grown-ups finally say, "I'm sorry," and life becomes good. Kids keep on hoping even when this alignment of the stars never happens. The ante on the price of admission is often raised by this hope—the "Maybe, maybe, if I do just this one more thing I will be loved" mantra. "I love you," these kids say to the parent who is indifferent, disengaged, angry, even dangerous. "You're the best parent in the world." This is not sycophantic flattery. These words are heart-felt pleas for love made by many small, insecurely attached human beings. It takes a long time for children to learn to hide their love away.

Losing hope and a belief in love is dangerous for a child. Children who have lost hope, whose learned helplessness in the face of abuse leads—while still young—to severe acting-out against others, suicidal behavior, or substance abuse, are more likely to be noticed by the child welfare system, or by the legal system, or both. They are the kids more likely to cope with abuse by becoming abusers themselves, what psychologists call "identification with the aggressor." Developing an internal working model of endless hope for change in inadequate caregivers is thus adaptive for children, because it allows them to stay connected. Having this hope can prevent them being sent to foster care or being locked up in an adolescent psych unit or a juvenile jail. Hoping against hope is, like its sibling betrayal blindness, a good-enough solution to a much-less-than-good-enough situation.

It's not usually the case that survivors are conscious of having this kind of hope. Nor is it necessarily obvious that this hope underlies your internal working model for dealing with the toxic payment system in your adult relationships. Survivors continue the pattern of their childhoods, hoping for something better in relationships that, to outside observers, are incurably toxic. "S/he's just going through another hard time, s/he doesn't intend to be mean to me," you say to your concerned friend. "Her/his boss is being so unfair. Of course s/he comes home and yells at me." Or, "S/he's not been feeling well, s/he'll be interested in sex again when s/he's feeling better." Only you've been saying that to yourself or your therapist or your good friend for the last six years.

When you're operating from the strategies of an endlessly hopeful baby, you ignore the data of experience in the present about how someone is behaving toward you. You masterfully hope against hope that you can pay enough of a price that this person will love you without hurting you too much—or at least not leave you. It's a reenactment of what you learned with your less-than-adequate caregivers. You can even be self-righteous about this by telling yourself how loyal and committed you are in the face of a difficult person.

Although attachment to an inadequate caregiver is an unfortunate necessity for a child's survival when that's all they've got, attachment in adulthood to a person who abuses, exploits, uses, demeans, mistreats, or neglects you runs counter to your survival. Your internal working model of relationships, which served you well enough in childhood, becomes a vulnerability to being willing to pay prices in adult relationships. Relationships that are reenactments are emotionally and physically draining. Humans pay prices not only in our psychological well-being but also in our general health status when we continue to engage closely with people who implicitly or explicitly convey to us that we are not welcome or worthy. Being in such relationships raises the risk for cardiovascular disease, type 2 diabetes, chronic obstructive pulmonary disease (COPD), addictions, and other diseases that arise from chronic stress and struggles with self-care.

You Can't Make Their Hearts Feel Something They Don't

Because it looks like an entry point for pain, survivors lash out at their own hope for others to change, calling the hope and themselves foolish because, "What's the point?" Please have compassion for your younger self. Honor your little bubble of hope and your ability to love the adults who hurt you as evidence of your emotional capacities. Your hope is proof that you made a fierce commitment to love, relationship, and connection with other humans at times and in places where it would have appeared to have made utter sense to many people to give up. It's the proof of your humanity.

I encourage you to cherish this place inside of yourself as evidence of your decency and your capacity to see the best self in those who repeatedly brought you their worst selves. Thank your hope for having gotten you this far. And then allow yourself to grieve its loss. Allow yourself to grieve for what never was and won't be—not with the adults who raised you, and perhaps not with people in your life today who expect you to keep paying prices for the dubious privilege of remaining connected to them. Grieve, too, for the pain of your younger self, who was swept into the lies that you could get the love you deserved if only you sacrificed enough of yourself.

What does it mean to grieve the loss of hope for what never was, never could be? It does not mean to give way to despair. Despair says, if you can't hope for your payments to make the relationship better, then, you wonder, what is there for you? Well, you *can* have emotionally-meaningful relationships in which you have reciprocity, love, decency, and equity. That's what's there for you. Despair involves taking as true the one thing that's not accurate at all—that you have to pay a price for connection, affection, attachment, and love. Despair feeds on that lie.

Hopelessness—the chronic stance of being unable to expect the good—is not the same as having grief for what never will be. For those of you who have had less-than-adequate attachment experiences, despair is a potent entrancing lure. Despair teaches us that there's nothing we can do but give up, feel terrible, accept defeat. Despair teaches us that we have no power, that we are helpless, because our only choice was to pay prices for connection and our prices were never enough. Despair is the guiding principle of avoidance of feelings. Grief teaches us that we've had a loss—period—and that feeling a feeling about that loss will heal us.

Learned hopelessness and learned helplessness often develop together. You've been taught despair through repeated unsuccessful attempts at attachment with people who are incapable of good-enough connection. Paying, paying, paying, paying, you collapse into despair when it seems as if no price is high enough. The first step in grieving impossible hope in any given relationship is being willing to admit that hope has already been dead with this person for quite a while. The prices you paid weren't inadequate. You simply didn't quite understand until this moment that attaching to an impaired adult was undoable, something in the same category as being a human who can flap their arms and fly.

Can't Help Themselves?

When you've held out hope while making payments to a relationship as if your life depended on it, telling yourself the truth means examining—clearly and without self-blame—the evidence of the excuses you've made for the other person's unwillingness to stop charging the price of admission. Survivors are masters at giving other people in their lives a version of what criminal law calls the "diminished capacity defense," referred to by the verbal shorthand "dimcap."

When criminal defendants plead dimcap they're trying to convince the jury and judge that they did the bad thing they did—which they're not denying having done—because of something outside of their control that made them incapable of acting otherwise. Dan White's infamous "Twinkie defense" was that he assassinated George Moscone and Harvey Milk because he had been eating Twinkies, which had messed with his blood sugar. He claimed that this made him unable to stop himself from walking purposefully into San Francisco City Hall and methodically stalking and shooting his victims.

That's an example of the worst use of the dimcap defense—a cold-blooded killer pretending that his actions weren't under his control and choice. (Worse, the jury bought it.) But dimcap isn't always used as a defense for someone trying to get away with murder. There are even times when dimcap is a good thing. It can be a necessary context for a jury to understand why an otherwise good person committed a criminal act. For example, if someone threatens your child, you may not be in a calm and stable enough state of mind to deal with the threat by not hurting that dangerous other person.

Many people who had less-than-adequate attachment experiences have been strenuously applying a dimcap explanation to their caregivers' behaviors to keep hope alive. An important step in giving up the fight for getting what you won't from someone is to stop excusing their bad behavior toward you on the grounds of their allegedly diminished capacities, whatever those inadequacies might be. Be sure that you're not arriving at this conclusion out of despair. Then hold the other person responsible, period.

Calling people to account doesn't mean that you think they don't have diminished capacities. They may be quite impaired in some way. You're simply not going to use this as a reason to keep hope going and stay in a situation where you pay prices for connection. I've known people who have been gravely wounded by life, people suffering with chronic pain and illness, people struggling to pay the bills and put food on the table, people carrying the burdens of a history of oppression, people who were themselves, like many of you, abused, neglected, denied safety in childhood. And they're all excellent parents, loving partners and friends, decent, caring, and giving. I hope some of you reading this book will recognize yourself in this description. (Hi, all of my current and former clients!) You haven't cashed in your ticket to behave other than honorably. You've rarely—if ever—pled dimcap on your own behalf although you had every right and reason to do so.

This is a stance of "both/and." You can compassionately observe that a person is impaired: "Yes, my father has suffered from depression his entire life." You can compassionately note that this impaired his capacities: "He was unable to be emotionally available to me, and encouraged me to entertain and please him to try to make himself feel better." You can judge that this wasn't an excuse: "That was not an inevitable outcome of his being depressed. Depressed parents have other choices than the ones he made." And, "Yes, my partner learned from his family of origin that violence was a way of solving problems. So he has repeatedly lashed out at me verbally when he was feeling stress and excused it as not so bad because, after all, he wasn't hitting me. That's still not okay. People who grow up in violent families are able to make other choices about how they handle being upset."

Cry You a River

When you're finally able to let yourself believe that there is no excuse for what was done to you, tears may start to fall. Allow yourself to feel sad today for the kid you were, the one who tried so hard. Let your tears flow for that kid, the one who has formed the adult you are, the one who is still trying so hard. Imagine that your younger self is sitting on your lap, or next to you on the couch. It can help to have a photo of yourself as a kid, back when you felt so powerful in a terrible way, so responsible for all of the bad stuff happening. Do this so that the reality of how little you were can get through to you in present time.

Hold that little one in the lap of your mind's eye and tell that kiddo that you're very sad, for example, that Dad was so depressed, and that you're even sadder that Dad couldn't just love this child for being in the world. Allow that sadness to permeate your being. Cry for and with that younger self. Let go of the hope of change in that relationship. Cry again. And then some more. If it helps to have someone there with you when you do this, lean into that person. If you don't have a human, lean into your dog or cat. Invest in a large supply of tissues. Silence the critic inside your head who's trying to tell you how ridiculous you look. If you are able to make noise when you cry, allow yourself to do that. Shake. Drip snot. Use up a whole box of tissues.

Now do this exercise again with regard to your present day pay-to-play relationships. Have that conversation with your more recent self: "I'm so sad that you believed that you had to put up with being yelled at so frequently just to have a husband. No one deserves that, just as no one deserved always having to perform to be loved as a kid. You didn't know you could tell him to stop yelling, did you?" Allow that sadness to fill you up, to spill over and out, to cleanse and nourish you. Let it clean out the guilt and shame and self-hatred so that you can begin to assess with as much clarity as possible the prices you are paying today. Do it again. And again. You'll likely need to return to this many times. Be sure to have plenty of tissues on hand. Why is this necessary? Because until you can feel, not just think, that you have a right to be loved without prices, you're probably going to continue to flirt with paying a few prices that are still pretty toxic to you.

This exercise is more challenging when your less-than-adequate caregiver was dangerous and disorganizing. Many people raised by parents who were worse than wolves have piled on dimcap excuses. Changing polarities from, "My parent had a terrible childhood, so of course he beat me" to, "It's never okay to beat a child, no matter how terrible your childhood was, and I did not deserve one moment of those beatings" may tempt you to skip the step of grief and go right to anger. Grief over the loss of hope for someone who has demonstrated that they will not change, and grief over the loss of what never was and likely never will be, leaves you feeling very vulnerable. Anger feels like a stronger, less exposed place.

Yet vulnerability and grief are both powerful and potentially healing. They are encounters with relational and emotional truths. The existential crisis engendered by realizing that your internal working model has been a source of so many difficulties can bring on despair if you avoid the cleansing power of grief. You risk despair if you try to skip the honest acknowledgement that as a human, you are vulnerable and in need and that you wish for emotionally-meaningful connections with others. So anger is a pathway to despair. Anger also keeps you connected to the person who harmed you. Anger is a relational experience—you are angry with someone, at someone. Grief allows you to let go. Sadness is about absence and loss, about a relationship no longer there.

Allowing hope about change in your caregivers to die allows you to tell yourself the truth about what you did not have. Allowing this kind of hope to die lets you know what was stolen from you by less-than-adequate attachment experiences. While painful, this can be surprisingly freeing. When you stop working hard to get what's not there, you can begin to have glimpses of what is actually available to you. That wound will heal from the inside out, from the bottom to the top. When you move through the grief and pain of betrayal and cease putting energy into hoping that one more piece of self-sacrifice might make the difference, you see will light shining in new places. Spaces can open up to experience being well loved in places that you were keeping reserved for the relationship that you're now grieving. There's now room to notice good-enough love and care walking in. Sometimes that kind of love and care has to knock very hard on your door. Initially it might be almost impossible to recognize those good-enough connections with people because your internal working model of attachment won't resonate at all with what was going on. Remember limbic resonance? You won't feel that at first with the good-enough connections.

This process of transformation wasn't—and isn't—magical. It was—and is—hard work to see and remain capable of seeing that you're out of the old patterns. You'll sometimes lose a grip on this knowledge and try to recreate a reenactment. You'll offer prices in these new relationships and get angry and upset when people won't take them from you. And then you'll remember again: "Oh, yeah, that's not what this person wants." You simply have to show up, be decent, keep your commitments as well as you're able, and be honest about the times when you've stepped on someone's toes and been a source of pain for them. Oh yeah. Simply that. When your internal working model insists that it's all way more complicated and requires you to perform emotional and mental contortions in a smog bank, it can feel odd to stand up straight and breathe freely. In the Biblical book of Exodus, Hebrew slaves who'd been recently freed from bondage complained vociferously that it wasn't as easy to find food as when their slave masters fed them. You won't have to wander 40 years in a relational wilderness to get over the habits of being emotionally enslaved, though.

I Believe in Love

There's a lyric in a song sung by the Dixie Chicks that perfectly celebrates the possibility of emotionally-meaningful relationships in which we need not pay prices, and where we can be reciprocal and human. They sing, "Silence stared me in the face and I finally heard its voice, it seemed to softly say that in love you have a choice."

The small people who you once were, struggling to connect in less-than-adequate attachment relationships with adults, did not have choices. Children are mostly stuck with the adults who brought them into the world. Thus, your internal working model of emotionally-meaningful relationships was one of having no choice other than paying prices in order to have something masquerading as love. You had to hold out impossible hope for the adults in your life, because all of your fantasies that you had been switched at birth and that your real parents would finally show up and rescue you were just that—fantasies. You believed in your broken little heart that these people raising you and hurting you were as good as it got.

For your adult self, though, the next line of the song is spot on. "In love you have a choice." In romantic love, in friendship, in the people with whom you associate in other than superficial ways, you have choices today that you may not yet notice or experience. The notion of choice—of choosing relationships with people who value the human being you are and require no more than basic decency, honesty, and willingness in order to connect with you—may still seem odd. What's available will seem unrecognizable, strange, or even initially somewhat repellant. It will feel "not like me."

Hey, You've Got to Hide Your Love Away

One of the ways that children in difficult attachment relationships survive is to dissociate their capacity to feel deep love. They come into my office as adults telling me that they are incapable of loving, that they go through the motions but have no experience of being moved emotionally. "I'm dead inside," Doug said. He had grown up with parents who were preoccupied with real and imagined physical illness, and would never touch or kiss him because of their irrational fears of contagion. He went on, "I know that Kim loves me. She's overflowing with it, she shines with it. I feel nothing. So I fake it. And after six years I'm beginning to wonder what's wrong with me, and when she'll figure out that I've been faking it.

I do love her, you know, as much as I know how to love anyone. I just don't feel anything. I'm too broken."

If this is you, the grief work that's ahead of you is for the baby and child you were who had to dissociate your love for your impaired grownups so that you could stop your tender young heart from becoming too broken to survive. This grief is not feeling sorry for yourself. This is not crying over spilled milk, or sitting on a pity pot, or any of the other shaming things that you've been told and tell yourself about your grief. This grief represents an honest confrontation with the damages done and the losses incurred by the carelessness or malice or incapacity of the adults who raised you.

Your grief is simply telling the emotional truth about the enormity of your loss. You had the experience of good-enough attachment taken from you before you knew that it might ever exist. You learned to believe that connection and love were entirely conditional or completely absent. These lessons have affected your life and relationship choices. Those are real losses for which genuine grief is the reciprocal and reasonable response, and the necessary step to clear out the pain and open up your heart to what is possible and available today.

What this grieving also does is convey a message to yourself that you *did* deserve good-enough attachment, that the love offered you by your caregivers should have carried no conditions, and that your existence on the planet should have been welcomed, not made into a problem. You can look at your depleted or impaired or dangerous parent and say, "You could have done better. You should have done better. I deserved better." In those moments you begin to develop the emotional knowledge that today you *do* deserve better. Not perfect (remember, no perfection in this world). Better. Good enough.

Take a breath. Dive in. Keep breathing. Use your psychic snorkel of mindfulness as you dive deeper. As you allow grief, you will reconnect with the loving small person who you were. Knowing that you are able to love can feel frightening, because it was once associated with so much pain. Here's an important piece of truth: Love always leads to loss. Even in a life-long loving relationship one person dies before the other. Our beloved four-legged companions all die too soon. But if you try to avoid loving with your whole heart, you'll feel loss anyhow. Plus, you'll feel regret, which is more painful and difficult to work through than any loss. Loss is different than the pain of being denied, pushed away, used, betrayed. The Yiddish poet Chaim Nachman Bialik poignantly wrote, "Alas for those who cannot sing; they die with all their music in them." Replace "sing" and "music" with "love" and "loving." Allow the grief, so that you can enlarge the space for your capacity to feel love. Grief lets you love as fully and openly as you could the day you were born.

The love and attachment adults can have in emotionally-meaningful relationships will never be the pure, wordless love of the securely attached infant-caregiver pair. But it will be good enough, and it won't come at the price of your well-being, your pocketbook, or your safety. It is real love—a love full of flaws, a love that is confused at times, a love that steps on toes. It's human, and it's good enough. And there will be moments when it gets close to the pure love of the securely attached child.

Don't Cry Now

Sometimes one of the effects of a history of undermined attachment is that you begin to grieve too soon for a loss that isn't actually happening. Because you're still trying to get out of the way before the other shoe drops, you prematurely declare a loss. You give up when you're in the midst of a conflict with someone. You stop paying attention to what's happening in the present. You put yourself into a trance of despair to avoid feeling pain. You let hopelessness define the meaning of what's happening with the other person. It's a crappy, and yet comfortable and familiar place for a survivor. It's your EPs coming out to run the show. Terrified of conflict, they whisper in your ear that you must go now, that all is lost. "Leave," they say, "before today's experiences expose the pain of our unhealed, undigested wounds."

Claire and Aisha had been having a low-level, and in Aisha's mind, minor conflict for several days over whether or not to attend an event that was important to Claire and somewhere between uninteresting and mildly aversive to Aisha. Aisha's level of discomfort and distress was palpable to Claire—so much so that she began to talk to herself about the importance of letting go, grieving what could not be, and making alternate plans for that evening. She told herself that she was being an adult who could handle disappointment, and imagined that Aisha would be pleased by her sacrifice "on behalf of the relationship."

Thus her surprise when Aisha asked, "Okay, what should I plan to wear for that fundraiser?" Claire stuttered with surprise and said, "Oh, I already made other plans. I was sure you didn't want to go." Aisha then became upset with Claire about having acted as if they had made a mutual decision about what to do. They hadn't, of course. Aisha had voiced her lack of interest, yet she'd never insisted that they not go. She understood that the event was important to Claire even if she herself thought it was a colossal waste of time.

Based on Aisha's honest opinion about the event, Claire's EPs had unilaterally assessed that she was demanding too much from Aisha. Her EPs convinced her that she was making a horribly unreasonable demand of Aisha and needed to give up going to the event in order to be loved. Claire was confused at Aisha's upset feeling. She thought she'd been an adult and made a sacrifice for Aisha. That it not only hadn't worked but had backfired became further evidence in Claire's mind of her inability to be a good-enough spouse. She withdrew emotionally, feeling hurt because Aisha had (once again) refused to appreciate her willingness to sacrifice, and feeling shame-drenched because she had somehow "made" Aisha even angrier.

Claire's response exemplifies prematurely giving up and grieving, and thus losing what didn't have to be lost. Claire and Aisha's story exemplifies the risk of actual relationship loss and disconnection when you can't tolerate sitting with the discomfort of hanging out in ambiguity or in the other person's displeasure. Many survivors do just this. You give up on what you want in a relationship with a person who, as it turns out, is perfectly willing to discuss a compromise, even if they're not happy about it. Surprise, surprise! People in your life would like to do things that they aren't necessarily thrilled about because they perceive that you want something and are willing to bend a little to support you getting it. They actually want to reciprocate with you.

In the family where you grew up, such reciprocity and willingness to bend on your behalf were both missing. The person doing the bending was almost always you, not the adults to whom you were endeavoring to attach. Your internal working model instructs you that the same will occur with the people in your adult life. So you grieve and give up before people in your life today have an opportunity to offer you reciprocity.

Don't Give Up This Fight

Conflict is an unwelcome surprise for survivors attempting to have healthy relationships. The presence of conflict violates the fantasies, conscious or otherwise, that you've had of finding a person to be in your life who will always agree with you, always be on your wavelength, never argue. These are the fantasies of being in the seamless infant-caregiver experience that was denied to you. Psychologist and researcher David Schnarch, an incisive observer of adult relationship struggles, has commented that some people expect a spouse or partner to behave therapeutically, to make up for everything difficult that happened to them, and to act more like an indulgent parent than an equal spouse, partner, or friend. I've seen that with couples where one or both people are survivors. When one person in an emotionally-meaningful relationship has this kind of unspoken expectation, conflict can become particularly intolerable and even feel like a betrayal of trust.

Your disappointment that this other person now expects you to show up, to stop paying prices, to simply be their equal and do your reciprocal fair share, is very much what that client of mine so many years ago felt when I brought up the whole "You're responsible for yourself now" theme. You're tired of being responsible. You want someone to do all of the work for once like you used to do. You're furious that true love and care isn't a perfect, seamless, warm blanket. The same client who was angry about taking responsibility once told me that the ultimate fantasy partner would be a therapist. Therapy isn't a reciprocal relationship, after all, and this person imagined that a therapist partner would have as few personal needs and demands and be as highly attuned as therapists are during work hours. Not so, folks. Just ask the spouse of any psychotherapist if you want to be disabused of that fantasy!

It's not that there's something wrong with you for wanting this. You were robbed of it when you were little. It's hard to start embracing the value of the good-enough adult relationships you deserve and can have today when they aren't the blissful ones of secure infant attachment that you've been unconsciously yearning for. You have more grieving to do so that you can fully embrace good-enough other adults in your life.

The difficult truth is that adult people who love one another well and relatively unconditionally still have conflicts with one another. Conflict emerges when there's a rupture in the fabric of connection, and such ruptures hurt—often intensely. Happily connected people don't always handle conflict well either. The rupture in connection that engenders conflict creates a certain amount of emotional dysregulation. Two of my good friends—who have been together for going on 26 years, through multiple moves and a life-threatening illness, and have a healthy, loving relationship on which they've worked and continue to work very hard—joke about what they call the "five-minute fight." As they described it at their 25th anniversary celebration, they start with "I" statements (the official proper way to fight that no one can hang on to for very long), move to "you" statements (the blame statements that all therapists tell you not to do and we all do anyhow), then to "always" and "never" statements (which, as you will see below, are considered problematic by researchers of relationships), and finally to "F" statements (cursing, in other words!). For five minutes they allow themselves to have an intense, caricatured horrible fight until they begin to crack one another up and find their excess funny. But for no longer than five minutes, they told their guests, because life is too short to spend on conflict.

The message of the five-minute fight is that conflict is inevitable, it's not inherently dangerous, and if you're going to behave badly in a conflict, keep the crappy stuff short, please. This idea that conflict is inevitable can be scary for people who lived through physical and emotional abuse in childhood. I'm not suggesting that you should adopt this strategy unless both parties truly know that the other isn't being either coercive or controlling. You can have the most appalling conflict for a very brief period of time and have it be survivable. A crappy fight can even open up the door to more clear, loving, and accurate communication about whatever it is that's the source of distress.

You can also conduct your conflicts according to rules set by therapists: emotions no higher than "4" on the 10-point scale, "I" statements, no sarcasm or contempt or defensiveness. You might find this a more tolerable strategy for subverting the message that all conflict is abusive and dangerous, or that any dissent means that you are bad and wrong and about to be dropped. The point is, conflict *always* occurs in an emotionally-meaningful relationship between adults because we *are* adults, with formed selves, opinions, boundaries (remember boundaries), and extreme humanness. In good-enough relationships where the price of admission is not silencing yourself, conflicts are unpleasant. They're not, however, inherently dangerous to a relationship. They simply suck to be in the midst of.

Another couple among my friends, both therapists who celebrated their 32nd wedding anniversary while I was writing, told me once that in the first 10 years they were together they had loud yelling fights daily. They still battle it out verbally at times. Both of them are brilliant, passionate, highly-opinionated people who get their feelings hurt easily by those they love. They credit their openness to the inevitability of fights for the strength and longevity of their relationship. Nothing is suppressed. Everything is out in the open, on the table to be dealt with. Each of them has sufficient skills at self-soothing, and each trusts that the other one loves her or him enough to get through the hurricanes that have blown through their marriage. Like that tropical storm in Hawai'i, their relational storms have nourished and fertilized the ground of their marriage.

When you're in a conflict, you don't control what the other person is doing or saying. This doesn't mean that you are powerless or out of control or being controlled by the other person. You do have enormous power within yourself. You *can* soothe yourself, talk to yourself, and use those skills of emotion regulation and distress tolerance that we talked about earlier in this book. Remind yourself that you have choices. You can initiate a self-talk narrative about yourself and the other person to remind yourself that the other person does generally like and respect you, and has your best interests at heart even if in the moment that's a little hard for you to notice.

One of the most empowering things you can do in a conflict is work hard to believe that the other person is acting without conscious malevolent intentions. That's such a grounding, centering, calming belief. In aikido, which is founded on the principle of peaceful resolution of conflict, we practice in our bare feet. Consequently we often step on one another's toes when we're training. No one ever assumes that it's other than an accident, even when, as sometimes happens, it breaks someone else's toe. Those moments are quite physically painful. I've broken a toe of my own in one such encounter, and acquired many other bruises and torn toenails. No one who hurt me ever intended me any harm. My training partner on the day I broke my toe was just moving where he was moving and his heel and my toe had a too-close encounter. We were having a genuine, close-up, no-holds-barred connection. Ouch!

So, too, we must believe in good intentions as we move into a conflict. Our emotional broken toe is hurting—a lot. The other person didn't mean to break it.

That person was simply moving clumsily through emotional space, close enough that you got stepped on. Ouch! It wasn't, "You were trying to hurt me on purpose," or "You like it when I'm in pain." Neither should be the case when you're no longer paying prices in a relationship. It can be quite challenging to take and maintain this perspective. If you were subjected to pain by the caregivers of your childhood, you may have noticed some of them enjoying your pain. So you expect sadism. It can be hard to believe that someone isn't enjoying your pain. But when you've assessed your current circumstances well, it's extremely unlikely that the people you've mindfully chosen to have in your life would have fun with your distress. Sadism would show up in all kinds of other places, and you refuse to pay that price.

This doesn't mean that someone can't be clueless. An otherwise loving and well-intentioned person might be slow to learn that you really, truly meant it that they were stepping on your toe. You might have to say, "ouch" more loudly, and repeatedly. In a relationship you don't pay prices for, you should expect that the other person believes that what they're doing is painful for you and wants to figure out how to stop doing that as soon as they can.

You can speak up for yourself in a conflict. Rather than be defensive, you can say when and if what's happening has crossed your boundaries and doesn't feel okay. You can say, "It's hard for me to hear what you're saying when your voice is this loud. I need you to be quieter, because I want to listen." You can say, "Asking me what kind of idiot would do something so stupid feels like an insult. I don't accept being insulted. Say it a different way, please." And it will still suck. Conflict isn't pleasant even if you follow all of the rules in every single one of the relationship books about "I" statements and not talking when you're above "4" on the 10-point scale. It's unpleasant even when you've empowered the heck out of yourself. But it's a necessary component of a good-enough relationship with another adult. Better to be prepared and to enter into conflict from the most grounded, self-loving, and effective place possible. When I step on the mat for aikido practice, I know I'm going to get thrown; I'm not surprised to find myself lying on the mat. A good-enough relationship is the mat where contact—and thus sometimes conflict—will happen. Don't be surprised by it.

To have connection you must give up the fantasies of a *seamlessly* warm and loving relationship. Two adults who do not always agree have a *genuine* warm and loving relationship. They will misunderstand one another, jump to conclusions, mishear and misinterpret each other, and be fully human with one another in many ways without requiring each other to pay prices. In good-enough families, kids have that kind of experience with their parents as they grow up. Conflict emerges when the kids increasingly become people with opinions of their own. Parents get mad, kids get mad, and in the end everyone loves one another. They're family and still connected. No one is shown the door, cut off, humiliated, starved, beaten up, or otherwise harmed because there was a disagreement. In a good-enough family, kids might lose their computer privileges for a period of time. They might be given an obnoxious extra chore. There will be logical consequences. And that'll be it.

Those of you who are parents may have a hard time with this aspect of your kids' normal development. Your kid is upset with you, and you walk into my office certain that you have failed as a parent. Your alleged failure is plunging you into despair, because being a good parent is one of the most important goals in your life. It's what Judith Herman, in her classic book, *Trauma and Recovery*, calls your survivor mission—the thing you were going to do perfectly to redeem what was done to you. You're surprised as hell when I tell you that your teen yelling at you about how much they hate you is the best evidence of your success that I can imagine. Kids are able to feel angry, and say some horrid things to their parents, when they feel securely attached and know that they will always be loved. They don't know until they're older that they can hurt your feelings; you're the parent, who they believe can handle anything. Because you've been a good-enough parent, your kids see you as strong and capable, not fragile and in need of constant care. Your kids feel cared for and trust your love for them, so they can say and do the kinds of things you were never safe to say or do.

Some conflicts in good-enough families are harder than others. When a kid uses drugs, when a parent is struggling with mental illness, when a kid grows up and converts to another religion, when dad starts to transition into a woman— these are all harder than usual. But they're all things that families with good-enough attachment histories weather. I know a parent who has struggled with bouts of psychosis since before their first child was born. In the intervening 30 years that kid received very powerful doses of good-enough attachment experiences. The parent recruited the assistance of extended family, therapists, and spiritual communities in order to ensure care and connection. Now a young adult, that child has become a passionate advocate for the rights of people living with psychosis. The process of encountering difficult life passages can deepen and strengthen the bonds in an attached-enough family.

I invite you to act like a well-enough-attached person and have conflicts with the people you love. The trick is to do it with skill and a commitment to not punish yourself or others when conflict emerges. Bring an open heart, skills at centering yourself, compassion, and your sense of humor. With those tools in hand, a conflict is fertilizer, not toxin.

What Not to Say

There are some things you should *not* bring to a conflict. Most of them are ways of relating that feel familiar if you grew up in a family where abuse occurred. Because you were on the receiving end of these not-okay ways of expressing disagreement or distress, you're at risk of behaving in those ways as well. In fact the more you insist you're nothing like that parent, the more likely you are to act like them. When you disowned a part of yourself because it reminds you of someone you'd rather not be like, you free that part of yourself to run amok. I often tell clients that I know that very kind people are capable of being nasty because I know that my father—who was a master of sarcasm and cutting remarks—lives on inside of me. That unfortunate inheritance—which I received from him along with my curly hair, a tendency to be argumentative, and a risk for developing melanoma— used to show up when I was hurt. Once I could look in the mirror and say hello to my father's face I was more able to be kind more of the time, even when I was angry.

Because the adults in your past labeled their behaviors as "arguments" or "discipline" or "talking sense into you," you grew up believing that what happens in a conflict always includes shaming, painful, and even dangerous experiences. Sometimes you've used those strategies with people yourself (I know I have), even though you hate that you've internalized these ways of relating that hurt or frightened you. Sue Johnson calls these patterns of problematic interaction in relationships the "Demon Dialogues," where the focus is on finding and placing blame, getting a rise out of the other person somehow—because *any* response is some response—or escaping from them as fast as possible.

No surprise, then, that you're averse to conflict because you believe in the very core of your being that once in an argument, you will either devolve into despised behaviors or be forced to deal with being treated badly yourself. For you, *all* conflict is a Demon Dialogue. There must be a victim and a persecutor. You will end up losing—no matter what—and you'll hurt more than when you started. Your EPs have a hard time knowing that a conflict is about dealing with a raised voice or ardent disagreement, with misunderstanding or clumsiness, with lousy timing or a hurt feeling, and not with being shamed, humiliated, and tossed away.

In my definition of healthy conflict, humiliation, shaming, sarcasm, cut-offs, and brutality are not conflict behaviors. They are actually ways of attempting to increase power over another person and avoid conflict. Conflict that contributes to a healthy connection with others is a vulnerable, not controlled, reciprocal exchange that attempts to solve a problem of rupture in the fabric of connection. Behaviors that masquerade as conflict are antithetical to problem solving and repairing a rupture. They're tactics to control other people through shame, guilt, terror, or devaluation—attempts to shut conflict down. They are taxes on a relationship, a toll-bridge with an evil troll.

That's not the kind of conflict that builds and strengthens healthy connections. If you were raised with emotionally or physically abusive, or neglectful caregivers, you may have never had a healthy conflict in your life; you've had something that masqueraded as a conflict, but was really someone trying to control someone else instead of resolving matters to a reciprocal, mutual conclusion. It was someone trying to make someone else pay a price for being merely human, not a bid to repair a rupture.

Lately He's Taken to Saying I'm Crazy

Sarcasm and its cousin contempt are dangerous to relationships; they deepen ruptures. Sarcasm isn't "being funny." It's a message about how worthless you are. Relationship researcher John Gottman has found that romantic couples who use contempt with one another have relationships that are more fragile, shorter-lasting, and rarely make it to the five-year mark.

Attacking the other person and criticizing that person's character is also a risky thing to do if what you want is rupture repair in a good-enough relationship instead of control of the other party. When you call someone names or label them, you can't have a good-enough connection. You know how lousy it feels to be treated like that, especially if you were on the receiving end of that kind of treatment when you were young. The admonition made by many couple therapists to talk about behavior you don't like without impugning the person engaging in that behavior is foundational to conflict being helpful rather than destructive.

Stating that a person "always" or "never" does something (unless you're expert at the five-minute fight, where you can get away with anything for five minutes) puts everyone into a box that is both inaccurate and explosive. The words "frequently" or "rarely" may not feel as viscerally satisfying in the middle of a shouting match, but are both more accurate and effective ways of calling attention to the other person's recurring behaviors. "Always" and "never" are EP words; in EP consciousness things are either entirely absent or interminable. And because EPs are almost always activated by whatever it is that began the conflict, it's important to self-soothe them out of their time warps. This allows you to describe how abandoned you feel today when the other person forgets to keep a commitment.

Reciprocal, growth-producing conflict requires a willingness to hear that you have done something that felt disrespectful, dismissive, or hurt the other person's feelings, leaving that person feeling dropped, ignored, or unimportant. We have to be willing to know we have been otherwise fully and totally human and imperfect. Growth-producing conflict also requires that you not brush feedback aside simply because it's so painful to hear that your human imperfections have been a source of distress. This is particularly challenging for you because you were not granted opportunities to simply be human when you were young. Feedback about being imperfect was information that your less-than-adequate attachment might become even less adequate. You've likely had relationships as an adult where you paid prices for connection by being willing to be punished, shamed, or controlled for being human and fallible.

When someone is important to you, responding non-defensively to complaints requires an advanced level of skill in distress tolerance and emotion regulation. But it's a level you can obtain. You'll need to do a lot of self-soothing. You may need to take short breaks. You might want to put limits on when other people can offer you critical feedback. For example, I have learned that I don't bring my adult self to this process at all when I've just awakened. It's easier to hear difficult feedback and be non-defensive when feedback is offered at times when we are able to most effectively recruit our skills. Being willing to determine how to critique each other compassionately is one piece of evidence that you're learning how to create reciprocal responsibility for a relationship. When both people are responsible, there are shared commitments for handling the hard times that support the connection and don't feel punitive.

Resist the urge to distance, shut down, or immerse yourself in a narrative of having done nothing wrong when a person you care about lets you know that you have, in fact, stepped on their metaphorical toes. Leonard Cohen wrote a great line about the costs of defensiveness: "When you're not feeling holy your loneliness says that you've sinned." Or as some of my friends have said about their successful marriages, "We figured out that we could be right, or we could be happy. So be happy."

When you grew up in a family where someone had to be right and someone wrong—where blame was both inevitable and usually placed on you—the idea that you can do something displeasing to a person you care about and they will still like you, love you, and want to relate to you when the brief storm of their distress passes seems foreign at first, second, and one hundredth try. Yet it's quite possible. Willingness to be non-defensive isn't an invitation to another person to seize on your honesty and savage you with it. Openness is not showing a weakness that the other person will exploit to hurt or control you. Such transparency is, rather, an invitation to genuine closeness.

I don't enjoy being honest with people I care about when I've been less than perfect. I hate knowing that I hurt or disappoint people I love. Yet when I am able to muster the difficult skill of listening with an open heart, conflict is invariably over more quickly, and we become closer. I know that seems odd. The paradox is, when you can be vulnerable in a safe-enough context, greater closeness is a logical outcome. Openness leads to closeness. The amazing moments of wordless bliss that occur from time to time in good-enough romantic relationships are fed by healthy resolution of conflicts. Each person takes a risk to be known, seen, and imperfect—and this deepens connection.

Remember cut-offs from earlier in this book? They don't belong in a conflict either. Shutting everything down by walking away or refusing to interact may feel powerful. That's an illusion. A cut-off silences the other person and disconnects you. I've been on both sides of cut-offs in a family that specialized in them. They're a fortress into which you can go and have the illusion of safety. When you come out, though, conflict is still there. Then thing are worse, because the other person is now not only unhappy with the source of the conflict, that person is now also upset about being cut off. Sometimes people do dueling cut-offs, where each party retreats further and further into her or his respective corners until connection is strained to the breaking point.

"But I get flooded with emotions during a conflict, and I can't stay," you say. "I have to leave or I'll start acting badly." Well of course you get flooded emotionally. You've been avoiding these feelings for decades. A plunge into forbidden territory scares you, and your EPs show up and anticipate doom. The other person in a conflict may not see that you're overwhelmed, and be confused when you declare that there's nothing further to discuss. You're trying not to explode all over them. Instead, they feel abandoned and shut out. You might feel calm, but you're not; you're shut down, dissociated from painful emotions, and distant from the other person.

So what to do? You can choose neither to explode nor close down. Make an agreement about the use of time-outs, and use them wisely. Make it clear that no one is leaving for good. That's especially important to state clearly if deep wounds from childhood involve being abandoned or having things change abruptly for the worse. Having a mutually agreed-to time-out allows over-activated nervous systems to calm down and gives both people time to remember that they each want connection equally.

Create a "safe word"—a phrase that both parties agree means that a time-out is in order. It can be as simple as calling "time out" or holding up the "T" hand signal sports referees use; don't get more exotic than that. Agree how long a time-out will last. Leaving things open-ended or ambiguous will activate attachment-related states and can give you enough time to head back down the rabbit hole of avoidance. Either of those outcomes can make it seem that you're about to finally find out that there was a price on this relationship, and difficult to stay in the present. Most people can handle about 15 minutes before a time-out makes things worse. Fifteen minutes usually gets you back to a place where you're not flooded with stress hormones. Experiment with this; you might be able to do it in less time. If you find out that you need more, ask for more. Fifteen minutes is a suggestion, not a prescription.

There are themes to this discussion of what not to do. *Do* engage your behavior chain analysis. *Don't* use the findings to plead diminished capacity for yourself. That information is for later personal use, not to excuse today's missed mark. Yes, you were tired and forgot to run that errand. Yes, you were upset and snapped at the other person. Yes, you were distracted and forgot you'd been asked not to tell a mutual acquaintance about the illness they aren't ready to make public. In the families in which you grew up, pleas of dimcap were your attempts to lessen the blow. That didn't work then. Only the adults had their bad behavior excused. Pleading dimcap doesn't work now; it's a distraction from hearing that you missed a mark. Instead of pleading dimcap, soothe yourself using emotion regulation and distress tolerance skills. Breathe. Save behavior chain analysis for later; its purpose is to help you change, not to give you a free pass to avoid fair feedback.

When you don't have to be perfect to have connection, you can stop explaining why you aren't perfect. You aren't. It's as simple as that—and it's almost intolerably difficult to stop apologizing for being imperfect. That's going to be okay. Eventually it will feel less difficult. You know the theory that it takes 10,000 tries to master something? Conflict is like that. Allow yourself to be a beginner who is struggling. Don't expect it to be fun or easy. Keep your eyes on the prize of improved connection and intimacy. Speak up and take a time-out if you're slipping down the rabbit hole of self-hatred.

Conflict is contact. Avoidance of conflict is avoidance of connection. Conflict also sucks. You have to continuously practice skills of emotion regulation, self-soothing, and interrupting the narratives that attempt to turn distress with each other into evidence that there is a price for this relationship. You have to tolerate someone else's distress, not use it to feed the demons of self-hatred. You have to accept that you matter enough that your actions can hurt someone without seeing yourself as the bad guy. You have to hang on to your knowledge that conflict has the potential to deepen the quality of connection. As Sue Johnson says, "In the best outcome (injuries) become integrated into couples' attachment stories as demonstration of renewal and connection." Repaired ruptures are places where you can return and say, "Remember when? Remember how we got through this and were even better than before?"

What you don't have to do when you're open to conflict is grieve. What conflict helps to sustain is commitment to connection. Coming back after conflict with an open heart demonstrates willingness to hang in there and work things out. In the families you came from, commitment to reengage and feel difficult emotions was usually absent. If one of your caregivers was distressed by your behavior, they didn't work things out—instead, they penalized you by withdrawing or acting out.

Conflict doesn't mean that love is absent. Quite the contrary. It means that two people are trying to make connection better by working through things that are obstacles to connection flourishing. Conflict means you can say, "I don't like what you did," or "That hurts a lot," without an inherent risk of disconnection or punishment. When you let go of the fantasy of seamless connection, you can let the good-enough connection that you have be its gloriously imperfect self. The corollary is that *you* can be your gloriously imperfect self. You're not required to pay the price of perfection to be admitted to a good-enough, emotionally-meaningful relationship.

EPILOGUE
Happy Enough Together

"The real thing is gonna steal your unhappy ending."
Maia Sharp

I end this book, as I began it, with a lyric from the song "Real Thing." (You can hear Maia Sharp sing it on YouTube at https://www.youtube.com/watch?v=4EOrivg1_rA). I had a huge "aha" moment the first time I heard it. Maia Sharp was singing to me, to you, to all of us who've been "Waiting for the punch line, knowing that the joke's on you," and who now stand in the middle of an emotionally-meaningful relationship that isn't being played by your old rules. You aren't being required to pay prices. You aren't being used, dumped, abandoned, and betrayed. The joke isn't happening; the other shoe isn't dropping. "Maybe it's just the real thing," she sings. It's the polar opposite of "I can't make you love me if you don't." Instead it's, "Okay, you do love me, for me, as me, no hidden prices, no tax, no penalty. Not necessarily easy, and no special added toll because of who I am." The real thing has snuck in without you noticing and is changing the ending of the story.

What steals your unhappy endings is a realization that there is no legitimate price of admission to emotionally-meaningful relationships. Not having a price of admission doesn't mean that relationships are simple or free from conflict. You have to work at having the real thing. You don't get to be happy together forever like love songs promise without putting your heart, soul, and intention into co-creating that happiness. No one gets a unicorn. Genuine intimacy *is* possible and entirely worth having. Because your childhood threw down emotional boulders, your path to intimacy is often painful and rocky. It's a lot like taking a hike on a difficult trail to get to a special hidden beach. The trail looks impossible at times. It's rough and slippery. Take the trail—even if you fall and skin your knee along the way. The hike is entirely worth it. Once you get there all you have to do is walk into the water to see gorgeous coral and fish that you can find nowhere else.

When you decide to proceed in life as if good *is* true, and systematically apply the lessons of this book, you increase your chances of having more of the "real thing" in your life. You'll feel a lot of happiness. You'll have moments of bliss, of vulnerable, open-hearted connection, joy in attachment. You'll also have a lot of banal good-enough times. You'll be bored sometimes. You'll be impatient sometimes. You'll be sad and pissed off and frustrated sometimes. The other person will likely feel these emotions as well. Sometimes one of you will be a pain in the behind to the other one. It's all normal. You're not missing what's promised in love songs and movies. You have the real thing, and it's nourishing and tasty. It's not a gourmet five-course meal every day. Gourmet food is pricy. Enjoy the low-cost home cooking you get by having a long-term seat at the table of love.

The real thing in a relationship is balance and reciprocity, honesty and decency, commitment and consistency. The real thing is other people being there for you as much as you are for them. The real thing is having a right to make mistakes. The real thing is about making clean amends, free of dimcaps and excuses, and free of fear that honesty will be used as a weapon against you. It's about love and care and friendship and emotional intimacy. It's not a unicorn. It's a real creature, the iridescent parrot fish swimming through blue waters off the beach you hiked so long and hard to get to.

One of the challenges for people who've been deprived of secure attachment is that you've been promised a unicorn. You've been listening to love songs—and the love they sing of is not what adults have with each other. Instead, you've been hearing a version of the blissful state that only happens for infants experiencing secure infant attachment. No wonder love songs sell so well! They misdirect you to a unicorn hunt. Most love stories are pretty much the same: "Love means never having to say you're sorry" was the theme of one that sold millions of copies in the 1960s. Because you didn't have good-enough love, you had no way to know that the songs and stories were a distortion.

Well, folks, blissful, wordless mind-reading connection is a unicorn. Love means being willing to say that you're sorry when your actions have initiated a rupture in connection and care. Yes, the terrible wounds to attachment can sometimes challenge people close to you. There's no shame in that fact. You might not be easy, but you're not high maintenance. You bring at least as many gifts to relationships as challenges. Ultimately you're no more and no less difficult than any other human being.

Love means accepting amends from someone when you're the one who's been hurt, and assuming the other person's best intentions. Expecting someone to never hurt you is a mythical beast. Attachment in adult life isn't the same as the infant-caregiver variety. It's a different good thing. Its value is that adult relationships are conscious and intentional and full of choice. Someone chooses you every bit as much as you choose them. People in your life trip, stumble, and fall on you emotionally. Don't close your heart when this happens. Accept their apologies without exacting a price from them.

When We're Sixty-Four

Like me, some of you are well into the second half of life. You may have been in a long relationship where you've paid prices the entire time. It's scary for you to imagine that those prices might not have been necessary It's nearly impossible to comprehend that your friend, spouse, or partner never was—and still isn't—interested in you continuing to pay. It's even scarier to find out that you weren't making it up. You know what those prices are. You're ready to stop paying them. And you sincerely believe that the minute you stop you will be entirely alone in the world.

I can hear you say, "This is all fine and good, Laura, this not paying prices thing, but what about the reality of life? I'm too old to start over. And now—thanks to reading this book—I'm too angry and upset with what I've been doing in relationships not to shake things up. Don't leave me hanging here. This is scaring me."

I'm not going to apologize for waking you up from a trance of despair. You were already awake enough that you picked up this book and kept reading. You're ready to make changes in your life. Of course you're frightened. You've not yet tested the hypothesis that says that you're a valuable, lovable human being.

You're right. It can be more difficult to make new connections as we get older. Opportunities for meeting people shrink. Well-established friendship circles seem to have no space for another person. Romantic relationships are challenging to initiate (although they're not easy for younger folks, either).

This is all true. But it's not necessarily true that this is a barrier to having the toll-free relationships you deserve. I've seen people in the second half of life stop being willing to pay prices and have good—as well as challenging—outcomes. I've seen people create new or better emotionally-meaningful relationships after 50. People who do these things aren't special or lucky. They've been persistent and committed to an emerging belief that they deserve quality connections with others, and they've been willing to do a little psychological bungee jumping in the process—leaping off the bridge believing that the bungee will hold and keep them from smashing to the metaphorical ground.

You won't necessarily be dumped or left alone in the world when you begin to retract prices you've been paying in long-standing relationships. Renegotiating relationship agreements can be risky. Pay attention to the risks inherent in the status quo that you've been ignoring. It's likely that you'll be a little inaccurate in your assessments of some people some of the time. You'll probably over-estimate the risks of change and underestimate those of stasis. Don't forget to look at both types of risks.

There are some relationships where it's quite clear that a price of admission is required. Those relationships exist in name only. You can tell, if you're honest with yourself, when you've been doing life support on a dead connection. But you really don't know how most of the people in your life are doing to respond when you change. Your EPs speak loudly, saying, "Don't take the risk! He'll hate you forever! You'll be alone and it'll be your fault!"

Start with small renegotiations. Do one small, powerful thing. Identify one price that you've been paying. Communicate—without blame or shame—your unwillingness to continue paying it. Don't assume that the other person asked or required you to pay a price, even if you believe that they did—they may not have. You've learned from reading this book that you've imposed prices on yourself even when no one asks. Don't blame anyone else. Simply be clear that you realize that what you've been doing isn't good for you, isn't good for the connection between the two of you, and you're going to do things differently now. Notice the emphasis: **The price is good neither for you nor the relationship. The price is also not good for the other person**.

Thad had given up going to concerts because Arliss didn't enjoy live classical music. Crowds annoyed her, and she preferred listening to music on headphones in the quiet of her own home. Thad had given up going because he believed Arliss had told him that her feelings would be hurt if he prioritized going to a concert over spending time together. So, with trepidation, the first topic in his "not paying this price of admission any longer" adventure was to tell Arliss he had decided he missed going to concerts and was going to begin attending the local classical music series again. "Oh honey, I'm so glad you're going to do that," was Arliss' response. "I can imagine that you've missed that."

"You mean you don't want me to stay home?" Thad was confused. In one moment Arliss had disrupted 30 years of beliefs and self-sacrifice. She explained, "Well maybe sometimes, yes, but you know, that's something we can work out. Like, if it was on our anniversary or my birthday, I wouldn't want you going to a concert without me. Remember, that's why I was cranky about it years ago when the Boston symphony was in town on my birthday. But why not go other times? You used to enjoy that so much when we were dating. I never did understand why you stopped going."

Thad was flummoxed. He had to work hard not to beat himself up internally for having paid a price for so many years—a price that Arliss had not needed, wanted, or appreciated. He had misunderstood her and given himself an unnecessary loss. It took large doses of self-compassion for Thad to accept reality and buy the tickets. He had been mistaking her for his parents.

Thad's retraction of the price of admission was difficult relationally because it made Arliss aware of dynamics in their marriage that she had sensed but not quite understood until that moment. She was upset to learn that Thad had been framing her actions as being like his parents, who she had never liked very much and who she thought treated Thad badly. The couple needed to clear the air to be able to reach a new, more solid ground with one another.

And Some You Lose

Gayle had a different experience when she told her close friend Rae that she'd noticed that she (Gayle) had always picked up the check when they ate out together. It was a habit that started when they first met. Gayle was employed as a paralegal and Rae was a single parent who was in the same paralegal program from which Gayle had graduated. Gayle had come to speak to Rae's class and became Rae's professional mentor and—she thought—friend.

Now, 15 years later, things were different. Both women had good jobs. Rae's son was grown and on his own. Gayle had started to feel twinges of resentment about Rae's assumption about who paid the check. She decided to take a risk and ask Rae how she'd feel if they each paid for their own meals, or maybe took turns covering the costs.

What happened next was unpleasant. Rae turned red and sputtered to Gayle, "So, you think I've got it good now? Let me tell you, you have no idea how much debt I have! If you really want to spend time with me, you'd better be willing to help me out, because otherwise what's the point for me? I mean, you were a good mentor to me when I first got into the business, but really, Gayle, you can be so boring sometimes, talking on and on about the latest case you're working on."

Gayle was shocked. She would have understood if Rae were uncomfortable or even a little defensive; she'd expected that. The last thing she planned for was being attacked for asking to renegotiate the terms of their relationship so that it would be more reciprocal and equal. She paid the bill, got up, and left abruptly before she could say anything to Rae that would make the situation worse. On her way home she vacillated between tears of pain and rage. How dare Rae say such hurtful things to her!

When she arrived home to her husband she was fuming. He hugged her and validated her feelings that Rae's response had been extreme. He told her that it reminded him of listening to Gayle's father. Alden had an unhealthy streak of narcissism that made it almost impossible for him to admit that he had ever needed someone, or that he could have behaved differently or better in a situation. "Remember when he had surgery and your mom was helping him? When she asked him if he wouldn't mind answering the door for the UPS guy while she went out to run an errand? He blew up about how he wasn't her fucking servant and he knew that she didn't care if he reinjured himself by answering the door. Mostly he was just ashamed by needing her to wipe his butt."

Gayle found this feedback helpful. The hypothesis that Rae had been responding out of shame and wounded self-regard led her to feel compassion. It didn't lead her to let Rae off the hook. As a legal professional she knew the diminished capacity defense only too well, and she wasn't going to apply it to Rae. But because they had a long history, she was going to offer compassion and give Rae another chance.

I call this the "compassionate three strikes" rule. When you've been playing the game with someone for a long time, that person gets a few chances to respond better to your proposal to end the payment plan. People don't get off the hook for an initial bad response. They simply get a little more room for being truly—and deeply and painfully—human and adjust to your proposal.

Gayle called Rae. The voicemail message she left when Rae didn't pick up said, "I think something I said was hard for you. I worry that perhaps something felt shaming to you. I can't imagine another reason for you to have reacted the way you did to my reasonable proposal. Can we talk about it?"

Gayle waited a week. When she didn't hear back from Rae, she called again. This time she defined a boundary. "It's been a week. I haven't heard from you. If I don't hear from you in another week I will read your silence to mean you don't want to remain in our friendship any longer. If that's the case, I'm very sad for both of us. We've been good friends to each other. Please call me."

Rae never called. Gayle was incredibly saddened by the loss and all the layers of meaning that it had. She struggled with an inner narrative telling her that if she'd only kept her mouth shut and kept paying the price of admission and the literal price of their meals out, she'd still have her friend. It took a lot of commitment to remind herself that if this had truly been the price all along, Rae was not her friend, but simply someone pretending to be one in exchange for mentorship and meals. The rift was a lasting one. When she crossed Rae's path at professional meetings, Rae walked away.

She also reminded herself that with Shireen, another colleague/friend whom she had mentored, she had the same discussion with positive results. Shireen had said, "Well, I'm embarrassed to admit that I let this happen for so long. I appreciate that you brought this up. It feels kind of weird, doesn't it? It feels kind of weird to be talking about it. You know, Gayle, that's what I really value in you. You talk about the hard stuff, even if it feels weird. How about we start by paying our own way from here on? And let me pick this one up, okay?" When they got up to leave, Shireen gave Gayle a hug, something that hadn't happened in the 10 years they'd known each other. Honesty had increased their trust and closeness.

Sometimes when you stop paying prices, you find out that they were unnecessary. Sometimes you discover that the other person really was a toll bridge. A lot of times you'll realize that both were happening. It's rarely an either/or situation. You can't always be sure. Sometimes you can predict the outcome, and sometimes you'll be surprised.

Start with a request that seems small and reasonable to you—going to the concert alone, paying only your fair share of a cost, sharing housework more equitably. Send up a trial balloon. It should be something that you assess as relatively low-risk so that if things go poorly, your EPs don't take over more firmly than before. Ask for something you want and can tolerate not getting well enough that you can regroup, then continue to roll back prices. Investigate, be curious, pay attention to what is happening right now, in the moment when you withdraw payment. Soothe yourself when you do this so that your EPs don't take over and distract or deflect you from your goal of no more prices. When you are able to soothe yourself skillfully and be in the present moment, you can feel compassion for the other person's difficulties with your changes without losing your resolve to persist. You can feel with and for the other person at the same time you feel with and for yourself.

Rabbi Hillel's saying, "If I'm not for myself, who will be for me? If I'm only for myself, what am I? If not now, when?" must be your mantra. You can apply the compassionate three-strikes rule with people who struggle with this updated version of yourself. Let the other person be human and confused by what's happening. Be kind and caring with them when they're upset without going into a rescuer role and starting a reenactment. Be mindfully self-protective so that you don't allow yourself to become a victim. Soothe your own upset feelings about unskillful responses so that you don't become a persecutor. When others flail, step out of the way so you can see what they see; don't withdraw and turn into a disengaged bystander.

If it's hard for you to be around others struggling with your changes, resist the urge to shut the process down by declaring defeat too soon. Let the "real thing" steal your unhappy endings even when it takes some time to do that. Unhappy process is not unhappy ending. That's a conflict, remember? Change requires patience. Use the assessment skills you've been developing. Is someone upset because you've painted them in a not-very-flattering light? Is someone in pain because they genuinely love you and it hurts them to learn that you thought they required payment? Or are they furious that you've finally figured out that you're worthy of love and are doing their best to cow and coerce you back into the old way of doing things?

At first glance, these two very different responses might seem similar. Both parties may be upset—perhaps angry, maybe blaming—for a bit, and may not be able to regulate emotions very well. You might be reminded of the unpredictable and volatile adults who were your attachment figures. You may be tempted to let the EPs take over and give old familiar meanings to someone else's actions.

Slow yourself down. Breathe. Be curious. Hang on to yourself. Take care of yourself, but don't start by giving up the fight. You've had this connection for a while. As long as you're not at risk of being harmed physically, you can tolerate a few more weeks or months of assessment. Go to therapy together if you can.

A neutral third party can help you each see and hear one another more clearly and effectively.

Know when to say "game over." Seek out consultation during this process from a friend, a therapist, a 12-Step sponsor, or a spiritual director whose investment is not in keeping the relationship together but in your wholeness. Ending a long-standing relationship is a big decision with emotional, social, and financial consequences; if that's your choice, you want to make it wisely, not impulsively. Having help with the decision will increase the chances of a better outcome.

If this is upsetting the applecart of your marriage, this might be an excellent time to engage the services of a couples therapist. Look for one who is familiar with attachment literature as it applies to relationships. Your therapist doesn't need to be an expert in emotionally-focused or Imago therapy, even though those are the two best-known models of couples therapy that consider attachment dynamics directly. Most important is that your therapist should be experienced and knowledgeable enough about effects of attachment wounds on adult relationships to be able to understand that your problems aren't only about communication. They need to understand the attachment patterns that one or both of you brings to the relationship. There are websites in the Resources section for EFT and Imago therapists in the U.S. and Canada, and a discussion of what to consider when choosing a therapist. If you live elsewhere, you can find a good therapist using an internet search engine.

Such a Bargain!

Get support to keep stripping out prices from relationships; don't try to go it alone. You'll empower yourself by getting help. You won't do this perfectly. You'll learn to separate out unicorn fantasies from prices. Think about how good it feels when you find something you really want at a bargain price. Good-enough relationships are like that. It's a pretty good bargain to put up with someone who bores you with their stamp collection or to compliment their cooking when that person is otherwise loving and decent.

Don't insist on purity; you'll both make mistakes. Do insist on being loved for precisely who you are. Figure out what the right bargains are. It might be an okay decision to continue to relate to someone who doesn't handle anger well as long as they made a meaningful commitment to learn to handle it better. Agreeing to stick around and work together to have a better connection is a healthy thing you can do for and with people you love. **A bargain is different than a price.** When you stop paying toxic and damaging prices, you'll find that the bargains you agree to give you and the relationship a chance to repair and improve. A bargain doesn't require you to be blind to betrayal, put up with chronic ill-treatment, be used, or exploited.

Your part of the bargain is to show up willingly and accept yourself as a human being with all of your warts and foibles. Your part means being open-hearted and gazing with a compassionate eye on yourself and others. To keep bargains in healthy relationships you have to let go of perfection and unicorns.

You'll never get the secure attachment from your caregivers that you deserved as an infant, and you won't get it from another adult. What you *can* get—if you're willing to make these changes—is the real thing. You *can* have the good-enough, attached-enough, loving connections with other adults in your life that you deserve. You get good-enough love and care and commitment. Good-enough is your human birthright. Stop paying prices, and welcome yourself to the toll-free zone.

APPENDIX
Attributes of a Powerful Person

Throughout this book I've invited you to consider how to empower yourself. What follows is a very detailed description of how people can be powerful. I think of power as happening in four ways: Somatic power (in our bodies), Intrapersonal power (in our relationships to ourselves), Interpersonal Power (in our relationships with others and the world around us), and Spiritual/Existential Power (in our capacity to make meaning in life). This is not a prescription; it is an evolving list of ways in which people empower themselves in the world, a list that some other people who grew up with other-than-adequate attachment experiences have found helpful as they learn to stop paying prices in relationships.

Somatic Power

The powerful person is in contact with her/his body; the body is experienced as a safe enough place, accepted as it is rather than forced to be larger or smaller than it would be if adequately nourished. If its size or shape creates a lack of safety for a person, change of size or shape happens in the service of safety. There is connection with bodily desires for food, sexual pleasure, and rest; no intentional harm is done to one's own body or that of others. A powerful body requires neither the ability to see, hear, walk, or talk, nor is it necessarily free of pain or illness, nor strong or physically fit. Body modifications reflect moves toward power and congruence, and personal construction of self. You have compassion for your body.

Intrapersonal Power

The powerful person knows what she or he thinks; thinks critically and can change her or his mind; is flexible, not suggestible, yet open to input. This person trusts intuition, and also is able to find external data for validation of intuition; knows feelings as they are felt. Feelings are a useful source of information about the here and now. There is an absence of numbness, and the presence of aliveness. There is the ability to experience powerful emotions, to contain affect so as to feel it and still function, to be able to self-soothe in ways that are not harmful to self or others physically, psychosocially, or spiritually.

Interpersonal Power

A powerful person is more interpersonally effective than not, can have desired impacts on others more of the time than not; has no illusions of control; forgives self and others, and is appropriately self-protective; is differentiated and clearly defined, yet flexible. An interpersonally powerful person is capable of forming relationships that work more of the time than not with other individuals, groups, and larger systems and is able to create and sustain intimacy, to be close without loss of self or engulfment of other, and to be differentiated without being distant or detached; able to decide to end relationships when those become dangerous, toxic, require prices of admission or become excessively problematic; this person is able to remain and work out conflict when that's a possibility. This person enter roles in life— parent, partner, worker—most often from a place of choice, intention, and desire, not accidentally, although she or he welcomes serendipity and the opportunity to encounter the new.

Spiritual/Existential Power

The powerful person has systems of meaning-making that assist with responding to the existential challenges of life, and that have the potential to give a sense of comfort and well-being; sense of own heritage and culture integrated into identity in ways that allow for better understanding of self; is aware of the social context and can engage with it rather than being controlled by it or unaware of its impact; has a raison d'etre, and is able to integrate that into important aspects of her or his daily life; access to capacities for creativity, fantasy, play and joy; has a sense of reality that is alive, not fixed and concrete.

Resources

Attachment

- Behavior Chain Analysis: http://ptsd.about.com/od/selfhelp/ht/fxanalysis.htm. A nice discussion of why trauma can lead to problematic behavioral patterns and how to observe yourself mindfully to make changes.

- Daniel J. Siegel. *The Developing Mind.* This book does a nice job of reviewing and making accessible for the general reader some of the last two decades of research on attachment and the development of self.

Betrayal Trauma and Cheater Detectors

- Janis Spring Abrams, & Michael Spring. *After the Affair.* For some of you, the price of admission has involved being betrayed by a spouse's affair. My colleagues who are infidelity experts speak most highly of this book as a helpful guide to getting through that with your boundaries and sense of self in better shape.

- Campbell's Danger Assessment Scale for women in abusive relationships can be found at: https://www.dangerassessment.org/about.aspx. This instrument was developed by amalgamating information from homicides that occurred in the context of an intimate relationship and comparing those relationships to ones in which violence, but no death, occurred. Use this scale to assess your level of risk if physical violence has become part of your relationship.

- Gavin de Becker. *The Gift of Fear.* I think that anyone who's been taught to silence and dissociate from their feelings about other people will benefit from this book. De Becker, because of being a childhood trauma survivor himself, really gets the ways in which having to not know what you feel helps you to survive childhood and creates risks later in life.

- Paul Ekman. *Telling Lies.* His most accessible book for the general public. Ekman reviews his research and offers very clear information and examples of what to look for so as to detect deception from people's facial expressions. If you know you have a hard time reading faces, then this book can bring your skill level up.

- Jennifer Freyd. *Betrayal Trauma: The Logic of Forgetting Childhood Abuse.* Her first book, it contains a full description of the research that led to betrayal trauma theory.

- Jennifer Freyd & Pamela Birrell. *Blind to Betrayal: How We Fool Ourselves That We Aren't Being Fooled.* This book does a great job of illustrating how betrayal blindness works and pointing out paths to taking off the blinders.

- Martha Stout. *The Sociopath Next Door.* This is one I wish I'd read before I had a sociopath come into my life 20 years ago. Helpful in development of your assessment skills.

Childhood Trauma and Recovery

- Adverse Childhood Experiences Study—The ACE Study is the largest (17,000 children) study of the long-term health and mental health consequences of childhood adversity. Difficult reading, and it helps many survivors to see that their struggles are normal for people who've had their experiences. http://www.cdc.gov/violenceprevention/acestudy/

- Ellen Bass & Laura Davis. *The Courage to Heal.* One of best resources for adult survivors of childhood sexual abuse. Recently revised to include new research on trauma, it's full of advice from other survivors about how to move from surviving to thriving. Best read when you're past the remembering/knowing/re-appraising stage of recovery.

- Eliana Gil. *Outgrowing the Pain.* A very short book that many survivors have found to be a helpful introduction to the shared concerns of others like them.

- Judith Lewis Herman. *Trauma and Recovery.* Widely acknowledged as one of the very best books about complex trauma, a concept that the author proposed in this book. So many trauma survivors of my acquaintance, both colleagues and clients, have talked about how life-saving and validating this book was for them.

- Mike Lew. *Victims No Longer.* This is the brother book to *The Courage to Heal,* written for men who have survived childhood sexual abuse. Revised in 2004, this book does an excellent job of addressing the gender dynamics that are particular for male survivors.

- Alice Miller. *The Drama of the Gifted Child.* Essential reading for people who, in the absence of physical or sexual abuse, experienced emotional abuse or exploitation by a caregiver. Miller has a number of other, longer books, but this short volume is a must-read.

- Francine Shapiro. *Getting Past Your Past.* This is the first self-help book by the inventor of EMDR. Full of ideas about how to heal from trauma using some of the insights derived from three decades of EMDR practice.

Eye Movement Desensitization Reprocessing

The EMDR International Association, http://www.emdria.org, has a list of therapists who are certified in EMDR. This means that they have gone through many hours of rigorous training and received additional consultation. These are folks who know how to use this therapy well, and they are located everywhere in the world.

Faith, Religion, and Trauma

• Faithtrust Institute: http://www.faithtrustinstitute.org. Faithtrust Institute is an interfaith organization dedicated to the prevention and treatment of sexual and intimate partner violence using the foundation of religious faith. An excellent resource for locating faith-based information on survivor issues, including for survivors of abuse by clergy.

• Marie M. Fortune. *Sexual Violence: The Sin Revisited.* Fortune, an ordained United Church of Christ minister, is the founder of the Faithtrust Institute. Her work on the interface of religion and trauma may be especially helpful to survivors for whom faith is important.

• Marie M. Fortune & Joretta Marshall. *Forgiveness and Abuse: Jewish and Christian Reflections.* This book draws on the two faith traditions to explore questions of how and whether to forgive abuse by someone in the family.

•Harold Kushner. *When Bad Things Happen to Good People.* Although not formally a religiously-based book, this classic is very informed by its author's many years as a congregational rabbi. Helpful for people of faith struggling with the "Why me?" questions.

Grief and Loss

• Anne Brenner. *Mourning and Mitzvah.* While written from the Jewish perspective, the author makes a number of excellent suggestions about how to create rituals for grieving that could be adapted and applied by people who are not Jewish.

• Melba Colgrove. *How to Survive the Loss of a Love.* This is a classic. While it's specifically about the ending of a romantic relationship, the dynamics that the author explores are pretty pertinent to all forms of loss and grief.

• Joan Didion. *The Year of Magical Thinking.* Didion's powerful memoir of the year after her beloved husband died suddenly. Her grief was raw and unvarnished. Helpful to see that this kind of grief is simply human.

Mindfulness and Compassion

- Audio Dharma. Their introduction to meditation series can be found here: http://www.audiodharma.org/series/1/talk/1762/

- Additionally, this site has a number of talks on loving-kindness meditations, called Metta meditations. These are valuable supplements to basic meditation skills for survivors: http://www.audiodharma.org/talks/?search=metta

- Also very valuable is a series of four talks by Daniel Bowling on the practice of listening, which supports your skill in trusting yourself in your assessment of other people. They can be found at the top of this page: http://www.audiodharma.org/talks/?search=listening

- Brene Brown. *The Gifts of Imperfection*. The title says it all. You might want to check out her TED talks online, too. She's a great speaker and is eloquent about the value of daring to be vulnerable with other people. Her newest book, which speaks in depth to the falling-down-and-getting-up adventure, is called *Rising Strong*.

- Jon Kabat-Zinn. *Full Catastrophe Living*. The go-to book for understanding the value of mindfulness as a source of reducing stress, physical pain, and emotional distress.

- Jack Kornfeld. *A Path with Heart* and *The Art of Forgiveness, Lovingkindness, and Peace*. Kornfeld has been one of the great translators of Buddhist traditions of mindfulness for Western audiences.

Relationships and Relationship Patterns

- John Gottman's books are worth reading after you've developed your skills at self-compassion and emotion regulation. I've found that survivors don't get as much use from them before doing that personal internal work. So go check his work out when you're ready.

- Dee Graham, Roberta Rigsby, & Edna Rawlings. *Loving to Survive*. This book contains one of the clearest explanations of the dynamics by which a traumatic attachment to one's intimate abuser occurs, and discusses how people entrapped in this way can free themselves. While they use the problematic construct of "Stockholm Syndrome," their application of it is actually appropriate as they discuss relationships with people who are both loved and feared.

- Harville Hendrix. *Getting the Love You Want*. This is a classic self-help book for couples that does a pretty good job of exploring how childhood patterns lead to problematic adult attachments. The author also offers a comprehensive series of exercises that couples can do, on their own, to heal those patterns in relationship.

- Sue Johnson. *Hold Me Tight: Seven Conversations for a Lifetime of Love.* This is the very readable self-help book by the founder and author of *Emotion Focused Therapy for Couples*, which is eye-opening and effective stuff. It dovetails very nicely with this book because of the strong emphasis on attachment dynamics in relationships. Look for a Hold Me Tight™ seminar for couples if you live in a major metropolitan area in the U.S. or Canada. Attending it can be well worth your while. It's not therapy, and it doesn't require you to talk in a group, but it will give you support and coaching for thinking about attachment in your relationship with a spouse or partner.

- Harriet Lerner has written a number of books about the "dance" of relationships. *The Dance of Anger*, her first book, and *The Dance of Intimacy*, are both short, easy reads that take issues of gender and culture into account in describing how family dynamics can affect the capacity to relate to other people.

- Thomas Lewis, Fari Amini, & Richard Lannon. *A General Theory of Love.* A charming little volume that explores the ways that our neurobiology affects our choices in relationship. References to it turn up in a lot of other people's books about relationships.

- David Schnarch. *Passionate Marriage* and *Intimacy and Desire: Awaken the Passions in Your Relationship.* Schnarch's work is particularly helpful if you're struggling with sex, and if you're having a hard time letting go of the unicorn fantasy of a healthy relationship.

Skills Training Models

- Suzette Boon, Kathy Steele, & Onno van der Hart. *Coping with Trauma Related Dissociation.* This workbook can be a better first step in skills training if you are living with dissociative identity disorder and other forms of dissociative coping strategies.

- The DBT Self-Help website: http://www.dbtselfhelp.com/index.html. This site is by and for people living with the detritus of less-than-adequate attachment experiences, so it's by and for you. It has a wealth of resources, including many worksheets that are helpful for studying and practicing skills like distress tolerance and emotion regulation.

- Marsha M. Linehan. *Dialectical Behavioral Therapy Skills Training Module.* In 2011, the *New York Times* printed the story of Marsha Linehan, who courageously discussed how she had put together DBT in order to help people like herself who struggled with emotions and relationships. Read her story at: http://www.nytimes.com/2011/06/23/health/23lives.html?pagewanted=all&_r=0

Somatic Therapies, Trauma and the Body

These links provide you with information about three trauma-informed body-oriented healing methods, as well as links to practitioners who have trained in the modality.

• Bessel van der Kolk, *The Body Keeps the Score.* Van der Kolk is one of the people who founded the field of modern trauma studies, and who, parallel to Judith Lewis Herman, described the effects of complex childhood attachment trauma. This, his latest book, is an integration of what he's learned from his clients over the last 40 years and includes a lot of material about accessing the body as a resource for healing.

• Generative Somatics: http://www.generativesomatics.org/

• Sensorimotor psychotherapy:
https://www.sensorimotorpsychotherapy.org/referral.html

• Somatic Experiencing (SE): http://www.traumahealing.org/about-se.php

Trauma and Memory

I've included this section even though it's not precisely on topic because many survivors doubt the accuracy of the terrible things that they've always remembered, and doubt even more those things where the recall of memory was delayed. Here's some science for you.

• Christine Courtois. *Recollections of Sexual Abuse.* Written for professionals, this book nonetheless does an excellent job of reviewing the research on trauma and memory, and goes into some detail about what can be helpful in therapy.

• Kenneth Pope & Laura S. Brown. *Recovered Memories of Abuse: Assessment, Therapy, Forensics.* Although written for a professional audience, this book may be helpful for some survivors who wish to have a more thorough grounding in the science of memory for trauma.

Finding a Therapist

After reading this book you might have decided that you or your relationship (or both) could benefit from therapy. Here's some ideas about how to get therapy that'll be helpful. Many state, provincial, or local organizations of psychologists, counselors, and social workers have referral services that are free to the public. You can find your local organization by typing such search terms as the name of your state or city, psychological association, psychiatric society, clinical social work society, or counselor association, into your favorite search engine. Sexual assault centers or programs for victims of intimate partner violence often have names of therapists who are knowledgeable about trauma. If you belong to a religious organization, your clergy person may have the names of therapists.

In addition, there are several commercial websites, both national and local, that offer lists of therapists. Few of these sites do any sort of formal screening. The therapists who advertise there are free to make whatever claims they want about themselves. Use your assessment skills to check people out if you're going this route.

In fact, use those skills no matter what. I once went to a therapist who my best friend loved. He was horrible for me, and I left quickly when I figured that out. When choosing a therapist, it's important to find out not only what her or his credentials are and whether this person is covered by your insurance, but also how it feels to you to work with this person, and whether or not this therapist has an understanding of the effects of childhood maltreatment and abuse. Years of experience may be less important than a therapist's knowledge of trauma and ability to be connected to and compassionate with you. Pay attention to your gut. Any therapist saying they have a miracle cure that no one else has is misrepresenting her or himself. There are no such miracle cures. No therapist should ever suggest having a sexual relationship with you, borrowing money from you, or going into business with you. No therapist should try to make friends with you outside of therapy, or trade your services for theirs.

A really useful book to read as a way of identifying what can be most helpful in therapy John Norcross' *Psychotherapy Relationships That Work*. It reports findings of research that aggregated half a century of studies of psychotherapy outcome and identifies the ingredients of the secret sauce that makes therapy work well.

If you'd rather read a book or watch a movie than see a therapist, read *Self-Help That Works,* by John Norcross and his colleagues. They've reviewed a lot of different self-help books, in addition to memoirs, movies, and fiction relevant to a very wide range of topics. They include both their picks and their pans.

National Psychotherapy Resources

- Therapists practicing Acceptance and Commitment Therapy (ACT), a mindfulness-based therapy, can be found at: https://contextualscience.org/civicrm/profile?gid=17&reset=1&force=1

- EFT Couple therapists who have done the EFT certification training can be found at: http://www.iceeft.com/index.php/find-a-therapist

- Therapists who practice Functional Analytic Psychotherapy, which helps deepen people's ability to take risks and be vulnerable in relationships, can be found at: http://functionalanalyticpsychotherapy.com/find-a-fap-therapist/

- Practitioners of Imago Couples therapy, which also attends to dynamics of attachment, can be found at: https://pub.imagorelationships.org/FindATherapist.aspx

- Information about Schnarch's Crucible method with couples can be found at: http://crucibletherapy.com/

Trauma-Specific Psychotherapy Resources

- International Society for the Study of Trauma and Dissociation: http://www.isst-d.org. ISST-D is the home for research and training on complex trauma and dissociation. It publishes a journal and an online newsletter, and presents an annual conference. It also offers an online training program for professionals wishing to acquire competence in the treatment of dissociation. ISST-D has a referral list of therapists.

- International Society for Traumatic Stress Studies: http://www.istss.org. ISTSS is a multidisciplinary, international organization that publishes a journal and newsletter, and offers an annual conference as well as online continuing education for professionals.

- Sidran Foundation: http://www.sidran.org. In addition to having many written resources for survivors and therapists and offering training for therapists and other first responders, Sidran has long maintained a national referral network of therapists.

About the Author

Laura S. Brown received a Ph.D. in clinical psychology in 1977 from Southern Illinois University at Carbondale, and has been a practicing clinical and forensic psychologist in Seattle since 1979. She specializes in treating survivors of childhood trauma and training other therapists. She is a Diplomate of the American Board of Professional Psychology (ABPP). Her career has included the publication of 12 books for professionals, 150 professional articles and book chapters, and six training videotapes, including two specifically devoted to the treatment of survivors of childhood trauma.

Dr. Brown has received many awards from her colleagues, including the American Psychological Association's Award for Distinguished Professional Contributions to Public Service, the Sarah Haley Award for Clinical Excellence from the International Society for Traumatic Stress Studies, the Distinguished Award for Lifetime Achievement in Trauma Psychology from the APA Division of Trauma Psychology, and the Elizabeth Hurlock Beckmann Award for being an inspirational educator. She has served on the faculty of three universities, and leads workshops around the world on trauma treatment and feminist therapy. In 2000, she was the on-site psychologist for the reality TV show *Survivor* in Australia.

Laura first wrote for the general public when she published *Your Turn for Care: Surviving the Aging and Death of the Adults Who Harmed You* in 2013. She lives in Seattle with her spouse. Since 2003, she has been a student of the martial art aikido, in which she was training for the rank of black belt at the time she finished this book. You can read more about her at www.drlaurabrown.com.

Made in the
USA
Middletown, DE